THE

LAW OF MANDAMUS

AND THE

PRACTICE CONNECTED WITH IT,

WITH AN

APPENDIX OF FORMS.

By HALSEY H. MOSES,
COUNSELOR-AT-LAW.

Fred B. Rothman & Co.
LITTLETON, COLORADO
1981

Library of Congress Cataloging in Publication Data

Moses, Halsey H.
The law of mandamus and the practice connected with it, with an appendix of forms.

Reprint. Originally published: Albany : W. Gould, 1878.
Includes index.
1. Mandamus--United States. 2. Mandamus--United States--Forms. I. Title.

KF9037.M6 1981	347.73'77	81-12112
ISBN 0-8377-0838-9	347.30777	AACR2

THE

LAW OF MANDAMUS

AND THE

PRACTICE CONNECTED WITH IT,

WITH AN

APPENDIX OF FORMS.

By HALSEY H. MOSES,
COUNSELOR-AT-LAW.

ALBANY:
WILLIAM GOULD & SON,
LAW BOOKSELLERS AND PUBLISHERS
1878.

PREFACE

THE law of mandamus, although a necessary and important branch of the jurisprudence of the country, has heretofore been, to some extent, inaccessible to a large majority of the practicing lawyers, for the reason that it has lain scattered through the many reported decisions of the various State and federal courts of this country and of England. Besides the difficulty and labor of hunting up the law applicable to a particular case, even when the books were at hand, very few lawyers either own or have access to, a sufficiently extensive library. And notwithstanding it is a branch of the law not as often resorted to as some others, yet every practitioner is liable, any day, to be called upon to aid a client in securing his rights through the instrumentality of this remedy.

The lawyer who has had little or no practice in this branch of the law, and who has not had at command an extensive law library to consult, has no doubt felt the convenience it would be to the profession if the authorities bearing upon this subject were collected together and arranged in some accessible form. This work was undertaken with that object in view. Being of the opinion that the speculations of even the most learned of men, unless they occupy such an official position as will cause their opinions to be regarded as authoritative, are of but little importance to those who are seeking to know simply what the law is, we have been content to present, almost exclusively, the conclusions of those whose adjudications are entitled to be regarded as authority.

And while there are, no doubt, imperfections and mistakes, and many important matters overlooked, yet we hope and trust that the profession, and the judiciary, will find the work a great convenience to them in the performance of their professional and official duties.

HALSEY H. MOSES.

WARREN, O., *October 1st*, 1866.

TABLE OF CONTENTS.

CHAPTER V.

MANDAMUS TO CLERK OF COURT.

CHAPTER VI.

MANDAMUS TO THE SECRETARY OF STATE.

CHAPTER VII.

MANDAMUS TO THE SECRETARY OF WAR AND NAVY.

CHAPTER VIII.

MANDAMUS TO THE POSTMASTER-GENERAL.

CHAPTER IX.

MANDAMUS TO THE SECRETARY OF THE TREASURY.

CHAPTER X.

MANDAMUS TO GOVERNOR.

CHAPTER XI.

MANDAMUS TO AUDITOR OF STATE.

CHAPTER XII.

MANDAMUS TO ATTORNEY-GENERAL.

CHAPTER XIII.

MANDAMUS TO CANVASSERS.

CHAPTER XIV.

MANDAMUS TO STATE TREASURER.

CHAPTER XV.

CHAPTER XVI.

CHAPTER XVII.

CHAPTER XVIII.

CHAPTER XIX.

CHAPTER XX.

CHAPTER XXI.

CHAPTER XXII.

PROCEEDING.

CHAPTER XXIII.

THE APPLICATION.

CHAPTER XXIV.

THE ALTERNATIVE WRIT.

CHAPTER XXV.

THE RETURN.

CHAPTER XXVI.

THE PEREMPTORY WRIT.

CHAPTER XXVII.

WHAT COURTS MAY ISSUE THE WRIT.

CHAPTER XXVIII.

JUDGMENT UPON PETITION FOR MANDAMUS REVISABLE IN ERROR.

CHAPTER XXIX.

COSTS IN MANDAMUS.

APPENDIX.

TABLE OF CASES.

A.

B.

C.

G.

H.

I.

J.

K.

P.

S.

T.

U.

V.

W.

THE LAW OF MANDAMUS.

CHAPTER I.

INTRODUCTION.

To simply define and declare what are the rights of the citizen, is not the only object of civil government, and meets only a part of the wants of a people.

An equally important branch of the civil and criminal jurisprudence of a civilized nation, is the remedy provided by law for those who have been deprived of their rights. And that remedy which comes nearest to restoring to the injured party that of which he has been deprived, approaches nearest to a perfect remedy.

In many cases it is impracticable to restore to the party the thing he has lost, or to put him in possession of that which is illegally withheld from him. As, for instance, where one's trees have been cut down, or where the title to lands, purchased with a warranty of title from the vendor, proves to be in a third person. In such cases it is impossible for the law to restore to the party his trees, or to secure to him a title to the lands; but must be content to do the only thing practicable, award to him such damages as will compensate him for the injuries received. But if the vendee failed to obtain a title to the lands, not because the legal title was rightfully in some other person than the vendor, but because there was a defect in the instrument of conveyance, by which means the title did not pass to him, but remained in the vendor, the law affords the more complete remedy of compelling the vendor to fulfill his obligation, by making a full, complete, and adequate deed of conveyance.

In order to maintain a system of government which will be able to secure to the citizen his rights, it is necessary to have persons appointed, or chosen, to administer the law. And when persons are thus clothed with the power, and have assumed the duties of a public officer, they have taken upon themselves the obligation to perform those duties; and if they neglect or refuse to do so, any person whose rights are thereby injuriously affected, is entitled to demand relief. The remedy provided by our system of law, as well as that of England, is a process issuing from the judicial branch of the government, which seeks to compel the officer to go forward and do that which is enjoined upon him by the position he holds. This process is denominated a writ of mandamus; and when there is a right to execute an office, perform a service, or exercise a franchise, more especially if it be a matter of public concern, or attended with profit, and a person having such right is wrongfully kept out of possession, or dispossessed of such right, and has no other specific legal remedy, the court will interfere by mandamus, upon reasons of justice and upon reasons of public policy, to preserve peace, order and good government. (3 *Stephens' Nisi Prius*, 2292.)

It is substantially a civil remedy for the citizen who has been deprived of his right, although the case is commenced, and prosecuted, in the name of the State. The State, however, is only nominally a party.

It will therefore be observed that it is one of the remedies resorted to when a person desires to be placed in possession of a right illegally and unjustly withheld from him. It does not award damages as a compensation for an injury, but it seeks to give the thing itself—the withholding of which constitutes the injury complained of.

In every well constituted government the highest judicial authority must necessarily have a supervisory power over all inferior or subordinate tribunals, magistrates, and all others exercising public authority. If they commit errors, it will correct them. If they refuse or neglect to perform their duties, it will compel them. In the former case, by writ of error; in the latter, by mandamus.

And generally, in all cases of omission or mistake, where there is no other adequate, specific remedy, resort may be had to this high judicial writ. It not only lies to ministerial, but to judicial officers. In the former case it contains a mandate to do a specific act; but in the latter only to adjudicate, to exercise a judgment, or discretion, upon a particular subject.

The office of the writ of mandamus is very extensive. It has been said that "it is the supplementary remedy, when all others fail."

Its origin dates far back in the history of English jurisprudence. It was invented because public justice and good government demanded it; and it has been from that time used, and by legislative enactments fostered and improved, because the wants of a progressive people required it. If in England it is one of the flowers of the King's Bench, in America it is one of the gems of our judicial system. By its aid the servants of the government can be kept in subjection to the sovereign will—the citizen admitted or restored to the post of honor or profit to which he has been chosen by his countrymen, and the enjoyment of a franchise granted to him by his government.

CHAPTER II.

GENERAL NATURE OF THE WRIT OF MANDAMUS.

A writ of mandamus, at common law, was a command issuing in the King's name, from the court of King's Bench, and directed to any person, corporation, or inferior court of judicature within the King's dominions, requiring them to do some particular thing therein specified, which appertains to their office and duty, and which the court of King's Bench has previously determined, or at least supposes to be consonant to right and justice. (2 *Black. Com.*, 110.)

In England, it is denominated a prerogative writ because the King, being the fountain of justice, it is interposed by his authority, and transferred to the court of King's Bench to prevent disorder from a failure of justice, where the law has established no specific remedy, and where in justice and good government there ought to be one. It is a writ of right, and lies where there is a right to execute an office, perform a service, or exercise a franchise; and a person is wrongfully kept out of possession, and dispossessed of such right, and has no other specific legal remedy.

It is also grantable where a person has a legal right to insist that a certain act shall be done, the performance of which is, by law, made the duty of a public officer.

In England, no court but the King's Bench has power to issue it. That court derives its power to issue the writ from its high and peculiar powers. And these high and peculiar powers were possessed by the court of King's Bench, because the King originally sat there in person, and aided in the administration of justice. And according to the theory of the common law, the King is the fountain of justice, and where the laws did not afford a remedy, and enable the individual to obtain his right, by the regular forms of judicial proceedings, the prerogative powers of the sovereign were brought in aid of the ordinary judicial powers of the court, and the mandamus was issued in his name to enforce the execution of the law.

And although the King has long since ceased to sit there in person, yet the sovereign is still there in construction of law, so far as to enable the court to exercise its prerogative powers in his name; and hence its powers to issue the writ of mandamus, the nature of which is described by calling it extra-judicial, and one of the flowers of the King's Bench.

The peculiar powers of the court of King's Bench are clearly stated in 3 *Black. Com.*, 42, as follows:

"The jurisdiction of this court is very high and transcendent. It keeps all inferior jurisdictions within the bounds of their authority, and may either remove their proceedings to be determined here, or prohibit their progress below. It superintends all civil corporations in the kingdom. It commands magistrates and others to do what their duty requires, in every case where there is no other specific remedy."

"It protects the liberty of the subject by speedy and summary interposition. It takes cognizance both of criminal and civil causes; the former in what is called the crown-side, or crown-office; the latter in the plea-side of the court."

But in America, the authority to issue the writ of mandamus, does not exist as a prerogative power of the courts, but is derived by grant from the government, through the constitution, or legislative enactments. And when the power has been granted in general terms to a court, it is to be governed by the common law rules, as to when it is proper to be issued. (*Kentucky* v. *Dennison*, 24 *How.* [*U. S.*] *Rep.*, 66. *In the matter of James Turner*, 5 *O. R.*, 543.)

As it was a remedy introduced to prevent disorder from a failure of justice, in pursuance of the principles of the common law, it ought now to be used upon all occasions where the law has established no specific remedy, and where in justice and in good government there ought to be one. If there be a right and no other specific remedy, this writ should not be denied by our courts. It may be stated as a general principle that this writ is only granted for public persons, and to compel the performance of public duties. (3 *Stephens' Nisi Prius*, 2291.) It can be resorted to only in those cases where the matter in dispute, in theory, concerns the public, and in which the public has an interest. The degree of its importance to the public, is not, however, scrupulously weighed. (1 *Swift's Digest*, 564.) A mandamus gives no right, not even a right of possession, but simply puts a man in a position which will enable him to assert his right, which in some cases he could not do without it.

In order to lay the foundation for issuing a writ of mandamus, there must have been a refusal to do that which it is the object of the mandamus to enforce, either in direct terms, or by circumstances distinctly showing an intention in the party not to do the act required. (3 *Stephens' Nisi Prius*, 2292. *Redfield on Railways*, 441. *Note* 5.)

And although the power to issue a mandamus is not in America regarded as a prerogative power, yet the writ so far partakes of the nature of a prerogative writ, that the court has the power to issue or withhold it, according to its discretion. And if issued, it would manifestly be attended with hardship and difficulties, the court may, and even should refuse it. (*Ex-parte Fleming*, 4 *Hill*, 581.)

But this discretion is not an arbitrary one; it is a judicial discretion; and when there is a right, and the law has established no specific remedy, this writ should not be denied. (*The Proprietors of St. Luke's Church* v. *Slack*, 7 *Cushing's Rep.*, 226.)

CHAPTER III.

MANDAMUS TO INFERIOR TRIBUNALS.

The writ of mandamus is a proper remedy to compel inferior tribunals to perform the duties required of them by law. But it will not be granted unless the petition alleges facts sufficient, if proved, to show that such court has omitted a manifest duty. It must contain not only the affirmative allegations of proceedings necessary to entitle the party to the process prayed for, but it must also be averred that other facts, which would justify the omission complained of, do not exist. (*Hoxie* v. *County Commissioners of Somerset*, 25 *Maine*, 333.)

It was at one time doubted whether the writ would lie to an inferior court, commanding it to sign a bill of exceptions. But the case of *Ex-parte Crane et al.*, 5 *Peters' Rep.*, 189, decided that it did. That case was a motion made in the Supreme court of the United States, for a writ of mandamus to be directed to the Circuit court for the southern district of New York, in the second circuit, commanding the said court, "to review its settlement of the proposed bills of exceptions, and to correct, settle, allow and insert, in the said bills, the charge delivered to the said jury in each case, or the substance thereof." The court after quoting from Blackstone's Commentaries, where he says that it is the peculiar business of the court of King's Bench to superintend all other inferior tribunals, and therein to enforce the due exercise of those judicial or ministerial powers with which the crown or legislature have invested them; and this not only by restraining their excesses, but also by quickening their negligence, and obviating their denial of justice, proceeded to say, "It is, we think, apparent that this definition, and this description of the purpose to which it is applicable by the court of King's Bench, as supervising the conduct of all inferior tribunals, extends to the case of a refusal by an inferior court to sign a bill of exception, when it is an act which appertains to their office and duty, and which the court of King's Bench supposes to be consonant to right and justice."

"Yet we do not find a case in which the writ has issued from that court. It has rarely issued from any court; but there are instances of its being sued out of the court of Chancery, and its form is given in the register. It is a mandatory writ, commanding the judge to seal it if the facts alleged be truly stated; '*si ita est.*' * * * That a mandamus to sign a bill of exceptions is warranted by the principles and usages of law, is, we think, satisfactorily proved by the fact that it is given in England by statute; for the writ given by the statute of Westminster the second, is so in fact, and is so termed in the books. The judicial act speaks of usages of law generally, not merely of common law. In England it is awarded by the chancellor; but in the United States it is conferred expressly on this court, which exercises both common law and chancery powers; is invested with appellate powers, and exercises extensive control over all the courts of the United States. We cannot perceive a reason why the single case of a refusal by an inferior court to sign a bill of exceptions, and thus to place the law of the case on the record, should be withdrawn from that general power to issue writs of mandamus to inferior courts, which is conferred by statute."

It was also so ruled in the case of *Delavan* v. *Boardman and White*, 5 *Wend.*, 132.

But where, by statutory provision, or the practice of courts, bills of exceptions are required to be tendered at the trial, or at least during the continuance of the term, the court cannot be compelled to sign and seal it at a subsequent term. (*Sikes* v. *Ransom*, 6 *Johnson's Rep.*, 279.)

And where the return to an alternative mandamus commanding the judges of a court of common pleas to sign and seal a bill of exceptions or show cause, showed that the bill of exceptions was not tendered to the judges at the trial, but was presented to them individually at different times after the court had adjourned for the term, the court above refused to grant a peremptory mandamus, because the facts on which a bill of exceptions is taken must be reduced to writing at the time, and presented distinctly to the court during the trial, or at least during the continuance of the term. (*Midberry* v. *Collins et al.*, 9 *John.*, 345.)

But where the motion for a mandamus is for the purpose of compelling the judge to sign a particular bill of exceptions, and the cause shown is that the bill presented did not contain a true statement of the facts, a peremptory mandamus will not be granted. (*State of Ohio* v. *Todd et al.*, 4 *Ohio Rep.*, 351. *Ex-parte Bradstreet*, 4 *Peters' Rep.*, 105.) The power of determining whether a bill of exceptions is true or not, is vested in the judges to whom it is presented for signature.

But where the return to the mandamus showed as a reason for not signing and sealing the bill of exceptions offered to them, that it did not contain certain documentary evidence, but it averred they would have signed it had it contained those documents, it was decided that these reasons alone are not sufficient without showing further that those documents composed a part of the testimony upon which their own opinions rested, and which was related to the facts in the bill, and that the counsel were apprised of this cause of refusal, and had an opportunity to supply the defects of the bill. (*The State of Ohio* v. *The Judges of Clermont County*, 1 *Western Law Journal*, 358.)

Every court, in the exercise of its supervisory and protecting charge over its records, and the papers belonging to its files, has the power to direct the clerk to correct not only clerical errors, but such errors as may arise from any fraudulent or improper alteration or mutilation of its files or records. And the exercise of this power is obligatory upon them, and if they refuse to exercise it, mandamus lies against them.

Therefore, where an alternative writ of mandamus was issued out of the Supreme court at the instance of Hollister and Smith, directed to the judges of the District court, commanding them to cause an order to be made (or show cause why they refuse so to do), directing the clerk of said District court to correct the record in a certain action which had been tried in said court, in which action said Hollister and Smith were defendants, by restoring to the bill of exceptions signed, sealed and filed in said case as a part of the record thereof, certain material words which, as was alleged, the judge of the court of Common Pleas, who presided at said term of the District court, had improperly stricken out of the bill of exceptions, outside of the court room, after the final adjournment of the court, without personal consultation with either of the judges of said court, and without the knowledge or consent of Hollister and Smith or their attorneys, and which alteration as was alleged, was not the act of the District court.

To this writ, it was among other things returned that, two of the judges of the Common Pleas, holding the District court at the time the bill of exceptions mentioned in said writ was signed, were Messrs. Otis and Starkweather, whose official terms had since then expired, and they no longer held the office of judge. And that, "the judges of the Common Pleas now holding the District court for said county, say they know nothing about the facts set forth in said writ of mandamus, and, as judges, have no power over the clerk in the premises, and can make no order that he is bound to obey."

Bartley, C. J., in delivering the opinion of the court, said: "Every court of record has a supervisory and protecting charge over its records, and the papers belonging to its files;

and may at any time direct the correction of clerical errors, or the substitution of papers in case the originals are purloined or lost; and, in the exercise of the same authority, in case the records, or files should be fraudulently or otherwise improperly altered or defaced, may direct their correction and restoration to their original condition. And in making such corrections, the clerk is under the control and authority of the court."

"Two of the judges, it is said, have no knowledge of the facts touching the alleged alteration of the bill of exceptions. This is no legal excuse for not doing the act directed, when they have the unquestionable authority to direct the relators and other parties interested to produce their proofs in relation to the matter. The personal knowledge of the judge is not essential to the correction of a clerical error. He may inquire into the matter and inform himself by competent evidence, and act upon that, as he acts upon proof given in court in the performance of other judicial acts."

A peremptory mandamus was awarded. (*Hollister & Smith* v. *The Judges of the District court of Lucas county*, 8 *O. S. R.*, 201. *See also True* v. *Plumley*, 36 *Maine Rep.*, 466.)

The writ may be addressed to subordinate judicial tribunals, requiring them to exercise their functions and render some judgment in cases before them, when otherwise there would be a failure of justice from a delay or refusal to act. But when the act to be done is judicial or discretionary, the court will not direct what decision shall be made. (*The People* v. *Judge of Wayne county*, 1 *Manning's* [*Mich.*] *Rep.*, 359. *In matter of Turner*, 5 *O. R.*, 542.)

In the case of *James Turner*, 5 *O. R.*, 542, the court say, there is no doubt that the writ may issue, commanding an inferior court to act, and proceed to judgment, yet it will not prescribe what judgment to give. Yet when the party for whom a verdict is found, will not move for judgment, the other party may pray for judgment against himself. And when he thus prays for judgment against himself, to the intent that he may bring a writ of error, he is entitled to have it so rendered against him as matter of right; and if the court refuse or neglect to proceed, a mandamus will be granted to compel the court to give judgment. (*Fish* v. *Weatherwax*, 2 *John. Cases*, 215.)

And so where the court of Common Pleas had arrested judgment for the alleged insufficiency of the declaration mandamus will not lie to compel the court to vacate the rule so arresting judgment. The course is for the party against whom the rule is made to apply for judgment against himself, and then bring error. If the court of Common Pleas refuse to give judgment against him, the court above will then interfere by mandamus. (*Ex-parte Bostwick*, 1 *Cowen's Rep.*, 143.)

So where a verdict has been obtained in an action, on which the court refuses, or delays to give judgment, a mandamus may issue. (*The People* v. *The Judges of Cayuga*, 2 *John. Cases*, 68. *Strange*, 113, 392. 1 *John's Cases*, 279, 181. 19 *John. Rep.*, 147.)

And in Massachusetts it has been granted to compel the Court of Sessions to enter the verdict of a jury in the assessment of damages. (9 *Mass.*, 388. 5 *Ib.*, 435.)

And to compel a probate court to issue his warrant for the arrest of an insolvent who refused to obey the order of the court.

The case of *Kimball et al.* v. *Morris, Judge, &c.*, 2 *Met.* (*Mass.*) *Rep.*, 573, was a petition asking the court to exercise its supervisory power over the proceedings of the judge of probate, in a matter pending before him in a case of insolvency, arising under the statute, by directing a writ of mandamus to issue, requiring the said judge to issue his process for the arrest and imprisonment of one Davis, the alleged insolvent, for refusing to obey the order of said judge requiring said Davis to appear before him at a meeting of the creditors, and to produce a schedule of his debts, and submit himself to an examination on oath. The statute provided that, "the debtor shall at all times, before the granting of his certificate as hereinafter provided, upon reasonable notice, attend and submit to an examination on oath, before the judge and the assignee, upon all matters relating to the disposal of his estate," &c. It also provided that, "in case the debtor, after being duly notified to appear at the time and place appointed for said meeting for such purpose, shall unreasonably neglect and refuse so to do, it was the duty of the judge of probate to issue his warrant to a proper officer, commanding him to arrest and commit such debtor to the common jail, to remain in close custody until he shall obey the said order of the said judge, unless he shali be released therefrom by the supreme judicial court, or some justice thereof, on a writ of *habeas corpus* pursuant to law." The petition for a mandamus was sustained, and an alternative writ issued, requiring the probate judge to issue such warrant, or to show cause for refusing so to do.

It may also be granted to compel the judge of a District court of the United States, to sign a judgment rendered by his predecessor in office. (*Life Ins. Co.* v. *Wilson*, 8 *Peters' Rep.*, 291.)

In that case, judgment had been rendered in the District court of the United States for the eastern district of Louisiana, in favor of the plaintiff. By the law of Louisiana, and the rule adopted by the District court, a judgment without the signature of the judge, cannot be enforced by execution; neither is it a final judgment, on which a writ of error may issue for its reversal. And after the rendition of the judgment, three days were allowed by the law, within which to move for a new trial; and if no new trial shall have been granted, the judge was required to sign the judgment at the expiration of this time. Judge ROBERTSON, who was judge of the court at the time the judgment was rendered, died without signing it, and was succeeded by Judge HARPER. About six years after the rendition of the judgment, and four after the death of Judge ROBERTSON, a notice was filed in the clerk's office, to the defendant, that at the next term, application would be made to the District judge, on behalf of the plaintiff, to sign the judgment. A motion to that effect was made, which was overruled by the court, on the ground that a judgment by the practice of that court, was not complete, and therefore no judgment at all, until signed by the judge; that the successor of Judge ROBERTSON could not sign the judgment without making it his own, thereby pronouncing on the rights of the parties whose cause he had never heard. A motion was then made in the Supreme court of the United States for a writ of mandamus, to be directed to the District judge, commanding him to sign the judgment.

Mr. Justice McLEAN, delivering the opinion of the court, said: "But the District judge is mistaken in supposing that no one but the judge who renders the judgment can grant a new trial. He, as the successor of his predecessor, can exercise the same powers, and has a right to act on every case that remains undecided upon the docket, as fully as his predecessor could have done. The court remains the same, and the change of the incumbent cannot and ought not, in any respect, to injure the rights of litigant parties."

The court also decided that the act of signing was a ministerial and not a judicial act; that the plaintiff had a right to be placed in such a posture as would enable him to proceed to another trial, or to take out execution on his judgment. The writ of mandamus was therefore allowed.

A mandamus may also be issued to an inferior court, commanding that it reïnstate a cause dismissed, and proceed to try and adjudge the same according to the rights of the case. (*Ex-parte Bradstreet*, 7 *Peters' Rep.*, 647.)

And where the court below order proceedings to be finally stayed, upon suggestions of the attorney for the United States, in a case in which the United States are not a party, the Supreme court will order a mandamus *nisi*, in the nature of a *procedendo*. (*Livingston* v. *Dorgenois*, 7 *Cranch*, 577.)

So where an inferior court make an order in a case which is in violation of the plain legal rights of one of the parties, and by virtue of such order refuse to proceed further in the case, the inferior court can, on mandamus, be compelled to vacate the order. Therefore, where an appeal had been taken from a magistrate's court to the court of Common Pleas, and the bail required by statute had been given, and where, under a general rule of the court of Common Pleas requiring additional bail in cases of appeal, a rule had been entered staying the proceedings in the case by reason of non-compliance with such general rule, it was held that the court of Common Pleas had no power to make a rule as to bail on appeal different from the statutory requirements; and, therefore the Superior court, on mandamus, ordered the rule to be vacated, and that the court proceed with the case. (*The People* v. *The Judges of Washington County*, 1 *Cowen*, 576.)

So, a court having appellate jurisdiction from an inferior court, and which has refused to entertain an appeal of a case, may be compelled to do so by writ of mandamus from a higher court. (*Ex-parte Henderson*, 6 *Florida*, 279.)

And in New Jersey, where an appeal was taken from the judgment of a justice to the Common Pleas, and the appeal bond had been delivered; and the justice, either from the want of opportunity or forgetfulness, as he himself stated, did not send up the proceedings to the court on the first day of the term; and the appellant, perceiving that the justice had not sent up the proceedings as was required of him by law, went to the house of the justice and procured from him the transcript, appeal bond and proceedings, and brought them into court during the term, but after the first day, when they were duly filed. The next following term the court dismissed the appeal, and assigned the following reason for so doing: that the transcript of the justice was not filed on the first day of the court next after the judgment was given by the justice below. The court above ordered a mandamus, because the act requiring the appeal papers to be sent in on or before the first day of the term is only directory to the justice. (*The State* v. *The Judges of Bergen*, 2 *Pennington's R.*, 541.)

But where, as in Ohio, the statute provides that the party appealing shall file in the court above, a transcript, on or before a certain day of the next term, and he neglects to do it until after the time designated, and for that reason the appeal is dismissed, it is doubtful whether a mandamus would be granted to compel the court to reïnstate the cause. In such a case it would be the appellant's own neglect that it was not filed in time.

But if, on demand, the justice should refuse to furnish the appellant with a certified transcript, a mandamus would be granted to compel him to do so.

And in the same State, where a court of common pleas dismissed an appeal for want of the necessary affidavit, a mandamus was allowed to reïnstate the case. The affidavit, which had been made, and which in other respects was sufficient, having been written on the back of the appeal bond, the court above granted a mandamus, observing: "The court of Common Pleas no doubt dismissed the appeal in this case in consequence of what was said by this court in the case of *Freas* v. *Jones*, 3 *Green's R.* 20; but on one or two occasions since that case was decided, we have expressed an opinion that the objection ought to be to the bond and not to the affidavit. The party, by putting his affidavit on the bond, has in effect deprived his adversary of the benefit of it. For the court of Common Pleas cannot deliver the bond to the appellee for prosecution, without delivering with it the affidavit also, which ought not to be done. If the objection had, in this case, been made to the bond, the appellant might immediately have substituted a new one; but another affidavit would have come too late. Let a mandamus, therefore, issue as prayed for."

And where an appeal was dismissed because the appeal bond was not sealed, and by statute it was provided that "the court may permit the appellant to substitute a new one, in the place of the appeal bond filed and sent up by the justice," a mandamus was allowed to compel the court to permit an appeal bond to be substituted, and the appeal reïnstated. (*Garrabrant* v. *McCloud*, 3 *Green R.*, 462.)

But a mandamus will not be granted to restore an appeal which was dismissed because there was no subscribing witness to the appeal bond, unless the appellant and his surety had offered, instanter, to re-execute the bond in the presence of one or more witnesses, or to substitute a new bond. (*Thorpe* v. *Keeler*, 3 *Harrison* 251.)

A peremptory mandamus has been granted to a court of Common Pleas, commanding them to reinstate an appeal dismissed for want of prosecution at a special term after demanded. (*Ten Eyck* v. *Farlee*, 1 *Harrison*, 269.)

These cases seem somewhat to conflict with the rule that error, and not mandamus, is the proper remedy where the court has made an erroneous decision; and also, with the case of *The King* v. *The Justices of Monmouth*, 7 *Dowl. & Ryl.*, 334, where the Court of Sessions had quashed an appeal, and a motion for a mandamus was denied by the King's Bench, for the reason that, "where the sessions forbear to give any judgment at all, this court will interpose to compel them to go on and pronounce judgment; but where they have actually given judgment, even under a mistake of law, this court has never yet interposed to disturb their decision." The court further said: "If we were to grant this application, we should be opening a door to continued litigation, and enormous expense, in every case where the propriety of the decision of the sessions might be questioned, either on the ground of mistake in law or fact. There seems to be no authority for such a proceeding; and as our predecessors have not recognized its propriety, we are certainly not disposed to take a step which is so pregnant with mischievous consequences."

In the case of *The Commonwealth* v. *The Judges of Common Pleas of Philadelphia county*, the question was whether a mandamus would lie for such purpose. The court held that although they might command an inferior judge to proceed to judgment, yet they had no power to compel him to decide according to the dictates of any judgment but his own. And that upon this principle it would be improper for them to issue the writ, as the court of Common Pleas had already given judgment according to their own convictions. The court say: "There is another reason; a writ of error lies in this case, and therefore a mandamus cannot issue. The rule is, that a writ of error lies in all cases, when a court of record has rendered final judgment, or made an award in the nature of a judgment. The striking off the appeal is certainly in the nature of a judgment, making an end of the cause by the act."

If the above cases decided by the Supreme court of New Jersey were correctly determined, they must rest on the principle that where an inferior judicial tribunal declines to hear a case upon a preliminary objection, and that objection is purely a matter of law, a mandamus from a superior court will be granted, if the inferior court has misconstrued the law. This doctrine is maintained by the court in the case of *Castello* v. *St. Louis Circuit court*, 28 *Miss.* (7 *Jones'*) *Rep.*, 259.

A mandamus may also issue to an inferior court, commanding it to send up papers on appeal. (*The Trustees of the Wabash & Erie canal* v. *Johnson*, 2 *Ind.* [*Carter*] *Rep.*, 219.)

In that case, Johnson petitioned the Board of Trustees of the Wabash and Erie canal, to have his damages assessed for injury occasioned by taking his land. In this petition he prayed to have the assessment made according to the provisions of the statute in such case made and provided. The appraisement was made by the appraisers appointed for the purpose. Johnson appealed to the Circuit court, and required the board to certify the cause to that court, which they refused to do, claiming that Johnson had no right to appeal. A mandamus was granted, compelling them to certify the cause.

And where the judgment of a Circuit court is reversed, and the proceedings up to a certain point are set aside at the costs of the defendant in error. and the cause is remanded for further proceedings; if the Circuit court refuse to render a judgment for costs according to the mandate, the Supreme court will grant a rule to show cause why a mandamus should not issue. (*Jared* v. *Hill*, 1 *Black.* [*Ind.*] *Rep.*, 155. *Post.*, 39.)

And when a court of inferior jurisdiction, not possessing the power to grant new trials, nevertheless undertakes to do so, the writ will lie to compel a judgment. (*Haight* v. *Turner*, 2 *Johns*, 371. *The People* v. *The Justices of Chenango*, 1 *Johns Cases*, 180. *Ferman* v. *Murphy*, 2 *Pennington*, 747.)

And in the case of *The People* v. *Niagara Common Pleas*, 12 *Wend.*, 246, it was determined that where a court of Common Pleas set aside a report of referees on the merits, and erred in so doing, a mandamus will be granted directing the Common Pleas to vacate the order setting aside the report of the referee.

But in a State where the error could be reached by a proceeding in error, it is somewhat difficult to determine upon what principle the decision can be sustained. And in the case of *The People* v. *The Judges of Oneida Common Pleas*, 21 *Wend.*, 20, it was decided that a mandamus does not lie to a court of Common Pleas, directing the vacation of a rule of that court, setting aside a report of referees, although the

Common Pleas in the decision made by them clearly erred; and the case of *The People* v. *Niagara Common Pleas*, above cited, was substantially overruled. Judge COWEN, in a separate opinion announced in this case, declared his unwillingness to consent to the granting of a mandamus, for the purpose of disturbing any judicial decision whatever, of an inferior court or magistrate.

Mandamus has also been held to be a proper remedy to compel an inferior tribunal to grant, or vacate an order for a new trial, where the granting of such order is not a matter of discretion with such court, but depends upon fixed principles and rules.

Therefore, in the case of *The People* v. *The Superior court of the City of New York*, 5 *Wend.*, 114, it was conceded that a Superior court would not, by mandamus, interfere, or attempt to coerce, the discretion of an inferior court when it is not, and cannot be governed by any fixed principles or rules; yet where it has exercised its discretion in a matter which is governed and controlled by well established rules, and has erred therein, a mandamus may be granted. And as it appeared in that case, that the court below had granted a new trial in violation of a well settled rule that a new trial will not be granted where the newly discovered evidence consists merely of additional, or cumulative facts and circumstances relating to the same matter or point, which was principally controverted upon the former trial, a mandamus was allowed to vacate the rule granting such new trial.

But there is no standard by which the weight of conflicting evidence can be ascertained. Different courts and juries, and individuals would entertain different opinions upon the subject, and each must judge for themselves. Therefore applications for new trials on the ground that the verdict is against evidence, are addressed to the discretion of the court, and cannot be controlled by mandamus.

In *ex-parte Bailey*, 2 *Cowen*, 479, a motion was made in

the court below for a new trial on various grounds, and among others, that the verdict of the jury was against the weight of evidence. The motion was refused, and upon an application for a mandamus, the court above observed, that though in extreme cases it might interfere, and control inferior courts upon questions of fact, presented in the form of a motion for a new trial, yet it is a remedy which should be used very sparingly. A contrary course would draw before the court an examination of those questions which address themselves merely to the discretion of the inferior court. It would be perpetually appealed to for the adjustment of rights undefined by law. This would result in an endless conflict of opinion upon questions, which must from their very nature be finally determined by the court below, because they cannot be reached by the rules of law; and although the superior court may think the inferior court erred, yet it will not interfere. The writ was therefore refused.

In the case of *The People* v. *The Superior court of the City of New York*, before cited, it was also held that where the evidence is all upon one side, and clear and satisfactory it ceases to be a matter of discretion; that there is no room for difference of opinion; and it would be an abuse, not an exercise of discretion, to refuse a new trial, and a court above might, and ought to interfere. It was also maintained that if an inferior court should deny to a party the benefit of an established general rule of practice, not depending at all upon circumstances, the court above should interfere, and compel the inferior court to conform to such rule.

The decision in this case, so far as relates to the power of a superior court to control inferior courts in granting or refusing new trials, was somewhat shaken in the subsequent cases of *The Judges of the Oneida Common Pleas* v. *The People*, 18 *Wend.*, 79, and *The People* v. *The Judges of Dutchess Common Pleas*, 20 *Wend.*, 658, in which cases the former decision was reviewed and condemned, as going beyond the correct rule.

The proposition maintained in those cases is, that the office of a mandamus is merely to put an inferior court, magistrate, or ministerial officer in motion; but that when discretionary, or judicial powers have been exercised upon a matter within the jurisdiction of the inferior court or magistrate, although in making the decision the tribunal has mistaken either the law or the fact, or both, and whether there be a remedy by writ of error, certiorari, &c., or not, the superior court cannot compel a change of determination by mandamus.

The case of *The People* v. *The Judges of Dutchess Common Pleas* was heard on motion for a peremptory mandamus, on return to an alternative writ, requiring the judges of the court of Common Pleas to vacate a rule quashing an appeal. And although it was held that the Common Pleas erred in ordering the appeal to be quashed, yet a peremptory writ was denied, on the ground that the court did not possess the power to review judicial errors of any kind, by mandamus.

But where, on a demurrer to a declaration for the cause that the caption of the declaration was of a day anterior to the occurring of the cause of action, a court of Common Pleas gave judgment for the plaintiff, and also allowed him to amend his declaration so as to cure the defect, and at the same time refused leave to the defendant to plead to the amended declaration, a mandamus was awarded, directing the Common Pleas either to vacate so much of their order as gave the plaintiff leave to amend, or so much thereof as refused the defendant leave to plead. (*The People* v. *The New York Common Pleas*, 18 *Wend.*, 534.)

And where a motion to set aside the report of a referee is denied, the party who thinks himself aggrieved may, according to the practice in some States, have a review by writ of error, as to all questions of law involved in the decision, but not as to questions of fact. The decision of the court of original jurisdiction upon questions of fact is just as final and conclusive when a motion is made to set aside a report of referees, as it is on a motion to set aside the verdict of a jury. And where a rehearing has been denied, if the party wishes to bring error, a case, or statement of the facts, must be prepared and inserted in the judgment record; and a mandamus will lie to an inferior court compelling it to make a statement of facts, and say what conclusions of fact the referees were warranted in drawing from the evidence.

But a superior court cannot, by mandamus, undertake to control the court as to what particular facts the case shall contain. (*The People* v. *The Justices of the*, *&c.*, 20 *Wend.*, 663.)

A mandamus will not be granted to a court acting under a special commission which has expired by its own limitation, previous to the motion for the writ. (*The People* v. *The Monroe Oyer and Terminer*, 20 *Wend.*, 108.)

And in the case of *ex-parte Ostrander*, 1 *Denio*, 679, it was held that where an inferior court erroneously dismisses an appeal, the error cannot be corrected by mandamus, although the party has no other legal remedy.

In the case of *ex-parte Koon et al.*, 1 *Denio*, 644, it was also held that a mandamus will not lie to compel a judicial tribunal to set aside a decision which it has made. That was where a cause had been heard before referees, who reported for the plaintiff for a certain sum, who declined to receive it, and about thirteen months afterwards died. After the death of the plaintiff, the defendant made application to the court of Common Pleas to grant a rule to the effect that the representatives of the deceased plaintiff might file a record, and perfect judgment on the report, and upon their default therein, that the defendant might, within two terms after the plaintiff's death, perfect such judgment *nunc pro tunc*, which was granted.

A motion was then made, on behalf of the executors of Koon, the deceased plaintiff, for a mandamus to compel the Common Pleas to discharge the rule. BEARDSLEY, J., said: "After such great delay, for which no excuse appears, this court would have denied the application made in the court of Common Pleas, as altogether out of time, and that without looking at the question of power to aid the party applying, or entering at all into the merits of the particular application. But we disclaim all right to control the decision of the court of Common Pleas, in a case like this, by a writ of mandamus. If that court has authority, at this late day, to perfect a judgment, as the rule assumes, it will do so according to its own rules and practice, and to its own sense of propriety and justice; and if, on the other hand, it has no such power, the aggrieved party will be entitled to redress by writ of error, or other appropriate remedy. That court has passed upon the question before it, and the result of which complaint is now made, is a judicial determination. If that is erroneous, it is a judicial error, which cannot be corrected by writ of mandamus. The writ is appropriate to compel subordinate courts to proceed and determine cases pending before them. It also lies to correct many errors of ministerial officers, and even those of courts when in the exercise of mere ministerial functions. But in no case does it lie to compel a judicial tribunal to render any particular judgment, or to set aside a decision already made."

And where, by statute, it is made unlawful for persons other than Indians to settle on certain lands, and it is still further required that any judge of the court of Common Pleas, on complaint made to him, and on due proof of the fact of such settlement, to issue his warrant to the sheriff, requiring him to remove the intruders, and upon the hearing of such complaint by a judge of the court of Common Pleas, the judge refuses to issue his warrant, his decision upon the matter is final and conclusive, so far as concerns the remedy by mandamus. (*The People* v. *Tracy*, 1 *Denio's Rep.*, 617.)

This remedy has been employed to compel a court of inferior jurisdiction to admit or restore an attorney; but it is doubtful whether it can properly be extended to this purpose. There are authorities, however, showing that it has been allowed to restore one to an attorney's place in an inferior court. Because, it was said, his is an office concerning the public justice; and he is compellable to be an attorney for any man; and has a freehold in his place. (*Bacon's Ab.*, *tit. Mandamus.*)

And in the case of *The People* v. *The Justices of Delaware*, 1 *John's Cases*, 181, the Supreme court directed the restoration of an attorney who had been removed from his office, by a court of Common Pleas. But this decision seems to have been made on the ground that as there was an act of the legislature providing that if the court of Common Pleas removed an attorney from office, he could not be admitted to practice in the Supreme court; and, it was said, to allow the Common Pleas to thus disqualify an attorney of that court, would be giving it the power of superintending and controlling the officers of the Supreme court.

A different rule however seems to have been laid down in the case of *The Commonwealth* v. *The Judges of Common Pleas of Cumberland county*, 1 *Serg. & Rawle*, 87.

A mandamus was there refused to compel a court of Common Pleas to proceed to examine a person applying to be admitted as an attorney, notwithstanding the Supreme court was satisfied that he came within the rule of the Common Pleas.

Their refusal was put upon the ground, that the admission of an attorney is not a ministerial, but a judicial act, and therefore not the subject of this writ.

The case of *ex-parte Burr*, 9 *Wheaton's Rep.*, 529, was a motion for a rule to show cause why a mandamus should not issue to the Circuit court for the District of Columbia, commanding that court to restore Burr, an attorney of that court, who had been suspended from practice for one year by order of that court.

Chief Justice MARSHALL, in delivering the opinion of the court, said that the application was a very unusual one, and one upon which the court felt considerable doubts; and without directly deciding the question, declared that the court was not inclined to interpose unless it was in a case where the conduct of the Circuit or District court was irregular, or was flagrantly improper.

Mandamus is also a proper remedy to compel an inferior court to grant the usual legal process to enforce a judgment. Thus, in New Jersey, where a justice of the peace entered a judgment against a defendant, and afterwards made a conditional order that the judgment should be opened upon the payment of costs by the defendant on a certain day, and notwithstanding the defendant neglected to pay the costs on the day prescribed, the justice refused to issue execution after being requested by the plaintiff so to do, a mandamus was granted to compel him to perform this duty. *Terhune* v. *Barcalow*, 6 *Halst.*, 38. *Land.* v. *Abrahams*, 3 *Green.*, 22.)

So where it is the duty of the judge, in allowing an appeal, to take security on the appeal, in the sum decreed; if this is not done the appellant is not entitled to a *supersedeas* of any process necessary to carry the decree into effect; and the court is bound, on application of the plaintiff, to issue such process. If it refuses to do this, the appellate court will issue a peremptory mandamus commanding that the decree be carried into effect. (*Stafford* v. *Union Bank of Louisiana*, 17 *How. U. S. Rep.*, 275. *Stafford* v. *New Orleans Canal and Banking Co.*, 17 *How. U. S. Rep.*, 283.)

And it has also been decided that a mandamus may be issued to the clerk of an inferior court, commanding him to issue an execution. (*The People* v. *Gale*, 22 *Barb.*, 502. *But see* 10 *Cal.*, 333.)

And in Alabama it has been decided that if a judicial officer, before whom a prisoner is brought on *habeas corpus*, improperly refuses to hear and decide on the evidence adduced touching his guilt, mandamus lies to compel a hearing. (*Ex-parte Mahone*, 30 *Ala.*, 49.)

And in the same State it has also been held, that the wife has a right to a support out of her husband's estate, pending a suit for divorce against him, and also to such sum as is necessary to procure solicitors to conduct the suit for her; and when this right is denied by the chancellor, at any time before final alimony is set apart to her, a mandamus will be awarded from the Supreme court, to compel him to make the necessary order, as there is no other adequate and specific remedy. (*Ex-parte King*, 27 *Ala. Rep.*, 387.)

It may also be issued, to an inferior court, directing it to enter judgment on the report of a referee. (*Russell* v. *Elliott*, 2 *Cal. Rep.*, 245.)

But it is said that it is not the proper remedy where an inferior court refuses to enter a judgment for costs, as the party complaining has a right to appeal from such defective judgment, or he may resort to his action for the costs. (*Peralta* v. *Adams*, 2 *Cal. Rep.*, 594. *Ante*, 31.)

And in Illinois, where the declaration in a civil action contained a special count on a note, and the common money counts; a copy of the note was filed in due time, but no bill of particulars under the common counts. The defendant moved a continuance, upon the ground that the declaration had a special count, and the common counts, and there was no account filed with the money counts. The plaintiff entered a cross motion, to file a stipulation that he only sought to recover, on the note, and to proceed to trial. The Circuit court overruled the cross motion, and continued the cause. The Supreme court, on application of the plaintiff, awarded a peremptory writ of mandamus, to compel the circuit judge to grant the plaintiff's cross motion. (*The People* v. *Pearson*, 1 *Scam. Rep.*, 460. *Ib.*, 475.)

And in a suit against the maker and indorser of a promissory note, sued jointly, under a statute authorizing the holder to proceed against several parties to a bill or note in one action, where a general verdict is found for the defendant, if on a motion for a new trial, the court are of opinion that the verdict is wrong as to the maker, but right as to the indorser, they should permit the verdict to stand as to the latter, and allow him to enter judgment thereon in his favor, and grant a new trial only as to the maker; and when, instead of doing so, a court of Common Pleas sets aside the verdict as to both defendants, a Superior court has power to award a mandamus directing the Common Pleas to vacate the order for a new trial, as it regards the indorser, and to proceed and render judgment in his favor. (*The People* v. *The New York Com. Pleas*, 19 *Wend.*, 118.)

And where a change of venue was granted in a capital case, by consent of parties, to another county; and after the case was removed, the State moved the judge of the court of the county to which it was removed to dismiss the cause from the docket for want of jurisdiction, which the court allowed, and remanded the prisoner to the county in which the indictment was found, for the reason that the defendant had not complied with the statute by filing his petition to the Circuit court of the county where the indictment was found, verified by affidavit, for a change of venue; and also because the consent of parties could not give jurisdiction to the Circuit court of the county to which the cause was sought to be removed. The reasons were held to be insufficient, and a peremptory mandamus was awarded, requiring the Circuit court of the county to which the cause was removed to proceed and try the cause. (*The People* v. *Scates*, 3 *Scam.* [*Ill.*] *Rep.*, 351.)

Where a judge of an inferior court has entered upon the hearing of a plaint, and from the evidence adduced before him has decided that he has no jurisdiction to adjudicate between the parties, a mandamus will not lie commanding him to hear and determine it, even although he may be wrong in point of law. This rests upon the principle that where jurisdiction depends upon the existence of certain facts, which must be determined upon by the weight of evidence, the inferior court's decision cannot be reviewed in a mandamus proceeding. But it would be otherwise if, in a case in which the inferior court has jurisdiction, it refuses to hear the cause upon the mistaken notion that it has no jurisdiction to do so in respect of some preliminary matter. (*Milner*, *ex-parte*, 6 *Eng. Law and Equity Rep.*, 371.)

Therefore, in a case where the goods on A's premises having been seized in execution on a judgment against him in a county court, B put in the following claim in respect to them: "I give you notice, that by a certain indenture dated, &c., between A, of the one part, and me of the other part, reciting, &c., A did grant, convey and assign unto me all the household goods, furniture, personal estate and effects whatsoever of him, the said A, then, or at any time thereafter during the continuance of the said security, about his house, brewery and premises, &c., I do hereby claim, all and singular, the goods and chattels mentioned and intended to be assigned by the deed, and which were in the possession of A, upon the execution of the said deed, and which said goods and chattels, or some part thereof, have been seized and taken possession of by you by virtue of a certain writ, &c." On the hearing of the interpleader summons, the County court judge held that the notice and particulars of claim were insufficient, for want of an inventory specifying which of the goods and chattels seized by the bailiff were claimed by B, and consequently refused to adjudicate upon the claim. The court above made, absolute, a rule for a mandamus, calling upon the County court judge to proceed upon the interpleader summons, and to hear and determine upon the claim. (*Regina* v. *Stapylton*, 7 *Eng. Law and Eq. Rep.*, 390.)

And where a cause is improperly stricken from the docket, mandamus is the proper remedy to procure it to be reinstated. (*Ex-parte Low*, 20 *Ala. Rep.*, 330.)

And where a judge of an inferior court captiously refuses to hold a court at a time prescribed by law, and great injury would result therefrom, there being no other adequate specific remedy afforded to the party aggrieved, except a writ of mandamus, such writ should be issued by the Supreme court, if a proper application be made by the aggrieved party, at the proper time. (*Ex-parte Trapnall*, 1 *Eng.* [*Ark.*] *Rep.*, 9.)

But where, by law, it is required that bills of exception shall be taken and tendered to the judge for his signature during the progress of the trial, although he may sign them afterwards *nunc pro tunc;* and a bill of exceptions appeared to have been signed two years after the trial, it was held that they were rightfully stricken from the record by the appellate court, and a mandamus to the judge to sign the bill *nunc pro tunc* was properly refused, especially as it did not appear that the exceptions were taken during the trial. (*Sheppard* v. *Wilson*, 6 *How. U. S. Rep.*, 260.)

So where by law it is made the duty of an inferior court to grant letters of administration to a party entitled thereto, a mandamus will lie from a Superior court to compel it to do so. (8 *East's Rep.*, 407.)

But where by act of the legislature, a special commission is appointed, the duty of which is in its nature judicial, a Superior court will not collaterally review the doings of the commission, and hold as void the final determination made by it in the exercise of its judgment, although its action was strikingly injudicious; the same rule applying as in the case of subordinate courts, special tribunals, and magistrates, that their decisions can be reviewed only by certiorari, or writ of error, if no other mode of appeal is given by the statute creating such court. And where it is made the duty of certain officers to carry out the judgment of such special commission, and they refuse to do so on the ground that their action is highly improper and injudicious, they may be compelled to act, and carry out the judgment of the commission by mandamus, notwithstanding the court issuing the mandamus was satisfied that the special commission had thus acted injudiciously

Therefore, where by law it is made the duty of the county commissioners to lay out and establish highways, and when thus established it became the duty of the commissioners of highways to open and work them, the determination of such commissioners as to the location of a road, is in its nature judicial, and if the commissioners of highways refused to open and work the road, they may be compelled to do so by mandamus. (*The People* v. *Collins et al.*, 19 *Wend.*, 56.)

It has been held that a superior State court will not grant a writ of mandamus to an inferior State court, to compel such inferior court to permit a cause pending there to be removed to a Circuit court of the United States, giving as a reason that the latter court has itself the power to award the writ to the State court, when necessary to gain jurisdiction of the cause. (*The People* v. *The Judges, &c.* 2 *Denio Rep.*, 197.)

The contrary, however, seems to be the better doctrine. And in the case of *The State of Ohio* v. *The Court of Common Pleas of Fairfield County*, 15 *O. S. R.*, 377, this question was presented and distinctly decided. The relator had been sued in the court of Common Pleas of Fairfield county, for the unlawful and malicious assault, arrest and imprisonment of one Edson B. Olds. The relator, on entering his appearance in said court of Common Pleas, filed his petition, under the provisions of the act of Congress, approved March 3d, 1863, entitled "An act relating to *habeas corpus*, and regulating judicial proceedings in certain cases," in which petition he averred that the alleged arrest, imprisonment, &c., was during the rebellion, and was done by virtue of, and under color of authority derived from the Secretary of War, and the President of the United States, and praying that the cause might be removed for trial to the Circuit court of the United States to be held in the southern district of the State of Ohio.

The court of Common Pleas disallowed the prayer for removal, whereupon the relator moved in the Supreme court for a writ of mandamus to compel the court of common pleas "to accept the surety and proceed no further in the case." The allowance of the writ was resisted, among other things, on the grounds that the Federal court, and not the State court, had the power to issue it.

The court says: "It is objected in the second place, that the United States Circuit court, and not this court, is the proper tribunal to issue the writ of mandamus. It is unnecessary to decide whether the Circuit court has that power. If it has, it does not follow that this court has not, or that we should not exercise the power. I know of no good reason, either on grounds of convenience, comity, or State policy, if the jurisdiction is concurrent, as we suppose it is, why it should be refused by the State court, and left to the exclusive action of the Federal court. The power of this court would seem to be undeniable, from the plain reading of the law referred to. The act sought to be compelled is "an act which the law enjoins as a duty resulting from office." True, the law enjoining the act is an act of Congress, and not a statute of Ohio; but it is nevertheless, if constitutional, a law of Ohio. Nay, if there is any conflict, the State law must yield; for, by express constitutional provision, the Constitution of the United States, and laws made in pursuance of it, are the supreme law of the land, any thing in the laws of the State to the contrary notwithstanding. "If then, this law of Congress—or rather the fifth section of the law, which contains all the provisions reflecting upon the case in hand—is constitutional, and if the relator has conformed his case to its provisions, we have no discretion but to allow the writ, or disregard a plain duty enjoined by law." (*But see* 7 *O. S. Rep.*, 451.) Whether a United States court can grant a mandamus to a State court, to compel such State court to permit a cause pending in such State court to be removed to a Circuit court of the United States, when necessary to gain jurisdiction of such cause, is a question which has not yet been authoritatively settled; although from the two decisions last cited, as well as the practice in sundry cases not reported, it would seem that the Circuit court of the United States would, at least, have concurrent jurisdiction with the State courts, to compel such removal. (*Post*, .)

A mandamus will lie to compel the justices and the jury, summoned to assess damages for taking land for public use, to make return of their action in the premises; and if the justices have voluntarily parted with the verdict, they are still bound to recover the possession of it, and complete their duty. (*In the matter of the Trustees of Williamsburgh*, 1 *Barb.*, 34.)

And where it is the duty of referees, appointed by a county judge, to hear and determine an appeal from an order of commissioners of highways, laying out a highway—to proceed to hear the proofs and allegations of the parties, and to make and file their decisions in writing, affirming, reversing, or modifying the order appealed from, they have no power to dismiss the appeal, and refuse to proceed further, upon the ground that the order of the county judge was improvidently, or irregularly granted, or that the appellant had no right to bring an appeal.

And if the referees, instead of hearing and determining the appeal, dismiss the same, upon a preliminary objection, and thus in effect refuse to execute the trust committed to them, the remedy of the party is by mandamus, to compel the referees to proceed. (*The People* v. *Cortelyou et al.*, 36 *Barb.*, 164.)

So, a mandamus may be issued to an inferior court, compelling it to receive, and record a verdict; yet, if the proceedings be so irregular as to make the verdict a mere nullity, it should not be granted. (*Meacham* v. *Austin et al.*, 5 *Day's* [*Conn.*] *Rep.*, 233.)

But, as has before been said, a superior court will never by mandamus interpose to disturb the solemn judgment of an inferior court. Therefore, where it was sought to compel a District judge to issue a warrant to arrest an alleged deserter from the French naval service, under a treaty stipulation, it was the clear and unanimous decision of the court, that the District judge having acted judicially in deciding that the evidence was not sufficient to authorize his issuing a warrant, the Supreme court, however it might differ in opinion from the judge as to the sufficiency of the proof, had no power to compel him to decide according to the dictates of any judgment but his own. (*United States* v. *Lawrence*, 2 *Dallas*, 42.)

And in the case of *ex-parte Hoyt*, 13 *Peters' Rep.*, 279, the District judge for the southern district of New York had decided that the custody of goods, wares and merchandise, proceeded against, after a seizure by the collector of the port of New York, was in the marshal of the district, after process had issued by order of the court against the goods. A motion was made in the Supreme court of the United States for a mandamus to the District judge, to compel him to vacate the order made on this decision. The court held that a mandamus would not lie; Mr. Justice STORY, delivering the opinion of the court, after remarking that the court had authority given to it by statute to issue writs of mandamus in cases warranted by the principles and usages of law, said: "The present application is not warranted by any such principles and usages of law. It is neither more nor less, than an application for an order to review the solemn judgment of the District judge, in a matter clearly within the jurisdiction of the court, and to substitute another judgment in its stead. Now a writ of mandamus is not a proper process to correct an erroneous judgment or decree rendered in an inferior court. That is properly matter which is examinable upon a writ of error, or an appeal, (as the case may require,) to the proper appellate tribunal. Neither can this court issue the writ upon the ground that it is necessary for the exercise of its own appellate jurisdiction; for the proper appellate jurisdiction, if any in this case, is direct and immediate to the Circuit court for the southern district of New York. It has been repeatedly declared by this court, that it will not by mandamus direct a judge what judgment to enter in a suit; but only will require him to proceed to render judgment."

In the case of *ex-parte Whitney*, 13 *Peters' Rep.*, 404, the same doctrine was maintained. In that case, the judge of the District court of the United States for the eastern district of Louisiana, had, among other things, ordered that all the future proceedings in the case, which was then pending in that court, should be in conformity with the then existing practice of the District court, which practice was understood to mean the practice prevailing in the court in civil cases generally, in disregard of the rules established by the Supreme court, to be observed in chancery cases.

A motion was made in the Supreme court for a mandamus in the nature of a procedendo, to compel the court to proceed according to chancery practice.

Mr. Justice Story, in delivering the opinion of the court, said: "That it is the duty of the Circuit court to proceed in this suit according to the rules prescribed by the Supreme court, for proceedings in equity causes at the February term thereof, A. D. 1822, can admit of no doubt. That the proceedings of the District judge, and the orders made by him in the cause, which are complained of, are not in conformity with those rules, and with chancery practice can admit of as little doubt. But the question before us is not as to the regularity and propriety of those proceedings, but whether the case before us is one in which a mandamus ought to issue. And we are of opinion that it is not such a case. The District judge is proceeding in the cause, however irregular that proceeding may be deemed; and the appropriate redress, if any, is to be obtained by an appeal after the final decree shall be had in the case. A writ of mandamus is not the appropriate remedy for any orders which may be made in a cause by a judge in the exercise of his authority; although they may seem to bear harshly or oppressively upon the party. The remedy in such cases must be sought in some other form."

The same principle has been maintained in a number of other cases. (*Rex* v. *Justices of Wilts*, 2 *Chitty's R.*, 257; *The King* v. *The Justices of Cambridgeshire*, 1 *D. & R.*, 325; *Squire* v. *Gale*, 1 *Halst.* [*N. J.*] *Rep.*, 156; *Gray* v. *Budge*, 11 *Pick. Rep.*, 189.)

So, in Massachusetts, in the case of *Chase* v. *Blackstone Canal Co.*, 2 *Pick*, 244, the court say: "This writ lies either to compel the performance of ministerial acts, or is addressed to subordinate judicial tribunals, requiring them to exercise their functions, and render some judgment in cases before them, when otherwise there would be a failure of justice from delay, or refusal to act. But where a subordinate tribunal has acted in a judicial capacity, upon a question properly submitted to its judgment, a mandamus will not be granted to compel it to reverse its decision."

The law makes a distinction between the ministerial and judicial duties of judicial tribunals. In the former case, the particular duty imposed may be compelled; while in the latter case, the judicial officer can only be compelled to proceed and render some judgment. In the case of *Griffith* v. *Cochran*, 5 *Binney*, 103. TILGHAM, C. J., says: "The principles which govern the courts in issuing writs of mandamus, are well understood. Where a ministerial act is to be done, and there is no other specific remedy, a mandamus will be granted to do the act which is required. But where complaints are against a person who acts in a judicial, or deliberative capacity, he may be ordered by mandamus to proceed to do his duty, by deciding and acting according to the best of his judgment; but the court will not direct him in what manner to proceed. In New Jersey the same distinction was recognized.

In *Leving* v. *Inhabitants of Alloway's Creek*, 5 *Hals.*, 58, a mandamus was refused on the ground that "to officers a writ of mandamus may go to direct them how to proceed, and what to do; but a mandamus to a court, only to direct them to proceed according to law, and not how to proceed."

So, in Kentucky, in the case of *The County court of Warren* v. *Daniel*, 2 *Bibb.*, 573, it was decided that a mandamus is a proper remedy to compel an inferior court to adjudicate upon a subject within its jurisdiction where it neglects or refuses to do so; but where it has adjudicated, a mandamus will not lie for the purpose of reviewing, or correcting its decision. And where a ministerial duty devolves upon a judicial tribunal, and such tribunal construes it to be a judicial duty, and proceeds to act judicially in the matter, and gives judgment against the party moving such performance. and refuses to perform the duty, a mandamus lies to compel the performance. (*Delaney* v. *Goddin*, 12 *Gratt.*, [*Va.*] 266.)

Therefore, when it is made the duty of a circuit judge to appoint appraisers to assess damages under a statute relative to rights of way, such appointment is a ministerial act, the performance of which may be enforced by mandamus. (*Illinois Central Railway Company*, 14 *Ill. Rep.*, 353.)

So in the case of *Arberry* v. *Bearers*, 6 *Texas*, 457, it was also maintained that the process of mandamus lies to compel public officers and courts of inferior jurisdiction to proceed to do those acts which clearly appertain to their duty. If the act be ministerial in its character, obedience to the law will be enforced by mandamus, where no other legal remedy exists. But if the act to be performed involves the exercise of judgment or discretion, the Superior court cannot interfere to control or govern that judgment.

And therefore, where a statute required the Chief Justice of a certain county to order an election for a certain purpose, and directed that the election should be held, and the returns made in accordance with the laws of the State regulating elections, it was held that the Chief Justice, in receiving and estimating the returns, did not act in a merely ministerial capacity; and that a mandamus would not lie to compel him to receive and estimate certain returns which he had rejected.

So where by statute it was provided "that there shall be erected, built, or otherwise provided by the court of General Sessions of the Peace in every county within this commonwealth, at the charge of the county, a fit and convenient house or houses of correction, &c.," it was held that the duty was imperative and mandatory, and that there was no discretion given to the Sessions upon the subject, except that they be allowed a reasonable time to execute the duty; and as it appeared that more than twelve years had elapsed, a mandamus was granted compelling them to do their duty. (*Commonwealth* v. *The Justices of Hampden*, 2 *Pick. Rep.*, 414.)

So in the case of *Ruel Morse, Petitioner*, 18 *Pick. Rep.*, 443, the petitioner, being seized of certain land, over and through which a certain railroad was laid out and constructed, applied to the county commissioners to assess the damages sustained by him thereby. The commissioners reported that the company should construct and keep in repair a certain culvert, and pay to the petitioner $500. The petitioner considering the sum so assessed less than the amount he was entitled to receive, made application to the commissioners for a jury to assess damages. A jury was accordingly impanelled, who assessed the damages at $600, which verdict was duly returned to the court of Common Pleas and accepted by that court. The verdict and adjudication of that court were certified to the commissioners, and it was thereupon considered by them that the petitioner should recover of the railroad company the said sum of $600, without costs, on the ground that the amount assessed by the jury was not greater than the amount assessed by the commissioners. Thereupon the petitioner presented his petition to the Supreme court, praying for a rule on the commissioners to show cause why a writ of mandamus should not issue, commanding them to render judgment in the premises for the petitioner for the sum of $600, and for his costs. The court held that the awarding, or refusing costs was a judicial power for the commissioners to exercise according to their judgment of the merits; and also recognized the rule that a judicial tribunal may exercise ministerial functions, and in all such cases a mandamus will be granted when there is no other proper and adequate remedy. The court said: "Cases may be supposed in which such a remedy," (meaning mandamus to a judicial tribunal,) "would be proper and warranted by analogy. Some instances are mentioned in the case cited, as where a judicial tribunal declines taking cognizance of a case within its proper jurisdiction. So if a court having rendered a proper judgment, should refuse issuing an execution. And so where a judicial tribunal, having found all the facts necessary to a judgment, so that the judgment would be nothing but a conclusion of law upon those facts, the entering up of the proper judgment may be regarded as in its nature ministerial, and in the absence of any other remedy may be a proper subject for a mandamus."

And where, by legislative enactment, it was provided that the sufficiency of the affidavit to hold to bail, and the amount of bail to be given, should, upon application of the defendant, be decided by the court in term time, and by a single judge in vacation, the power of the court of thus deciding was held to be a judicial power; and when it has been exercised and a judgment passed, a Superior court cannot by mandamus command such inferior court to reverse its decision. (*Ex-parte Tayler*, 14 *How.* (*U. S.*) *Rep.*, 3.)

But where, by law, it was the duty of the county commissioners to adjudge on the question of damages, and if they found that the petitioner had sustained no damage, and he was dissatisfied and requested it, to issue a warrant for a jury to enable the petitioner to have their judgment revised in a due course of law, it was held that the issuing of the warrant, on the application of the petitioner, was a ministerial duty, and therefore a duty the commissioners could be compelled to perform by mandamus. (*Carpenter* v. *County Commissioners*, 21 *Pick.*, 287.)

And where a complaint was made before justices against one for keeping an illegal lottery, and it was alleged that the facts proved brought him within the statute, and rendered him liable to be punished as a rogue and vagabond; but the magistrate thought, erroneously as it was suggested, that the provision as to such punishment was repealed, and that no punishment then existed for the offense, it was held that however erroneous the decision of the magistrate might be, the court above could not review it on mandamus. (*Regina* v. *The Justices of Bristol*, 28 *Eng. Law & Eq. Rep.*, 160.)

In general every court must be the sole judge whether a contempt has been committed against it or not; and this exercise of its judgment is not liable to be controlled by the interposition of the writ of mandamus.

But if the civil rights of an individual become implicated, this remedy may be pursued. Therefore upon a motion for a mandamus to the justices of the general sessions of the peace of the county of Oneida, commanding them to attach and punish John Garter for non-attendance in that court as a witness; Chamberlain had been indicted for an assault and battery, which was tried at the February term of that court, 1825; he subpœnaed Garter to attend as a witness in his behalf; he neglected to appear and was attached; but was discharged by the court upon his answering to the interrogatories that no fees had been tendered to him. The court in which the motion for a mandamus was made, said they had looked into this subject and thought the distinction lay between misdemeanor and felony; that in the former case the defendant must tender his witnesses their fees, as in civil cases; but that in prosecutions for felonies they were compelled to attend without fees. They should have denied this motion at once, on the ground that it sought for a mandamus to compel an inferior court to punish for a contempt, had the matter rested there; for every court must be the sole judge whether a contempt has been committed against it or not; but as the private rights of an individual were also implicated, they had for that reason looked into the merits. (*Ex-parte Chamberlain*, 4 *Cowen*, 49.) And a Superior court will not grant a mandamus commanding the judges of an inferior court to do an act which may render them liable to an action; and under this principle a writ was refused to compel a magistrate to enforce a conviction when it was doubtful whether such conviction was good in consequence of the evidence not having been stated. (*Rex* v. *Broderip*, 5 *B. & C.*, 239, 7 *D. & R.*, 861.) Nor will it be granted when it may make costs for which there are no means provided for reimbursement. (*In re Lodge*, 2 *A. & E.*, 123.) Neither will a mandamus be granted to compel a magistrate to enforce a conviction for the plaintiff, where he had returned that the defendant was convicted of the penalty before him, and that the conviction was invalid in law. (*Rex* v. *Robinson*, 2 *Smith*, 274.)

Where a discretion is vested in any inferior court, and such court has exercised it, a Superior court cannot control such discretion by writ of mandamus. The writ when directed to an inferior tribunal, is a writ which seeks to compel action; it does not, however, point out to that court how it shall act in a matter over which it has a discretionary power. (*Lamar* v. *Marshall*, 21 *Ala.*, 772.)

A mandamus was therefore refused when asked for to be directed to an inferior court to compel it to discharge a rule of reference, as that was in the discretion of the inferior court. (*Ferris* v. *Munn*, 2 *New Jer.*, 161.)

So where an information was filed by the District Attorney, on behalf of the United States, against certain cases of cloth, seized as forfeited to the United States, upon the ground that the invoices under which the same were imported, were made by a false valuation, extension, or otherwise, to defraud the United States, and on an inquest by default in the cause, the cloths were condemned as forfeited to the United States; and where upon the refusal of the District court to set aside the default, a motion for a mandamus was made in the Supreme court, it was held that the application to set aside the default and inquest, was an application to the discretion of the District court, and therefore a mandamus would not lie to control the discretion of the court. (*Ex-parte Roberts* v. *Adshead*, 6 *Peters' Rep.*, 216.)

So where a motion was made for a mandamus to the judge of the District court of the United States, for the southern district of New York, "commanding him to restore to the record of the cause the plea of tender, filed in the cause by the defendant, and to proceed to trial, and judge thereupon according to law; and to vacate all rules and orders entered in the said court setting aside such plea as a nullity. The court held that the allowance of double pleas and defenses is a matter not of absolute right, but of discretion in the court, and as the courts constantly exercise a control over this privilege, and will disallow incompatible and sham pleas, no mandamus will lie to the court for the exercise of its authority in such cases, it being a matter of sound discretion, exclusively appertaining to its own practice. And as the record in the case furnished no positive means of information that the court did not order the plea to be struck from the record on that ground, the mandamus was refused.

If, however, the record should show that a good plea had been ordered to be struck off for the reason that it was held to be a nullity, whether mandamus would lie was a question not decided; but it was strongly intimated that it would. (*Ex-parte Davenport*, 6 *Peters' Rep.*, 661.)

So in the case of *Gray* v. *Bridge*, 11 *Pick. Rep.*, 189, where the court below had granted a new trial on the ground of certain newly discovered evidence, which evidence, it was contended, on the part of the petitioner, was not competent evidence, and for that reason prayed for a writ of mandamus to the court below to vacate the rule granting a new trial; WILDE, J., in delivering the opinion of the court said: "But in deciding this case, it is not necessary to consider the question as to the competency of the evidence, because we think it very clear that the court of Common Pleas had a discretionary power to grant a new trial if the justice of the case, in their opinion required it, and we ought not to attempt to control or coerce the discretion of the court. That the granting a new trial, like the granting a continuance, or taking of a default, rests in the discretion of the court, is fully established by all the authorities."

So in the case of *ex-parte Baily*, 2 *Cowen*, 479, a motion was made for a mandamus to the judges of the court of Common Pleas, commanding them to grant a new trial in a cause in that court between Baily, plaintiff, and one Stocker, defendant. The court, in deciding the case, said: "As to the remedy by mandamus, it may be proper to remark, that though in extreme cases we might interfere and control the court below upon questions of fact, presented in the form of a motion for a new trial, yet it is a remedy which should be used very sparingly. A contrary course would draw before this court, whenever one of the parties should be dissatisfied with the decision of the Common Pleas, an examination of those questions which address themselves merely to the discretion of that court. We should be perpetually appealed to for the adjustment of rights undefined by law. This would result in an endless conflict of opinion upon questions which must, from their very nature, be finally determined by the courts below, because they cannot be reached by the rules of law; and although we may think the inferior jurisdiction has erred, yet we will not interfere. It is true, that extreme cases may be supposed, which would form an exception to this doctrine. Where an action is brought on a promissory note, the execution of which is proved beyond all doubt, and yet the jury find against it, should the court below refuse a new trial, we might interfere; but it would be improper to do this in ordinary cases. Even where a verdict is plainly against law, yet the court may, many times, properly deny a new trial; as if the controversy be very trifling in its nature, or contemptible in amount."

The case of *ex-parte Caykendoll*, 6 *Cowen Rep.*, 52, seems to be one of those extreme cases which are exceptions to the general rule. In that case the court of Common Pleas had granted a new trial on the affidavit of three of the jurors, setting forth that they had made a mistake in their calculations in determining the amount of their verdict. A motion was thereupon made in the Supreme court for a mandamus to the judges of the Common Pleas commanding them to vacate the rule granting a new trial, and to give judgment on the verdict. The mandamus was granted on the ground that the judges of the court of Common Pleas erred in receiving the affidavits of jurors for the purpose of impeaching their verdict.

The setting aside of a judgment by default, is also a matter within the discretion of the court in which the judgment is rendered, and will not be disturbed by a proceeding in mandamus.

In *ex-parte Bacon & Lyon*, 6 *Cowen Rep.*, 392, the court of Common Pleas had set aside a regular judgment by default, against the defendant, in a cause in which the relators were plaintiffs, on the ground of merits, on payment of costs. A motion was thereupon made in the Supreme court for a mandamus, commanding the Common Pleas to vacate that rule.

The court say: "The Common Pleas must be their own judges, upon the circumstances before them, whether they will set aside a default upon the merits. This is so much a matter of discretion that we will not interfere by mandamus. The granting or refusal of such an application is governed by no fixed principles. No positive rule of law has been violated by the court below; nor can we fix bounds to their discretion upon this subject."

So in the case of *ex-parte Benson*, 7 *Cowen*, 363, which was on a motion for a mandamus to the judges of the court of Common Pleas, commanding them to set aside a rule to quash an appeal, taken by default against the relator, on motion of Brace and others, appellees. The motion was noticed for December term of the Common Pleas, 1826; and the hearing postponed to the next term, March, 1827. At this term, the relator's attorney was in Albany attending the Supreme court; and the postponement entirely escaped his recollection. On these facts, he moved the Common Pleas to vacate the rule, and hear the motion on its merits; but the motion was overruled.

The court, in giving its decision upon the motion, say: "Whether the Common Pleas would open the rule or not, upon the facts disclosed, rested entirely in their discretion; with which we have nothing to do. The question is not, whether we would have listened to the application, in a like case upon our rules of practice. The court below have their own rules; and so far as they rest in discretion and violate no rule of law, we uniformly refuse to interfere with them."

Mandamus does not lie from a superior court to correct the errors of an inferior court, if such errors can be redressed on appeal, or on proceeding in error. In the case of *The Bank of Columbia* v. *Sweeny*, 1 *Peters' Rep.*, 569, an application for a mandamus was made, to compel a Circuit court to withdraw an issue ordered by it to be made, and to direct a different issue to be made up, according to what the counsel for the relator supposed to be the proper construction of the statute. The motion was denied on the ground that the case did not differ in principle from any other case in which the party should plead a defective plea, and the plaintiff should demur to it; in which case it was said there was no doubt that the revising power of the court could be exercised only by a writ of error. The same principle has been applied in many other cases. (*Blecker* v. *St. Louis Law Commissioners*, 30 *Miss.*, 111. *State* v. *Judge of the Sixth District court of New Orleans*, 12 *La. An.*, 342. *Dunklin county* v. *District court*, 23 *Miss.*, 449. *State* v. *Judge of Kenosha county*, 3 *Wis.*, 809. *Ex-parte Williamson*, 3 *Eng.* [*Ark.*] 424. *State* v. *Mitchell*, *Const. Rep.*, 703. *Smyth* v. *Titcomb*, 31 *Maine*, 272.)

And a mandamus will not be granted to command an inferior tribunal to do that which it could not legally do without such mandate. (*The State* v. *The Judge*, 15 *Ala. Rep.*, 740.)

Neither will it lie to compel any officer to do an act which, without its command, it would not be lawful for him to do. (*Johnson* v. *Lucas*, 11 *Humph.*, 306.)

Nor will it be allowed, where, if granted, it would be unavailing to accomplish the object sought.

CHAPTER IV.

MANDAMUS TO SHERIFF.

The general rule, that a public officer can be compelled, by mandamus, to perform a duty enjoined by law, is applicable to the office of sheriff.

Therefore, where by law it is made the duty of the sheriff to keep his office at the county seat, mandamus is a proper remedy to compel him to do so. (*State* v. *Saxton*, 11 *Wis.*, 27.)

So, too, it has been held that mandamus lies where it is the only means of putting the plaintiff in possession of property which he is entitled to possess under a decree; and that although he has a civil action against the sheriff, or a criminal prosecution against him if he refuses to execute the writ, yet mandamus lies to compel the sheriff to execute it. (*Fremont* v. *Crippen*, 10 *Cal. Rep.*, 211.)

And where a writ of attachment was placed in the hands of a sheriff, who served it by taking the property into his possession and leaving a copy with the defendant; and while this writ was in the hands of the officer unreturned, the plaintiff in the action discovered that his claim, which was the subject of the suit, was not due, and directed the sheriff to erase his indorsement of service on the writ, and with that writ, without other alteration, attach the same property after the claim had become due, which the sheriff accordingly did, it was held that if the rights of the defendant in attachment had been essentially affected by the act of the officer, in erasing his first indorsement of service, he might be compelled to restore it, by writ of mandamus, so that the whole of his proceedings under the writ of attachment should appear upon the writ itself. (*Ward* v. *Curtiss*, 18 *Conn.*, 290.)

So, when a jailer refuses to deliver up the body of a person who has died while a prisoner in his custody, to the executor of the deceased, a mandamus has been held to lie, to compel him to do so. (*Reg.* v. *Fox*, 2 *Ad. & E., N. S.*, 247.)

But it must also be borne in mind, that to entitle a party to a writ of mandamus, it must be made to appear that he has a legal right to have something done by the party to whom he seeks to have the writ directed, and that he has no specific legal remedy, to which he can resort to compel the performance of this duty. And that, therefore, although the law may impose a duty upon the sheriff, which he neglects or refuses to perform, yet if the party applying for the writ has any other adequate means of redress, the writ will not be allowed. And, in the case of *The State* v. *Lawson*, 14 *Ark. Rep.*, it is left in doubt whether a writ of mandamus is the appropriate remedy to compel a sheriff to acknowledge a deed to the purchaser of lands at a judicial sale.

In the case of *The People* v. *Ransom*, 2 *Comstock*, 490, it was however substantially held, that mandamus would lie to compel a sheriff to execute a deed of conveyance to a purchaser of lands on execution. But in such case, as the alternative writ is in the nature of a declaration, it should set forth a good and substantial right to have the title. A like doctrine was maintained in *Van Rensselaer* v. *Sheriff*, 1 *Cowen's Rep.*, 501.

If a summons, or execution is placed in the hands of a sheriff to be served, and he neglects or refuses to serve it, the party in whose favor it was issued has a remedy by action against the sheriff, and therefore as an ordinary rule, a writ of mandamus would not lie to compel him to serve them. There may, however, be cases, where such remedy by action would be inadequate, in which case no doubt a mandamus would lie to compel the sheriff to perform his duty.

CHAPTER V.

MANDAMUS TO CLERK OF COURT.

Mandamus is the appropriate remedy to compel the clerk of a court to perform a ministerial duty imposed upon him by law, in all those cases, where the relator, whose rights are injuriously affected by the non-performance of the duty, has no other specific and adequate remedy.

It has therefore been held that the writ will lie to compel a clerk of the court to deliver the transcript on a writ of error, or appeal, if he illegally refuses to do so. (*Davis* v. *Carter*, 18 *Texas*, 400.)

But it will in no case be allowed against the clerk, unless it is clearly the legal duty of such officer to perform the act, and the party asking it has a clear right to its performance, and has no other adequate and specific remedy. (*Draper* v. *Noteware*, 7 *Cal. Rep.*, 276. *Williams* v. *Judge of Cooper county*, 27 *Miss.* [6 *Jones*] *Rep.*, 225. *State* v. *Jacobs*, 2 *Dutch.*, [*N. J.*] 135. *Morgan* v. *Monmouth, Plankroad Co.*, 2 *Dutch.*, [*N. J.*] 99. *Commonwealth* v. *Supervisors of Colley Township*, 29 *Penn. State Rep.*, 121.)

Neither can the discretionary powers of the clerk be controlled by mandamus. But where, among the official duties of a clerk, is that of approving and filing the bond of a sheriff, or other officer, he has no discretion other than to determine whether the security offered is sufficient; in all other respects, he acts in the matter as a mere ministerial officer. And if he withholds his approval of the bond, on any other grounds than the insufficiency of the security, he may be compelled by mandamus to approve and file the bond. But should his refusal rest on the ground of such insufficiency, his discretion in the matter cannot, in that manner, be controlled. (14 *Ind. Rep.*, 93.)

But where the party has another adequate and specific remedy against the clerk, mandamus will not lie. It has therefore been held, that if the clerk of the court refuse to issue execution on a money judgment, the plaintiff has a perfect remedy on the clerk's bond, and therefore cannot have a writ of mandamus. (10 *Cal. Rep.*, 333. *But see* 22 *Barb.*, 502.)

And where the election laws of a State direct the clerk of the court of Common Pleas, with two justices of the peace called to his assistance, to open and make abstracts of the several returns which shall have been made to his office, and also providing that in making such abstracts of votes, the justices and clerk shall not decide on the validity of the returns, but shall be governed by the number of votes stated in the poll-books; and the clerk and justices thus opening the returns, rejected, in good faith, a part of said returns, as illegal, and refused to incorporate them into the abstract exhibiting the result of the election, and thereupon declared one M. duly elected sheriff of said county, in conformity with the result of the abstract thus made, and gave him a certificate of election, where, if the votes rejected had been counted, the election for sheriff would have resulted in favor of I.; and he thereupon appealed to the court of Common Pleas to contest the election of M., and also caused an alternative writ of mandamus to issue out of the Supreme court, commanding the said clerk to immediately call to his assistance two justices of the peace of the county, to open and count the votes thus rejected, and deliver to him a proper certificate of his election to said office of sheriff, or to show cause why he refuses to do so; it was held by the court on hearing, that as the legislature had provided by statute that the correction of all errors, frauds and mistakes which might occur in the process of ascertaining and declaring the true expression of the public will, should be by appeal to the court of Common Pleas; and that the necessary steps for such appeal had already been taken, mandamus was not an appropriate remedy, and the peremptory writ was refused. One of the reasons given by the court for the refusal of the writ, was that the legislature had provided a plain and adequate remedy, and doubtless intended it as the specific and sole remedy, for errors in the counting and abstracting of the votes returned. (*Ingerson* v. *Berry*, 14 *O. S. R.*, 316.)

CHAPTER VI.

MANDAMUS TO THE SECRETARY OF STATE.

Where the heads of departments are the political or confidential agents of the executive, merely to execute the will of the President in cases where the executive possesses a constitutional or legal discretion, nothing can be more perfectly clear than that their acts are only politically examinable. But where a specific ministerial duty is assigned by law, and individual rights depend upon the performance of that duty, it seems equally clear that the individual who considers himself injured, has a right to resort to the laws of his country for a remedy, and that mandamus is a proper remedy.

Therefore, on motion for a mandamus, supported by affidavits showing that the applicant was, by the President of the United States, nominated to the Senate for their advice and consent to be appointed a justice of the peace of the District of Columbia; that the Senate advised and consented to the appointment; that a commission in due form was signed by the said President, appointing him a justice of the peace as aforesaid, and that the seal of the United States was in due form affixed to the said commission by the Secretary of State, that the applicant had requested the defendant, Secretary of State, to deliver said commission to him, who had not complied with such request, but had withheld the same, it was held that it was a plain case for a mandamus, either to deliver the commission, or a copy of it from the records. (*Marbury* v. *Madison*, 1 *Cranch's Rep.*, 137.)

And so where, by act of Congress authorizing the sale of public lands, it is provided that the purchaser, on paying his purchase money, becomes completely entitled to the property purchased; and on producing to the Secretary of State the receipt of the treasurer, upon a certificate required by the law, the President of the United States is authorized to grant him a patent; and it is further enacted that all patents shall be countersigned by the Secretary of State, and recorded in his office; if the Secretary of State should choose to withhold this patent, or the patent being lost, should refuse a copy of it, mandamus, no doubt, would lie to compel him to do it.

It was also held, in the same case, that "It is not by the office of the person to whom the writ is directed, but the nature of the thing to be done, that the propriety or impropriety of issuing a mandamus is to be determined. Where the head of a department acts in a case in which executive discretion is to be exercised, in which he is the mere organ of executive will, it is again repeated that any application to a court to control, in any respect, his conduct, would be rejected without hesitation. But where he is directed, by law, to do a certain act affecting the absolute rights of individuals, in the performance of which he is not placed under the particular direction of the President, and the performance of which the President cannot lawfully forbid, and therefore is never presumed to have forbidden; as for example, to record a commission, or a patent for land, which has received all the legal solemnities; or to give a copy of such record; in such cases, it is not perceived on what ground the courts of the country are further excused from the duty of giving judgment, that right be done to an injured individual, than if the same services were to be performed by a person not the head of a department."

The doctrine that mandamus lies, on the application of a private individual, and for his benefit, to compel the head of a department to perform a mere ministerial duty, where that duty is plain, seems to have been fully maintained in the case of *The Commissioners of Land Office* v. *Smith*, 5 *Texas*, 471.

CHAPTER VII.

MANDAMUS TO THE SECRETARY OF WAR AND NAVY.

The Secretary of War may also be compelled by mandamus to perform a ministerial act.

Therefore, where by law it is provided that the Secretary of War shall place on the pension list all persons whose names are contained in a report previously made by him to Congress, if he should refuse to do so, mandamus would lie.

But a distinction is made between the ministerial acts of one of the heads of department, and those duties required in the ordinary discharge of official duties, over which the officer is required to exercise judgment and discretion. While the former can be compelled by mandamus, the latter cannot.

Therefore, where by an act of Congress, passed on the 3d of March, 1837, the widow of any officer who died in the naval service, became entitled to receive out of the navy pension fund half the monthly pay to which the deceased officer would have been entitled, under the acts regulating the pay of the navy, in force on the 1st day of January, 1835;

the half pay to commence from the time of the death of such officer; and upon the death or intermarriage of such widow, to go to the child or children of the officer. And on the same day a resolution was passed by Congress, providing: That Mrs. Susan Decatur, widow of the late Commodore Stephen Decatur, be paid from the navy pension fund, a pension for five years, commencing from the thirtieth day of June, eighteen hundred and thirty-four, in conformity with the provisions of the act concerning naval pensions, and the navy pension fund, passed the thirtieth of June, eighteen hundred and thirty-four; and that she be allowed, from said fund, the arrearages of the half pay of a post captain, from the death of Commodore Decatur, to the thirtieth of June, eighteen hundred and thirty-four, together with the pension hereby allowed her; and that the arrearage of said pension be vested in the Secretary of the Treasury, in trust for the use of the said Susan Decatur; provided that the said pension shall cease on the death or marriage of the said Susan Decatur.

By the act of Congress of July 10th, 1832, the Secretary of the Navy is constituted the trustee of the navy pension fund; and as such, it was made his duty to grant and pay the pensions, according to the terms of the acts of Congress.

After the passage of the law and resolution of March 3d, 1837, Mrs. Susan Decatur, the widow of Commodore Decatur, applied to Mahlon Dickerson, then Secretary of the Navy, to be allowed the half pay to which she was entitled under the general law above mentioned; and also the pension and arrearages of half pay specially provided for her by the resolution passed on the same day.

The Secretary of the Navy doubted whether she was entitled to both, and referred the matter to the Attorney General; who gave it as his opinion that Mrs. Decatur was not entitled to both, but that she might take under either, at her election. The Secretary thereupon informed her of the opinion of the

Attorney General, offering at the same time to pay her under the law, or the resolution, as she might prefer. She elected to receive under the law; but it was admitted that she did not acquiesce in this decision, but protested against it; and by consenting to receive the amount paid her, she did not mean to waive any right she might have to the residue.

Sometime afterwards Mr. Dickerson retired from the office of Secretary of the Navy, and was succeeded by the defendant; and, in the fall of 1838, Mrs. Decatur applied to him to revise the decision of his predecessor, and to allow her the pension provided by the resolution. The Secretary declined doing so; whereupon Mrs. Decatur applied to the Circuit court for Washington county, in the District of Columbia, for a mandamus to compel him to pay the amount she supposed to be due to her. A rule to show cause was granted by the court; and upon a return made by him, stating among other things the facts above mentioned, the court refused the application for a peremptory mandamus. This decision the Supreme court was called upon to reverse; and in deciding the case, the court says: "In the case of *Kendall* v. *The United States*, 12 *Peters*, 524, it was decided in this court, that the Circuit court for Washington county in the District of Columbia, has the power to issue a mandamus to an officer of the federal government commanding him to do a ministerial act. The first question, therefore, to be considered in this case is, whether the duty imposed upon the Secretary of the Navy, by the resolution in favor of Mrs. Decatur, was a mere ministerial act.

"The duty required by the resolution was to be performed by him as the head of one of the executive departments of the government, in the ordinary discharge of his official duties. In general, such duties, whether imposed by act of Congress or by resolution, are not mere ministerial duties.

"The head of an executive department of the government, in the administration of the various and important concerns of his office, is continually required to exercise judgment and discretion. He must exercise his judgment, in expounding the laws and resolutions of Congress. under which he is from time to time required to act. If he doubts, he has a right to call on the Attorney General to assist him with his counsel; and it would be difficult to imagine why a legal adviser was provided by law for the heads of departments, as well as for the President, unless their duties were regarded as executive, in which judgment and discretion were to be exercised. If a suit should come before the court, which involved the con struction of any of these laws, the court certainly would not be bound to adopt the construction given by the head of a department. And if they supposed his decision to be wrong, they would, of course, so pronounce their judgment. But their judgment upon the construction of a law must be given in a case in which they have jurisdiction and in which it is their duty to interpret the act of Congress, in order to ascertain the rights of the parties in the cause before them. The court could not entertain an appeal from the decision of one of the Secretaries, nor revise his judgment in any case where the law authorized him to exercise discretion or judgment. Nor can it by mandamus, act directly upon the officer, and guide and control his judgment or discretion in the matters committed to his care in the ordinary discharge of his official duties.

"The case before us illustrates these principles, and shows the difference between executive duties and ministerial acts. The claim of Mrs. Decatur having been acted upon by his predecessor in office, the Secretary was obliged to determine whether it was proper to revise that decision. If he had determined to revise it, he must have exercised his judgment upon the construction of the law, and the resolution, and have made up his mind whether she was entitled under one only, or under both. And if he determined that she was entitled under the resolution as well as the law, he must then have again exercised his judgment, in deciding whether the half pay allowed her was to be calculated by the pay proper, or the pay and emoluments of an officer of the Commodore's rank.

"And after all this was done, he must have inquired into the condition of the navy pension fund, and the claims upon it, in order to ascertain whether there was money enough to pay all the demands upon it; and if not money enough, how it was to be apportioned among the parties entitled. A resolution of Congress requiring the exercise of so much judgment and investigation, can, with no propriety, be said to command a mere minsterial act to be done by the Secretary. The interference of the courts with the performance of the ordinary duties of the executive departments of the government, would be productive of nothing but mischief; and we are quite satisfied that such a power was never intended to be given to them. * * * We are, therefore, of opinion that the Circuit court were not authorized by law to issue the mandamus, and committed no error in refusing it." (*Decatur* v. *Paulding*, 14 *Peters' Rep.*, 497.)

And where the plaintiff made application for a mandamus against the defendant, the Secretary of the Navy, to compel the payment of arrearages of pay due him from the government as a commander in the navy of the United States, it was held by the court that if the plaintiff had made out a title to his pay, as an officer of the United States navy, a mandamus would not lie to enforce the payment.

Mr. Justice Nelson, in delivering the opinion of the court, said: "Besides the duty of inquiring into and ascertaining the rate of compensation that may be due to the officers under the laws of Congress, no payment can be made unless there has been an appropriation for the purpose. And if made, it may have been already exhausted, or prior requisitions may have been issued sufficient to exhaust it. The Secretary is obliged to inquire into the condition of the fund, and the claims already charged upon it, in order to ascertain if there is money enough to pay all the accruing demands, and if not enough, how it shall be apportioned among the parties entitled to it.

"These are important duties, calling for the exercise of judgment and discretion on the part of the officer, and in which the general creditors of the government, to the payment of whose demands the particular fund is applicable, are interested, as well as the government itself. For these reasons we think the writ of mandamus would not lie in the case." (*Brashear* v. *Mason*, 6 *Howard's* [*U. S.*] *Rep.*, 92.)

CHAPTER VIII.

MANDAMUS TO THE POSTMASTER GENERAI

It seems that the judiciary cannot direct or control the Postmaster General, in the discharge of any official duty, requiring the exercise of judgment or discretion; but the performance of a mere ministerial act, which he nor the President has any authority to deny, or control, may be enforced by mandamus.

Therefore, where the application for a mandamus set out certain contracts made between the relators and the late Postmaster General, upon which they claimed certain credits and allowances upon their contracts for the transportation of the mail. That credits and allowances were duly made by the late Postmaster General. That the present Postmaster General, when he came into office, re-examined the contracts entered into with his predecessor, and the allowances made by him, and the credits and payments which had been made;

and directed that the allowances and credits should be withdrawn, and the relators recharged with divers payments they had received. That the relators presented a memorial to Congress on the subject, upon which a law was passed for their relief; by which the solicitor of the treasury was authorized and directed to settle and adjust the claims of the relators for extra services performed by them; to inquire into and determine the equity of such claims; and to make the relators such allowances thereof, as upon full examination of all the evidence may seem right, according to the principles of equity. And that the Postmaster General be, and he is hereby directed to credit the relators with whatever sum or sums of money, if any, the solicitor shall so decide to be due to them, for and on account of any such service or contract.

It further set out, that the solicitor assumed upon himself the performance of the duty and authority created and conferred upon him by law, and did make out and communicate his decision and award to the Postmaster General; by which award and decision, the relators were allowed one hundred and sixty-one thousand five hundred and sixty-three dollars and eighty-nine cents. That the Postmaster General on being notified of the award, only so far obeyed and carried into execution the act of Congress, as to direct, and cause to be carried to the credit of the relators, the sum of one hundred and twenty-two thousand one hundred and two dollars and forty-six cents. But that he has, and still does refuse and neglect to credit the relators with the residue of the sum so awarded by the solicitor, amounting to thirty-nine thousand four hundred and sixty-two dollars and forty-three cents. And the petitioner prayed the court, to award a mandamus directed to the Postmaster General, commanding him fully to comply with, obey and execute the said act of Congress, by crediting the relators with the full and entire sum awarded in their favor by the solicitor of the treasury. One of the questions presented by the record was, whether the case was a proper one for a mandamus.

It was contended by the counsel for the Postmaster General, that it was a proceeding against him to enforce the performance of an official duty, and therefore an infringement upon the executive department of the government. Mr. Justice THOMPSON, in delivering the opinion of the court, said: "The act required by the law to be done by the Postmaster General, is simply to credit the relators with the full amount of the award of the solicitor. This is a precise, definite act, purely ministerial, and about which the Postmaster General had no discretion whatever. The law upon its face shows the existence of accounts between the relators and the Post Office department. No money was required to be paid; and none could have been drawn out of the treasury without further legislative provision, if this credit should overbalance the debit standing against the relators.

But this was a matter with which the Postmaster General had no concern. He was not called upon to furnish the means of paying such balance, if any should be found. He was simply required to give the credit. This was not an official act in any other sense than being a transaction in the department where the books and accounts were kept; and was an official act in the same sense that an entry in the minutes of a court, pursuant to an order of the court, is an official act. There is no room for the exercise of any discretion, official or otherwise; all that is shut out by the direct and positive command of the law, and the act required to be done is in every just sense, a mere ministerial act." It was therefore held that the mandamus would lie. (*Kendall v. The United States*, 12 *Peters' Rep.*, 526.)

CHAPTER IX.

MANDAMUS TO THE SECRETARY OF THE TREASURY.

The Secretary of the Treasury can be compelled by mandamus to perform a mere ministerial act, on which he has no right to exercise his judgment or discretion, and which is distinctly and clearly imposed upon him by law.

But he cannot, in that manner, be controlled in the general duties of his office, nor in those several and inherent functions or duties which may be implied as incident to his office. A mandamus, therefore, will not lie against a Secretary of the Treasury, unless the laws require him to do what he is asked in the petition to be made to do.

Therefore, where a mandamus was asked for by the plaintiff, as executrix, to direct the defendant, as Secretary of the Treasury Department, to pass to the credit of said estate a certain sum of money, and pay the same to the plaintiff as such executrix; and setting out, as grounds for the petition, that the United States had sued the testator in his lifetime, in the Circuit court of the United States for the eastern district of Pennsylvania, on certain post office contracts, and on the 22d of October, 1841, he pleaded a large set-off, and the jury, on the 6th of December ensuing, returned a verdict in his favor on the several issues which had been joined, and certified that the United States were indebted to him in a certain sum; and that on the 12th day of May, 1842, final judgment was rendered in his favor on this verdict, which has never been paid, but still remains in full force; and it was not pretended that there was any special law directing the entry of this claim on the books, or the payment of it either before or after the entry, it was held that a mandamus would not lie.

Mr. Justice WOODBURY, delivering the opinion of the court, said: "No officer, however high, not even the President, much less a Secretary of the Treasury or Treasurer, is empowered to pay debts of the United States, generally, when presented to them. If, therefore, the petition in this case was allowed so far as to order the verdict against the United States to be entered on the books of the Treasury Department, the plaintiff would be as far from having a claim on the Secretary or Treasurer to pay it as now. The difficulty in the way is the want of any appropriation by Congress to pay this claim. It is a well known constitutional provision that no money can be taken or drawn from the treasury, except under an appropriation by Congress. (*See Const., Art.* 1, *Sec.* 9 [1 *Stat. at Large*, 15].)

"However much money may be in the treasury at any one time, not a dollar of it can be used in the payment of anything not thus previously sanctioned. Any other course would give to the fiscal officers a most dangerous discretion. Hence, the petitioner should have presented her claim on the United States to Congress, and prayed for an appropriation to pay it. If Congress, after that, make such an appropriation, the treasury can, and doubtless will, discharge the claim without any mandamus. But without such an appropriation it cannot and should not be paid by the treasury, whether the claim is by a verdict or judgment, or without either, and no mandamus or other remedy lies against any officer of the Treasury Department, in a case situated like this, where no appropriation to pay it has been made." (*Reeside* v. *Walker*, 11 *How.* [*U. S.*] *Rep.*, 272.)

So, too, where the application for a mandamus set forth, substantially, that on the 19th of March, 1849, the relator had, with the advice and consent of the Senate, been commissioned, by President Taylor, Chief Justice of the Supreme court of the Territory of Minnesota, to which office there had been annexed (by the act of Congress organizing the territorial government), a compensation, or salary, of eighteen hundred dollars per annum, payable quarter yearly; that the tenure of the appointment was, by the language both of the act of Congress and of the commission of the relator, declared to be for the term and duration of four years from the date of the commission; that the relator having accepted his commission, was afterwards, namely, on the 22d of October, 1851, informed by J. J. Crittenden, acting Secretary of State, that the President had thought it proper to remove him from his office, and to substitute in his place another person; that the relator, insisting upon the tenure of his office according to the literal terms of the commission, preferred a claim before the first auditor of the treasury for the sum of $2,343, as compensation from the period of his dismission up to the expiration of four years from the date of his appointment; that the first auditor having rejected the claim in these words, "That Aaron Goodrich is not entitled to the salary claimed by him," an appeal was taken by the relator to the comptroller of the treasury, by whom the decision of the first auditor was sustained, and by whom, in adjudging it, it is remarked that "There can be only one Chief Justice of the Supreme court in the territory, and the President of the United States having thought proper to remove Chief Justice Goodrich, and having nominated, and, by and with the consent of the Senate, appointed Jerome Fuller, Chief Justice, in the room and stead of the said Chief Justice Goodrich, he, that is the comptroller, was bound to consider the said removal and appointment as legal;" and in consideration of the facts, and the law, his decision was that the United States were not indebted to the said Aaron Goodrich as Chief Justice of the Supreme court of the territory of Minnesota, and that the decision of the first auditor in the premises was confirmed and established.

Upon the foundation of the facts above recited, application was made to the Circuit court of the United States, for the District of Columbia and county of Washington, for a rule upon the Secretary of the Treasury, to show cause why a mandamus should not issue to compel the payment of the said salary, which was refused by the court. The case was thereupon carried to the Supreme court by writ of error.

Mr. Justice DANIEL, in delivering the opinion of the court, said: "The only legitimate inquiry for our determination upon the case before us, is this: Whether under the organi zation of the federal government, or by any known principle of law, there can be asserted a power in the Circuit court of the United States for the District of Columbia, or in this court, to command the withdrawal of a sum or sums of money from the treasury of the United States, to be applied in satisfaction of disputed or controverted claims against the United States? This is the question, the very question presented for our determination; and its simple statement would seem to carry with it the most startling considerations —nay its unavoidable negative, unless this should be prevented by some positive and controlling command; for it would occur, *a priori*, to every mind, that a treasury, not fenced round or shielded by fixed and established modes and rules of administration, but which could be subjected to any number or description of demands asserted and sustained through the undefined and undefinable discretion of the courts, would constitute a feeble and inadequate provision for the great and inevitable necessities of the nation.

"The government under such a regime, or, rather, under such an absence of all rule, would, if practicable at all, be administered not by the great departments ordained by the constitution and laws, and guided by the modes therein prescribed, but by the uncertain, and perhaps contradictory action of the courts, in the enforcement of their views of private interests. But the question proper for consideration here, has not been left for its solution, upon theoretical reasoning merely. It has already been authoritatively determined.

"The power of the courts of the United States to command the performance of any duty, by either of the principal executive departments, or such as is incumbent, upon any executive officer of the government, has been strongly contested in this court; and, in so far as that power may be supposed to have been conceded, the concession has been restricted by qualifications which would seem to limit it to acts or proceedings by the officer, not implied in the several and inherent functions or duties incident to his office; acts of a character rather extraneous, and required of the individual rather than of the functionary.

"Thus it has been ruled, that the only acts to which the power of the courts, by mandamus, extends, are such as are purely ministerial, and with regard to which nothing like judgment or discretion, in the performance of his duties, is left to the officer; but that wherever the right of judgment or decision exists in him, it is he, and not the courts, who can regulate its exercise.

"These are the doctrines expressly ruled by this court, in the case of *Kendall* v. *Stockton*, 12 *Peters' Rep.*, 524; in that of *Decatur* v. *Paulding*, 14 *Peters'* 497; and in the more recent case of *Brashear* v. *Mason*, 6 *How.*, 92; principles regarded as fundamental and essential, and apart from which the administration of the government would be impracticable. These principles, just stated, are clearly conclusive upon the case before us. The Secretary of the Treasury is inhibited from directing the payment of moneys not specifically appropriated by law. Claims against the treasury of the United States, like the present, are, according to the organization of that department, to be examined by the first auditor; from this office they pass, either under his approval, or by appeal from him, to the comptroller; and from the latter they are carried before the Secretary of the Treasury, without whose approbation they cannot be paid, and who cannot, even by the concurring opinions of the inferior officers of the department be deprived of his own judgment upon the justice and legality of demands upon public moneys confided to his care.

"Opposed to the claims under consideration, we have the decisions of three different functionaries; to each of whom has been assigned, by law, the power and duty of judging of its justice and legality. By what process of reasoning, then, the authority to make those decisions, or those decisions themselves, can be reconciled or identified with the performance of acts merely ministerial, we are unable to conceive; and unless so identified, as there could have been shown some power in the Circuit court, competent to the repealing of the legislation by Congress, in the organization of the Treasury Department—competent, too, to the annulling of the explicit rulings of this court, in the cases hereinbefore cited—the Circuit court could have no jurisdiction to entertain the application for a writ of mandamus in this instance. As no such power has been shown, nor in our opinion could have been shown, or even had existence, the decision of the Circuit court, overruling the application, is approved and affirmed." (*United States* v. *Guthrie*, 17 *How.* [*U. S.*] *Rep.*, 284.)

The principles thus applied in cases of mandamus to the heads of departments of state, are also applicable to cases of mandamus to all other officers of the government.

The rule to be gathered from all the cases decided in the Supreme court of the United States, governing mandamus to the officers of the government seems to be this. It cannot issue in a case where discretion and judgment are to be exercised by the officer, nor to control him in the manner of conducting the general duties of his office; it can be granted only where the act required to be done, is imposed by law—is merely ministerial, and the relator without any other adequate remedy.

This rule was applied in the case of *The United States* v. *Seaman*, 17 *How.* [*U. S.*] *Rep.*, 225, which was an application for a mandamus to the Superintendent of Public Printing of the two houses of Congress. By an act of Congress it was made the duty of the Superintendent to receive, from the secretary of the Senate, and the clerk of the House of Representatives, all matter ordered by Congress to be printed, and to deliver it to the public printer or printers. It also provided that when any document shall be ordered to be printed by both houses of Congress, the entire printing of such document shall be done by the printer of that house which first ordered the printing.

On the 31st of January, 1854, the Commissioner of Patents communicated to the Senate that portion of his annual report for 1853 which relates to arts and manufactures, which that body, on the same day, ordered to be printed; and on the following day it was communicated to the House of Representatives, who passed a similar order. This communication was delivered to the relator by the Superintendent.

On the 20th of March, 1854, the Commissioner communicated to both houses the agricultural portion of his report, which each house, on the same day, ordered to be printed, the order of the House of Representatives being first made.

The relator, printer to the Senate, claimed that the report of the Commissioner of Patents was but one document within the meaning of the act of Congress above referred to, and that by virtue of the order of the Senate of the 31st of January, 1854, he was entitled to the printing of the agricultural portion of the report, although the printing of this part was first ordered by the House of Representatives. The Superintendent, however, refused to deliver it; and the relator thereupon applied to the Circuit court for the District of Columbia for a mandamus to compel the delivery. That court was of the opinion that it had not jurisdiction of the case, and refused the mandamus; whereupon the relator brought a writ of error to the Supreme court. The Supreme court held, that before the Superintendent could exercise the authority vested in him, it was necessary for him to make inquiries. He must ascertain in which house the order to print was first passed. And even in that particular case to take oral testimony, before he could determine the fact of priority, as the order was passed in each house on the same day. That after he had made up his mind upon this fact, it was still necessary to examine into the usages and practice of Congress in making a communication in their proceedings as a document; and to make up his mind whether separate communications upon the same subject, or on different subjects from the same office, when made at different times, were, according to the usages and practice of Congress, described as one document, or different documents, in printing and publishing their proceedings. And as he was obliged to examine evidence, and form his judgment before he acted, it was not a case for mandamus.

CHAPTER X.

MANDAMUS TO THE GOVERNOR.

Mandamus will not lie to control the Governor in the discharge of his ordinary official duties, nor to compel him to perform any act over which he has the right to exercise his judgment or discretion. It has also been held that he cannot be compelled, by writ of mandamus, to perform a mere ministerial act devolved on him by the laws of the State. (*Low* v. *Towns*, 8 *Geo.*, 360; *People* v. *Bissell*, 19 *Ill.*, 229.)

In the case of *Mauran* v. *Smith, Governor*, recently decided by the Supreme court of Rhode Island, and reported in the

10th No. of the 5th Vol. of the American Law Register, 630 (N. S.), an application was made to the Supreme court for a mandamus to compel the Governor to convene a court martial, for the purpose of hearing charges and trying the relator thereon. The Governor had revoked the commission of the relator as adjutant general, and although the latter had, on the same day, demanded to be informed of the cause thereof, and to be tried by court martial, no action had been taken by the Governor for the space of twenty-one days. The statute provides as follows:

"Sec. 10. The commander-in-chief may revoke and cancel the commission of any officer and discharge him from the service in his discretion.

"Sec. 11. Such revocation, cancellation and discharge shall not be effectual if, within ten days after receiving notice thereof, such officer shall demand of his immediate superior to be informed of the cause thereof, and to be tried by a court martial.

"Sec. 12. If such demand be made, it shall be the duty of the officer on whom it is made to transmit the same to the commander-in-chief, who shall give such officer the required information, and see that charges are duly preferred, and that a court martial be convened to try the same."

The application was dismissed, the court holding that mandamus does not lie from a State court to the Governor to compel the performance of an official duty, even of a merely ministerial nature, where such duty is enjoined on him by the Constitution, or where, though imposed by statute, it is of such nature that he alone could perform it; and that it is immaterial whether the duty be of a political nature, or one pertaining to the Governor in his capacity as commander-in-chief of the military forces.

The reason upon which this decision is founded is that which is drawn from the division of the powers of government under the Constitution, into three coördinate depart ments, legislative, executive and judicial, each independent of the others, except in so far as one is subordinated to the other by the Constitution. That to hold that the ministerial duties of the executive may be compelled by the judiciary, is in effect to maintain, that to the extent of his ministerial duties, the executive is not the coördinate of the judiciary, but subordinate to it.

But the better doctrine seems to be, that the Governor is not an exception to the general rule that all public officers may, by mandamus, be compelled to perform an act clearly defined and enjoined by the law, and which is merely ministerial in its nature, and neither involves any discretion, nor leaves any alternative. (*Pacific Railroad* v. *Governor*, 23 *Miss.*, 353; *Colten* v. *Ellis*, 7 *Jones' Law* [*N. C.*], 545; *Chamberlain* v. *Sibley*, 4 *Min.*, 309; 7 *O. S. R.*, 372.)

In the case of *The State of Ohio, ex rel. Lewis Whiteman et al.* v. *Salmon P. Chase, Governor*, 5 *O. S. Rep.*, 529, the question, "Whether the Governor can be controlled in his official action by the authority of a writ of mandamus from the Supreme court," was presented and discussed for determination.

Bartley, C. J., in delivering the opinion of the court, said: "Can the chief executive officer of the State be directed or controlled in his official action by proceedings in mandamus? It is claimed on the part of the defense, that, inasmuch as the government is, by the Constitution, divided into the three separate and coördinate departments; the legislative, the executive, and the judicial; and inasmuch as each department has the right to judge of the Constitution and laws for itself, and each officer is responsible for an abuse or usurpation, in the mode pointed out in the Constitution, it necessarily follows, that each department must be supreme within the scope of its powers, and neither subject to the control of the other, for the manner in which it performs, or its failure to perform either its legal or constitititutional duties. This argument is founded on theory rather than reality. That each of these coördinate departments has duties to perform, in which it is not subject to the controlling, or directing authority of either of the others, must be conceded. But this independence arises not from the grade of the officer performing the duties, but the nature of the authority exercised. Under our system of government, no officer is placed above the restraining authority of the law, which is truly said to be universal in its behests, all paying it homage; the least as feeling its care, and the greatest as not exempt from its power. And it is only where the law has authorized it, that the restraining power of one of these coördinate departments can be brought to operate as a check upon one of the others. The judicial power cannot interpose and direct in regard to the performance of an official act which rests in the discretion of any officer, whether executive, legislative or judicial."

In *Marbury* v. *Madison*, 1 *Cranch Rep.*, 170, Chief Justice MARSHALL said: "It is not by the office of the person to whom the writ is directed, but the nature of the thing to be done, that the propriety, or impropriety of issuing a mandamus is to be determined. The constitutional provision declaring that 'the supreme executive power of this State shall be vested in the Governor,' clothes the Governor with important political powers, in the execution of which he uses his own judgment or discretion, and in regard to which his determinations are conclusive. But there is nothing in the nature of the chief executive office of this State, which prevents the performance of some duties merely ministerial being enjoined on the Governor. While the authority of the Governor is supreme in the exercise of his political and executive functions which depend on the exercise of his own judgment or discretion, the authority of the judiciary of the State is supreme in the determination of all legal questions involved in any matter judicially brought before it.

"Although the State cannot be sued, there is nothing in the nature of the office of Governor, which prevents the prosecution of a suit against the person engaged in discharge of its duties. This is fully sustained by the analogy of the doctrine of the Supreme court of the United States, in the case of *Marbury* v. *Madison*, 1 *Cranch Rep.*, 170. However, therefore, the Governor, in the exercise of the supreme executive power of the State, may, from the inherent nature of the authority in regard to many of his duties, have a discretion which places him beyond the control of the judicial power, yet in regard to a mere ministerial duty enjoined on him by statute, which might have been devolved on another officer of the State, and affecting any specific private right, he may be made amenable to the compulsory process of this court by mandamus."

"And when the issuing of a commission to one elected, or appointed to an office, is by law imposed as one of the official duties of the Governor, such duty is a mere ministerial act, which may be enforced by mandamus, should he neglect or refuse to issue it in a proper case." (*The State of Ohio* v. *Maffitt*, 5 *Ham.* [*O. Rep.*], 358.)

CHAPTER XI.

STATE OFFICERS.

MANDAMUS TO THE AUDITOR OF STATE.

The rule applied by the Supreme court of the United States, in cases of mandamus to the heads of departments for the federal government, is undoubtedly the rule which should be applied to the same cases against the heads of departments of State governments. And therefore while they may be controlled in the performance of a mere ministerial act, imposed upon them by law, they cannot in that manner be controlled by the courts, in the ordinary duties of their office, nor in those acts requiring the exercise by them of judgment and discretion.

In accordance with the principles thus stated, it has been held, that where by legislative enactment, a sum of money is appropriated to be paid to a person, and by law it is made the duty of the auditor of State to draw his warrant on the State treasury for its payment, and on the presentation of such warrant it is made the duty of the treasurer to pay the money; if the auditor refuse to do his duty in that respect, he may be proceeded against by mandamus. (*Divine* v. *Harris*, 8 *Monroe* [*Ky.*] *Rep.*, 440.)

It seems also that it will lie to compel the comptroller of the State to audit the accounts of a member of the legislature, for the daily compensation fixed by law. (*Fowler* v. *Peirce*, 2 *Cal. Rep.*, 165.) But he cannot be compelled to allow an account against the State, when he is clothed with the authority to pass upon the legality and justice of a claim. Therefore where the comptroller of State refused to pay a sheriff certain fees, to which he was entitled, and the sheriff petitioned for a mandamus; and it appeared that it was the duty of the comptroller to audit, adjust and settle the accounts of all officers, and also to decide upon the justice and legality of claims against, or by the State.

It was held, that as his official duty in that respect was not purely ministerial, but discretionary, the comptroller could not be controlled by the court in the exercise of his judgment and discretion, and that the relief of the sheriff was by memorial to the general assembly of the State and not by mandamus. (*Towle* v. *The State*, 3 *Florida Rep.*, 202.)

It appears also, that where there is a constitutional provision that no disbursements shall be made from the treasury except under sanction of a legislative appropriation, specifying distinctly the object to which it is to be applied, a return to a writ of mandamus, the object of which writ was to compel the comptroller to draw his warrant on the treasurer, in favor of the relator, for a sum alleged to be due to him from the State, for a portion of his salary as a former justice of the Supreme court, setting forth that no appropriation had ever been made by law for the payment of the relator's claim as required by the constitution, was, on demurrer, held to be a conclusive answer. (*The People* v. *Lorenzo Burrows*, 27 *Barb. Rep.*, 89.)

So, too, it has been held that although the auditor is the general accountant of the State, yet it is competent for the State to refer the settlement of accounts to other persons, by whose decision, in the scope of their authority, it will be bound; and the auditor cannot decline to issue his warrant to the treasury, because he thinks the claim unjust.

Therefore, where by law, making appropriations for certain printing, it was provided that all payments thereof shall be upon accounts certified by the secretary of State, which accounts, so certified, shall be sufficient vouchers for the auditor to draw his warrant on the treasury, it was held that the certificate of the Secretary of State, approving the accounts of the State printer for work done in accordance therewith, was conclusive on the auditor, and left him no discretion as to opening the accounts, though he should allege fraud and deception therein; and that if he refused to draw his warrant he might be proceeded against by mandamus. (*Danly* v. *Whitely*, 14 *Ark. Rep.*, 687.)

A distinction has been made between the judgment of an officer in a matter left to his discretion and his judgment as to the extent of his discretion under the law. And that, although the decision of an auditing officer, as to the amount of a claim which the law permits him to allow, is conclusive; yet his decision as to whether the claim is in its nature within the statute, is not so, but is reviewable on mandamus. (*State* v. *Hastings*, 10 *Wis. Rep.*, 518.)

And where an auditor refuses to perform an act enjoined upon him by a statute, for the reason that in his judgment the law is null and void by being unconstitutional, the courts may, if the statute be decided to be constitutional and valid, compel, by mandamus, the auditor to go forward and perform the duty.

Therefore, where, by a general banking law of the State, it was provided that "The auditor is hereby authorized and required to cause to be engraved and printed, in the best manner to guard against counterfeiting, such quantity of circulating notes in the similitude of bank notes, in blank, of the different denominations herein authorized, as he may from time to time deem necessary to carry into effect the provisons of this act, and of such form as he may prescribe;" and it was also provided that "Whenever any company formed for the purpose of banking under the provisions of this act shall lawfully transfer to the auditor of State any portion of the public stock issued, or to be issued by the State of Ohio, or by the United States, such company shall be entitled to receive from the auditor an equal amount of such circulating notes, of the different denominations, registered and countersigned as aforesaid;" and it was shown that the relator, a banking company, had organized and tendered to the auditor—lawfully transferred to him, twenty thousand dollars of public stocks of the State of Ohio, it was held by the court that the law unquestionably specially enjoined as a duty upon the auditor of State, that he cause such notes to be printed, countersigned, numbered, and registered, and receive said stocks lawfully transferred to him, and give said company its notes for circulation. And that if the auditor refused to do so, although on the ground that as the law had been passed under the old Constitution, it had, in his judgment, become abrogated by the adoption of the new Constitution, mandamus would lie to compel him to perform the duty, if in fact, the law was not so abrogated. (*Citizens' Bank of Steubenville* v. *Francis M. Wright, Auditor*, 6 *O. S. Rep.*, 318.)

CHAPTER XII.

MANDAMUS TO THE ATTORNEY GENERAL.

The attorney general is also subject to control, by writ of mandamus, in his mere ministerial duties in those matters where he has not the power of exercising his judgment or discretion. But in his case, as well as in others, the courts will not grant a mandamus when it would be fruitless and ineffectual to relieve the relator.

And by this is meant that the aid of the court will be refused where its writ will not finally avail the party, or protect his rights, and where he has no right to the ultimate relief to which his proceedings tend, or cannot redress his grievances in the proceeding which he seeks to institute.

Therefore a peremptory mandamus was denied in a case to compel the attorney general to certify that certain suits for penalties were duly instituted as by law required, and which certificate it was claimed it was his duty to give, in obedience to a law providing "that whenever costs are adjudged against the people of the State in any civil suit or proceeding instituted by any officer duly authorized for that purpose, it shall be the duty of the comptroller to draw on the treasurer for the amount thereof, upon the production of an authenticated copy of the judgment record, etc., and upon a certificate of the attorney general that such suit or proceeding was duly instituted, as by law required," where it was shown by the return of the attorney general that no appropriation had been made by the legislature for the payment of such costs. For it was maintained that inasmuch as the money could not be paid out by the treasurer without an appropriation by the legislature, it would be of no avail to the relator if the comptroller's warrant was obtained; that if the attorney general should be compelled to give the certificate asked it could not avail the party, as it could not give him the relief to which his proceedings were designed to tend. (*The People* v. *Tremain*, 29 *Barb. Rep.*, 96.)

The same doctrine was maintained in the case of *Woodbury, petitioner*, v. *County Commissioners of Piscataquis*, 40 *Maine Rep.*, 304, in which case it was held that the writ will be denied where a person applies for it for the purpose of being placed in an office filled by an annual election, to which he alleges he was duly chosen, but illegally counted out, where it appears that before any effectual action could be had in the case, if the writ should be granted, the term for which the petitioner claims to have been elected will have expired. (*Williams, petitioner*, v. *County Commissioners*, 35 *Maine*, 345; *Howard* v. *Gage*, 6 *Mass.*, 462.)

Neither will courts attempt to compel any officer to do any act which he is not bound to do, or perform an act which will have no force when done. Therefore, a mandamus to compel the Secretary of State to issue a commission to one appointed by the Governor to the office of attorney general, was denied, upon it appearing that the Governor had no power to make the appointment. (*Collins, Secretary of State*, v. *The State*, 8 *Ind. Rep.*, 345.)

CHAPTER XIII.

MANDAMUS TO CANVASSERS.

Though each house of the legislative assembly can alone determine the right of its members to seats, yet mandamus lies to compel the canvassers to perform the ministerial act of giving their official certificate to the person who appears by the returns to have received the largest number of votes as a senator or representative. (*O'Ferrall* v. *Colby*, 2 *Min. Rep.*, 180.)

And where by law it is provided that where one is elected or appointed to an office by the general assembly, it shall be the duty of the speaker to give to him a certificate of his election; if they refuse to give him such certificate, they may be proceeded against by mandamus. (*State of Ohio* v. *Loomis*, 5 *Ham.* [*O. R.*], 358.)

So where the duty of a board of canvassers of an election is simply to receive and count the returns of votes, and not to judge of their validity, or of any fraud affecting them, that question being for another specially appointed tribunal, upon a case properly brought after the board have declared the result, the action of the board in this matter is ministerial only, and mandamus will therefore lie to compel them to perform their duty. (*State* v. *County Judge*, 7 *Clarke*. [*Iowa*] 186, *State* v. *Bailey*, *Ib.*, 390.)

And where the statute defining the duties of the board of examiners provided, that they should "examine the returns of votes transmitted to them, and if any person shall be found to have a majority of all the ballots" to give the person elected written notice of his election, it was held that they were not made a judicial tribunal upon the validity or the fact of the election in any other mode than by an examination of the returns made to them, according to law. That they were not required or authorized to hear witnesses, or weigh evidence; nor had they power to send for persons or papers. That if one result appeared upon the returns, and another was the real truth of the case, they could only act upon the former. And that as the return required by statute was a copy of the town record, signed by the selectmen, and attested by the town clerk, the board of examiners were not required by law to receive, examine, or treat as a return, any paper which did not appear upon its face, to be such a return. (*Luce* v. *Mayhew et al.*, 13 *Gray's Rep.*, 83.)

And where the general election laws of a State directed that the clerk of the court of Common Pleas, with two justices of the peace called to his assistance, should open and make abstracts of the several returns which shall have been made to his office, and that in making such abstracts of votes the justices and clerk shall not decide on the validity of the returns, but shall be governed by the number of votes stated in the poll-books, and that no election should be set aside for want of form in the poll-books, provided they contained the substance, it was held that the aggregate results of the returns, exhibited by the several poll-books, were to be ascertained by arithmetical calculation, and could not be controlled by the discretion of the persons performing the duty. That such counting of votes, making of abstracts, which exhibit the result, and giving certificates accordingly, were duties which fell within the province of a clerk and accountant, and admitted of no discretion, and were in their nature ministerial, and that, therefore, the performance of such duties might be enforced without assuming to control judicial discretion. (*Ingerson* v. *Berry*, 14 *O. S. Rep.*, 322.)

The same doctrine was maintained and applied by the courts of Massachusetts. (*Strong, Petitioner*, 20 *Pick. Rep.*, 484.)

CHAPTER XIV.

MANDAMUS TO STATE TREASURER.

The State Treasurer may also be controlled by mandamus in the exercise of his ministerial duties. And when the law requires him, upon the happening of a certain event, to go forward and do a certain act, his declining to act at once, when notified of the happening of such event, is equivalent to a refusal, and is sufficient ground for issuing a mandamus.

Therefore, where the charter of a government stock bank provided, that if said corporation should at any time, or under any pretense, refuse to pay any of its notes, the holder thereof might file his affidavit of the fact with the State Treasurer, who shall thereupon give notice that the bills of said bank would be paid at the Treasurer's office ; it was held, that it was the duty of the Treasurer, on such affidavit being filed, to act at once, without waiting for counter affidavits, and that declining to act at once was equivalent to refusal, and was sufficient ground for issuing a mandamus to compel him to give the prescribed notice. (*The People* v. *State Treasurer*, 4 *Mich.* 27.)

In *Houston* v. *Randolph*, 24 *Texas Rep.*, 317, however, it was held that mandamus would not lie to compel the State Treasurer to pay, in accordance with a warrant signed by the Governor and attorney-general, acting as the board of school commissioners, as he and not the judiciary, was the judge of his official duties.

This doctrine, however, can be extended only so far as relates to those general duties of the office, depending upon the Treasurer's judgment or discretion. For if the law imposed upon him some specific duty, if he should refuse to perform it, even if he thought he was not required by the law to do so, yet the courts would undoubtedly possess the power to compel him to act, by writ of mandamus.

CHAPTER XV.

COUNTY OFFICERS.

MANDAMUS TO COUNTY AUDITOR.

The writ has often been issued to compel county auditors to perform ministerial duties enjoined upon them by law, and to force them to act in those cases, even where they had a discretion as to how they should act in the premises.

The case of *Burnett* v. *The Auditor of Portage County*, 12 *O. R.*, 54, was an application for a writ of mandamus to the auditor of Portage county, to compel him to audit and allow an account against the county, amounting to eighty-eight dollars, for forty-four days labor performed as assistant appraiser of real property.

The law prescribing the duty of the auditor, provided, that he should settle all accounts, debts and demands, justly chargeable against the county, and which are not directed by law to be settled and allowed by some other person or tribunal, &c., "and for all demands against the county, the amount of which is fixed by law, he shall issue orders on the treasury of the county."

The compensation of assistant appraisers, was fixed by the legislature at two dollars for each day's services.

BIRCHARD, J. in delivering the opinion of the court, said: "If the amount of this account is fixed by law, and within the meaning of the act, the writ prayed for should be allowed; for in that case, the duty to be performed would be merely ministerial, and a writ of mandamus would be a proper remedy. So, if vested with a discretion, and the officer should refuse to act. In this case, however, the auditor has acted by rejecting the account. The proper remedy, if the account be just, and the auditor authorized to audit it, is an action of assumpsit against the county. It cannot be contended that the amount of the account is fixed by law, for the law only professes to fix the per diem at two dollars. This is but a rule for fixing the amount of the account; and whether it should be eighty-four dollars, or a less sum, depends entirely upon the amount of services performed."

Another objection to the allowance of the writ in this case, was that the statute made it the duty of each assessor, and deputy assessor, at the end of each week in which he shall have been engaged in the performance of his duty, to enter an account, in writing, of the number of days, or parts of days, he may have been engaged during the week, and at some stated meeting of the commissioners, to present such original account to them; to testify under oath to the accuracy of the account, and to answer such questions respecting the same as they may put to him.

It was therefore insisted by the court, that the account must be acted upon by the commissioners of the county, and they must be satisfied of the performance of the service, before the auditor could legally issue any order upon the treasury.

It seems clear that the auditor may be compelled, by mandamus, to perform any public duty specially enjoined upon him by some provision of law. But whether, from the circumstances of the case, he is thus enjoined by law, is, many times, a difficult question to determine.

Therefore, where the law provided "that all accounts, debts and demands, justly chargeable against any county, and which are not directed by law to be settled and allowed by some other person or tribunal, shall be examined and settled by the auditor of such county; and for all such just debts, accounts and demands, settled and allowed by the auditor, or settled or allowed by any other person or tribunal authorized by law to do so," it was doubted by some of the members of the court, whether the auditor could, by mandamus, be compelled to issue an order on the treasury for a sum allowed, and ordered by the court to be paid to the sheriff for expenses in boarding and caring for juries impaneled to try a person charged with murder.

A majority of the court, however, believed it to be a necessary incident to their authority to make a provision for the sustenance and care of juries when called to administer the criminal laws of the State in any county; and as the speediest way of reimbursing the sheriff for money advanced by him for this salutary purpose, they directed the county auditor to consider an account of this character, audited and allowed by the court, as "a just demand against the county, settled and allowed by a tribunal authorized by law to do so." (*The State* v. *Auditor of Hamilton County*, 19 *O. R.*, 116.)

Another case recognizing the doctrine that mandamus will not lie to compel the auditor of a county to draw an order on the treasurer of the county where the auditor has not the right to fix the amount to be drawn for, unless such amount has been ascertained and liquidated by the proper authority, is that of *The Commissioners of Putnam County* v. *The Auditor of Allen County*, 1 *O. S. Rep.*, 322.

The controversy in this case arose in reference to a claim set up by Putnam county against Allen county, for a sum of money which it was claimed was due from Allen to Putnam county, by virtue of the provisions of the statute creating the county of Auglaize. A large portion of the territory of Allen county was taken for the purpose of erecting the new county of Auglaize, and in order to compensate Allen county for the territory thus lost, a portion of Putnam county was added to Allen. The county of Putnam was largely indebted at the time, and in order to enable Putnam county to retain her capacity to pay off her debt, and to do justice in the premises, the legislature provided as follows: "That the commissioners of the counties of Allen and Putnam shall meet on or before the first Monday in April next, or within sixty days thereafter, and ascertain and determine the amount of the public debt of Putnam county, exclusive of that for the surplus revenue loaned to said county, and the proportion which the value of the taxable lands set off by this act to the county of Allen from the county of Putnam bears to the value of the taxable lands by this act remaining in Putnam county; and hereafter, each year until the public debt aforesaid shall be paid off and discharged, there shall be paid out of the treasury of Allen county, upon the order of the auditor thereof, to the treasurer of Putnam county, a sum which shall bear the same proportion to the amount raised in that year by Putnam county for the payment of the debt aforesaid, as the value of the taxable lands so set off as aforesaid bears to that of those so as aforesaid remaining in Putnam county, and the same shall be applied to the extinguishing of said debt, and for no other purpose; and it shall be the duty of the comissioners of Allen county to levy a sufficient tax to raise said sum."

Within the time prescribed by the statute, the commissioners of Putnam county met, having notified the commissioners of Allen county of the meeting. The commissioners of Allen county failed and refused to attend. The commissioners of Putnam county proceeded to ascertain the debt of Putnam county, and found that it amounted to over ten thousand dollars; and in accordance with the rule laid down in the statute, made a computation of what amount of this debt should be liquidated by Allen county. For the year 1849, Putnam county collected by tax $860.29, and paid off that amount of the debt. This required of Allen county, according to the computation made as above, to pay, as her propor t on, to the county of Putnam, $330. A demand was made on the auditor of Allen county to draw an order in favor of Putnam county for that amount; this he refused to do. An application was thereupon made for a mandamus to compel him to do so.

CALDWELL, J., in delivering the opinion of the court, said: "A question, however, arises. Whether this court, under the circumstances, can compel the auditor of Allen county, by mandamus, to issue the order for the amount claimed by Putnam county. The auditor of a county is a ministerial officer, except in such special cases as the Legislature may clothe him with discretionary powers. The county commissioners are the general legal representatives of the county. In this particular instance the auditor had no authority in determining the amount that was to be paid by Allen county; he was merely to draw an order for such amount as should be determined on by the commissioners of the two counties. The amount to be paid has never been decided in the way provided for by the statute. On the refusal of the commissioners of Allen county to meet with those of Putnam county, and to fix the amount, a right of action accrued to Putnam county, to recover from Allen such amount as might be found due under the rule of computation laid down in the statute. No provision is made for the commissioners of Putnam county alone fixing the amount. So that Allen county is not bound by the assessment thus made, although she is bound to pay so much as might be found due in an appropriate action. If the amount were fixed in the mode contemplated in the statute, or if it were liquidated by judgment, mandamus would be the proper remedy to compel the auditor to perform the ministerial act of drawing the order; but until the amount is thus liquidated, we think the auditor cannot be compelled to act; the time for his action has not arrived."

Mandamus also lies to compel a county auditor to enter upon the tax duplicate of the county, lands which should be thus entered, and which he neglects or refuses to so enter.

But the writ only lies when the officer is legally empowered to perform the judgment of the court. And therefore, when the duplicate for a particular year has gone out of his hands, and he has no further power or control over it, he cannot be compelled to so enter it, for it would be commanding him to perform an impossibility.

Neither can he be ordered to so enter it, before the time has arrived for making up the duplicate, for to do so is to assume that he will then, without coercion, refuse to perform his legal duty. (*The City of Zanesville* v. *Richards, Auditor*, 5 *O. S. Rep.*, 589.)

And so where the county auditor is about to do an official, ministerial act, in an illegal and incorrect manner, and in a matter of public right, mandamus will lie to compel him to do it in the manner pointed out by law. Therefore where the State board of equalization had ordered an addition of fifteen per cent. to the valuation of the real property of a certain county, and their acts and orders in the premises were null and void, and the county auditor was about to add said fifteen per cent. to the valuation of the land of said county, and to issue the duplicate for the tax on real property with the fifteen per cent. thus added, it was held that a mandamus would lie to compel him to certify the duplicate without such addition.

BLACKFORD, J. in delivering the opinion of the court, in the case of *Hamilton, Auditor of Marion County* v. *The State*, 3 *Ind. Rep.*, 452, said : "The next question is, whether a mandamus is the proper remedy in this case? We have no doubt as to this point. The order of the State board, as we have already shown, for the addition of fifteen per cent. to the valuation of the real estate in Marion county, is a nullity; it was consequently the defendant's duty, as the county auditor, to issue the tax duplicate without said additional per centage. That duty, which was a public one, the defendant refused to perform; and the proper remedy for the

State, to compel his performance of it, was by mandamus. The order aforesaid of the State board being null and void, the defendant had no discretion relative to the issuing of the duplicate. He was as much bound to issue it without the said addition of fifteen per cent. as he would have been, had the order for such addition not been made."

CHAPTER XVI.

MANDAMUS TO COUNTY TREASURER.

That a mandamus will lie to compel a county treasurer to pay an account legally chargeable to the county, and which has been audited and allowed by the proper authority, seems to be fully settled. (*The People* v. *Edmunds*, 19 *Barb.*, 472.) If however, he has not the funds to pay the account, or has it not in his power to provide them, the issuing of the mandamus would be an idle ceremony, and ought not to issue.

But if he might have had the funds, had he not misapplied them, he is as much bound to pay, as though he actually had them. Therefore, when public moneys are raised by taxation for specific purposes, and placed in the hands of the county treasurer to be paid out on the orders of certain auditing boards, and the treasurer pays out the money for other purposes than those for which the money was raised, he may, notwithstanding, be compelled to pay the orders drawn on him to satisfy claims for which the money was raised. (*The People* v. *Stout*, 23 *Barb.*, 339. *Huff* v. *Knapp*, 1 *Selden*, 65. *The People* v. *Edmonds*, 15 *Barb.*, 529, 12 *Barb.*, 607, 217. *Adsit* v. *Brady*, 4 *Hill*, 634.)

And where by law, and immemorial usage, the court is authorized to allow the fees of sheriff, and other executive and ministerial officers, while in attendance at their sessions, the determination of the court upon the amount of such costs and fees, is final and conclusive. And on presentation of a claim thus allowed, to the treasurer of the county, it is his duty to pay it, and if he refuses, a mandamus lies to compel him. An attempt on his part to exercise supervisory powers, is an assumption of authority. (*Baker* v. *Johnson*, 41 *Maine*, 15.)

A mandamus, however, will not be awarded to compel the county treasurer to pay an account audited and allowed by the proper auditing board, which was not a legal county charge.

In the case of *The People* v. *Lawrence*, 6 *Hill*, 244, the supervisors of the county of New York, audited and allowed to the relator his account for expenses incurred by him in defending himself as one of the special justices in the city of New York, on an impeachment and trial before the County court. The county treasurer refused to pay the account thus audited and allowed, and an application was made to the Supreme court for a mandamus to compel him.

Bronson, J., in delivering the opinion of the court, says: "Whatever appearance of justice there may be in charging the expenses of the account upon the county, it is enough for us to say, that this consideration addresses itself exclusively to the legislature. If this had been a case where the supervisors had authority to allow the claim, I agree that it would have been the duty of the treasurer to pay, without inquiring whether the account had been allowed upon insufficient evidence, or at too large an amount. But as the supervisors had no jurisdiction over the subject matter, and that fact appeared upon the face of the account, presented for payment, their act was a mere nullity, and it was the duty of the treasurer to withhold payment."

So, too, when the twelfth section of an act, defining the duties and liabilities of the officers of the city government of

New York—the organization of the courts therein, and the powers of the board of supervisors, declared that all work to be done, and supplies to be furnished for the corporation involving an expenditure of more than two hundred and fifty dollars, should be by contract, founded on sealed bids, or on proposals, made in compliance with public notice, for the full period of ten days; and all such contracts when given, should be given to the lowest bidder, with adequate security. And section fifteen of the same act declared, that no contract by the supervisors should be valid unless expressly authorized by statute, and such as are authorized must be made in the manner provided by the twelfth section of the act; and the relators were employed by the board of supervisors of the city and county of New York, to make certain repairs of books in the register's office, and their bill therefor was duly presented to the board of supervisors, and audited and allowed by them, at the sum of $2,644.50, it was held by the court, that the contracts were not such as could be made by the board in the manner they were made. That although the necessary expenses incurred in keeping the property of the county in repair, and to preserve it from decay, and keep it in a condition for use, is a proper and legal county charge, yet the board of supervisors could create no legal liability against the county by having this work done in direct violation of the provisions of the act; that no charge had thereby been created against the county, and that the court should not award a peremptory mandamus to the county treasurer commanding him to pay the accounts, but that it would even be its duty, on a proper application, to restrain him from so doing. (*The People* v. *Stout*, 23 *Barb.*, 349.)

CHAPTER XVII.

MANDAMUS TO COUNTY COMMISSIONERS.

The power of courts, in proper cases, to compel by mandamus the commissioners of a county to perform their duty, seems not to be questioned. It will not, however, be called into action on every trivial occasion; and although a peremptory mandamus will be awarded to compel the commissioners of a county to levy a tax for the satisfaction of a judgment against the county, should they refuse, or for a long time neglect to do so, yet they will not, when there has been no unnecessary, unreasonable or vexatious delay. (*Tillson, Jr.* v. *The Commissioners of Putnam County*, 19 *O. Rep.*, 415.)

And where subscription had been made by the commissioners of a county for stock in a railroad company, in pursuance of a statute authorizing the commissioners to so subscribe, and the county had thereby become absolutely bound by contract; and the commissioners, in pursuance of the law, having elected to deliver the bonds of the county to the company, in payment of the subscription, and afterwards, upon demand, refusing to do so, and showing no cause for such refusal, except that the law was of doubtful constitutionality, it was held that a writ of mandamus is the proper remedy to enforce the delivery, if the law was found to be constitutional. (*The C. W. & Z. Railroad Company* v. *The Commissioners of Clinton County*, 1 *O. S. Rep.*, 77; *English* v. *Supervisors*, 19 *Cal.*, 172.)

And when a claim is presented to the supervisors of a county, of such a character that it is their duty to proceed and act upon it, and they neither allow nor disallow it by any formal action, their conduct is equivalent to a rejection of the claim; and if their refusal to allow or disallow proceeds, from the opinion that the claim is not a legal one, and in the opinion of the court it is one which the county is legally bound to pay; they will be ordered to allow it. (*The People* v. *The Supervisors of Richmond County*, 20 *N. Y. Rep.*, 253.)

So in the case of *The State of Ohio* v. *The Commissioners of Clinton County*, 6 *O. S. Rep.*, 280, it was held that it is in general the duty of the commissioners of a county to ascertain, as near as may be, the amount necessary to pay the debts of the county, and to make an assessment for that purpose; and that mandamus will lie to compel the performance of such duty when neglected.

In that case the county commissioners had issued interest-paying bonds to a railroad company, in payment of subscription to the capital stock of the road. There was an agreement between the commissioners and the company that the latter should pay all the interest which "shall or may accrue on the bonds. The bonds were indorsed by the railroad company to the relator. The company paid the interest for three years, but failed to pay the fourth and fifth year's interest. The relator thereupon asked for and obtained a peremptory mandamus, requiring the commissioners, at their next session, to levy a sufficient amount of tax to pay the whole of the interest then due and unpaid.

It was held that in such case it was the duty of the county commissioners to ascertain whether the railroad company would pay the interest, and if not, the county being primarily liable, the board of commissioners should have made provision therefor. It was also held, that as it satisfactorily appeared that no fund or provision whatever had been made for payment at the treasury of the county, where the interest warrants were made payable, no proof need be made of demand of payment of the coupons before proceeding against the commissioners by mandamus; that in fact no demand was necessary.

A mandamus will undoubtedly lie to compel the county commissioners to accept and approve a sheriff's official bond, if such as is required by law, when it is made their duty to do so, and they neglect or refuse. But if the relator's election to the office of sheriff has been contested before the court of Common Pleas, and it was found by said court that the relator was not duly elected or entitled to the office, while such finding remains not reversed or set aside, mandamus will not lie. As it is a high prerogative writ, it will be awarded only in cases where there is a clear legal right, and the party has no other adequate remedy.

And the relator will not be entitled to the writ in such case, although he has filed his petition in error in the district court of the county to reverse said judgment of the court of Common Pleas, and has procured from one of the judges of the district court a writ of supersedeas. The petition in error and supersedeas does not vacate the judgment. The judgment retains its vitality and force until reversed or set aside. If reversed or set aside on the hearing of the petition in error, it of course ceases to be; but if affirmed, it is the judgment to be executed. (*The State of Ohio* v. *The Commissioners of, &c.*, 14 *O. S. Rep.*, 515.)

When county commissioners have a discretion and proceed to exercise it, courts have no jurisdiction to control that discretion by a writ of mandamus; but if they refuse to act, or to entertain the question for their discretion, in cases where the law enjoins upon them to do the act required, courts may enforce obedience to the law by a mandamus, when no other legal remedy exists.

As when the commissioners of a county refuse to allow a claim for services, as a county charge, if, in fact, it be a legal charge, the proper court may instruct and guide the commissioners in the execution of their duty by a writ of mandamus, and compel them to admit the claim as a county charge, or, in other words, set them in motion without controlling the exercise of their judgment and discretion as to the amount proper to be allowed. (*Hull* v. *The Supervisors, &c.*, 19 *Johns. Rep.*, 259; 18 *Johns.*, 242; 7 *Cowen*, 363; 3 *Mich.*, 475.)

So where it is made the duty of county commissioners to open and compare election returns, and to declare and certify who has the highest number of votes for a certain office, and the relator actually receives the highest number of legal votes, and the commissioners refuse to perform their duty by so declaring and certifying, they may be compelled to do so by mandamus; but when the election for a certain town was illegal, unauthorized and void, and the commissioners for that reason refuse to receive or count the returns from such town, mandamus will not lie to compel them. (*Ellis* v. *The County Commissioners*, 2 *Gray's Rep.*, 370.)

So, where a statute had charged upon the respective counties any deficiency which might arise upon the sale of land mortgaged to the commissioners of loans, and had directed that the amount should be raised by the board of supervisors; and the case of such deficiency having occurred in the county of Columbia, the attorney-general procured a mandamus to compel the supervisors to do their duty by raising the money to meet the deficiency. The question was presented by a demurrer interposed by the attorney-general to the return of the board of supervisors, and on the argument their counsel urged that mandamus was not the proper remedy, the county, as they contended, being liable to an action. The answer of the court to this position, as set forth in the opinion of Chief Justice SAVAGE, in giving judgment for a peremptory mandamus, was as follows: "Is this a proper case for mandamus? It has often been decided in England, and by this court, that a mandamus will not be granted when there is a remedy by action. The party asking for a mandamus must have a clear legal right, and no other appropriate specific remedy. (2 *Cow.* 444; 1 *Wend.* 325; 7

Tenn. R., 396, 404.) If an action lies in this case, then a mandamus should be refused; I think an action would not lie. The statute directs the supervisors to levy and collect the amount of the deficiency; it is a duty imposed upon those officers which should be performed by them; but for this neglect, the county in its corporate capacity, should not be punished, nor does any liability attach to the county to pay the money in any way other than that pointed out in the statute. Should it be thought that the offending supervisors ought to respond personally in damages, which is certainly very questionable, still there is no principle which would graduate the damages to the deficiency which would arise from the mortgage in question; and for aught the court can know, the money possibly might not be collected in that way. Besides, the law does not contemplate satisfaction in any other manner than by an assessment upon the taxable property of the county. An action, therefore, is not the appropriate and specific remedy." (*The People* v. *The Supervisors of Columbia County*, 10 *Wend.* 363.

This opinion, so far as it denies the liability of the county to an action may be somewhat questionable. Yet it has been approvingly cited as authority, "for holding that when a particular method of raising money for local public purposes is prescribed by statute, the party entitled to receive it, has a right to the full and perfect execution of the power conferred, which may be enforced by the writ of mandamus." (*The People* v. *Mead*, 24 *New York*, 123.)

And when money is collected of the taxpayers, and placed in the hands, or subject only to the order of the commissioners, for the purpose of being paid to certain creditors, in pursuance of specific statutory directions. and the commissioners refuse to make the appropriation, mandamus is an appropriate remedy, although an action might be maintained against the county. (*The People* v. *Mead, et al.*, 24 *New York*, 121.

But if the money had not been actually raised, and paid by the taxpayers into the treasury, and the commissioners, whose duty it is, refuse to credit and allow a legal claim against the county, and there is a perfect right of action against the county, there are cases favoring the view that mandamus will not lie. (*Ex-parte Lynch*, 2 *Hill*, 45; 1 *Tenn. Rep.*, 114; 2 *Cowen's Rep.*, 444; 1 *Wend.* 325; 10 *John.* 484; 10 *Wend.* 367; 6 *Hill*, 243; 12 *John.* 415; 19 *John.* 259; 1 *Kernan's Rep.*, 573.)

The case of *ex-parte Lynch*, 2 *Hill's Rep.*, 45, was an application for a mandamus to compel the supervisors of the city and county of New York to audit and allow the salary of an associate judge of the general sessions. The law organizing the court, provided a salary of $2,000, to be paid by the council, out of the city treasury, in quarterly payments. By a subsequent law "the mayor, recorder and aldermen of the city, as supervisors of the city and county of New York, are directed to audit and allow the judges' accounts for arrears of salary on or before the tenth day of July thereafter; and after that time quarterly, as such salaries might become due." It was maintained by the court, that an action might be sustained by the relator against the corporation, and that therefore mandamus would not lie to compel the supervisors to audit and allow the claim. This is certainly a strong case against the right to issue the writ in any case where an action can be maintained against the county, and at first thought, it may seem a little difficult to reconcile it with the case of *The State of Ohio* v. *the Commissioners and Auditor of Clinton County*, 6 *O. S. Reps.*, 280, before cited, and *The People* v. *Mead, et al.*, 24 *N. Y. Reps.*, 121. But a distinction may be made between compelling the commissioners to perform the specific duty imposed by statute, of ordering a levy to pay a claim, the amount of which is fixed, and its payment directly provided for by law, and the compelling them to audit and allow a claim not definitely fixed by law. In the former case, the law has fixed the amount to be paid. A suit and judgment could not make the obligation more obligatory or definite. And if put into judgment, would yet be in no better condition for compelling payment, without the aid of mandamus. In the latter case, however, as the amount is not definitely fixed by law, and the existence of the obligation, and the propriety of allowing it, depending upon facts and circumstances, the claimant should pursue his remedy by action. The case of *Burnet* v. *The Auditor of Portage County*, 12 *O. Rep.*, 54, before cited, seems to favor this distinction.

It seems unquestionable that a right of action for damages generally exists against public officers, who refuse or neglect to perform their duty, in favor of those persons whose rights are injuriously affected by such neglect of duty. But this remedy by action against the officers is of such doubtful and uncertain character as not to supersede that by mandamus. The unliquidated damages to be assessed by a jury would not necessarily be the amount due the party. (*The People* v. *Mead et al.*, 24 *N. Y. Rep.*, 120; *ex parte Lynch*, 2 *Hill's Rep.*, 45; *Strong, petitioner*, 20 *Pick. Rep.*, 497.)

In the case of *McCollough* v. *The Mayor of Brooklyn*, 23 *Wend.* 458, it was said by Judge BRONSON, that "although as a general rule a mandamus will not lie where the party has another remedy, it is not universally true in relation to corporations and ministerial officers. Notwithstanding they may be liable to an action on the case for a neglect of duty, they may be compelled by mandamus to exercise their functions according to law."

And in the case of *The People* v. *The Supervisors of Columbia County*, 10 *Wend.* 363, it was said that "should it be thought that the offending supervisors ought to respond personally in damages, which is certainly very questionable, still there is no principle which would graduate the damages to the deficiency which would arise from the mortgage in question; and for aught the court can know, the money, possibly, might not be collected in that way."

But in apparent opposition to this doctrine, see the case of *The People* v. *The Supervisors of Chenango County*, 1 *Kern. Rep.*, 573, it was at least strongly intimated by the court in that case that where the relator has a right of action against the officers or other person promoting the injury, that mandamus will not lie. The decision of the court in that case, however, was also based on another ground, namely: That the supervisors had no legal control over the delinquent parties to compel them to make restitution.

In that case town assessors had assessed the relator for his personal estate, when he was not a resident of the town at the time when the assessment was made. On such assessment the board of supervisors of the county imposed a tax upon the relator, which was collected by a seizure and sale of his property upon their warrant issued to the collector. The relator sought to compel, by mandamus, the supervisors to audit and allow a claim in his favor against the county, for the amount of the tax thus collected. It was maintained by the court that the assessors acted without jurisdiction in assessing the relator's property, and were liable, and might have been prosecuted for their acts, in subjecting the relator to the payment of an unfounded and illegal tax; that the relator had, therefore. a legal remedy by action. And the legitimate inference to be drawn from the reasoning of the court is, that in the opinion of the court the case was not such as should take it out of the general rule, that a party cannot have a remedy by mandamus when he has a legal remedy by action.

In the case of *Kendall* v. *Stokes et al.*, 3 *Howard's U. S. Rep.*, 87, the doctrine which seems to be maintained is, that when a public officer, whose duty it is to audit and allow an account, or perform any other ministerial duty, refuses to do so, the party who is entitled to the allowance is interested personally in the performance of the duty, may resort to his remedy by mandamus to compel the officer to perform his duty, or he may prosecute a suit for damages against such officer. And it is distinctly held that if he prosecutes his remedy by mandamus, it is a bar to his action for damages.

In that case Kendall, who was the Postmaster General, had refused to credit the defendants in error on the books of the Post office Department, with certain amounts to which they were entitled. They had sued out a writ of mandamus, and procured a peremptory writ compelling him to give the credit, which he had done; and afterwards they brought suit against Kendall to recover their damages, sustained by reason of his refusal to do so prior to the time of the issuing of the mandamus.

Chief Justice TANEY, in delivering the opinion of the court, said: "Now, the former case was between these same parties, and the wrong then complained of by the plaintiffs, as well as in the case before us on the fifth count, was the refusal of the defendant to enter a credit on the books of the Post-office Department for the amount awarded by the solicitor. In other words, it was for the refusal to pay them a sum of money to which they were lawfully entitled. The credit on the books was nothing more than the form in which the act of Congress, referring the dispute to the solicitor, directed the payment to be made. For the object and effect of that entry was to discharge the plaintiff from so much money, if on other accounts they were debts to that amount; and if no other debt was due from them to the United States, the credit entitled them to receive at once from the government the amount credited. The action of mandamus was brought to recover it, and the plaintiffs show by their evidence that they did recover it in that suit. The gist of the action in that case was the breach of duty in not entering the credit, and it was assigned by the plaintiffs as their cause of action. The cause of action in the present case is the same, and the breach here assigned, as well as in the former case, is the refusal of the defendants to enter this credit. The evidence to prove the plaintiff's cause of action is also identical in both actions. Indeed, the record of the proceedings in the mandamus is the testimony relied on to show the refusal of the Postmaster General, and the circumstances under which he refused, and the reasons he assigned for it. But where a party has a choice of remedies for a wrong done to him, and he elects one, and proceeds to judgment, and obtains the fruits of his judgment, can he, in any case, afterwards proceed in another suit for the same cause of action? It is true that in the suit by mandamus the plaintiff could recover nothing beyond the amount awarded; but they knew that when they elected the remedy.

"If the goods of a party are forcibly taken away under circumstances of violence and aggravation, he may bring trespass, and in that form of action recover not only the value of the property, but also what are called vindictive damages —that is, such damages as the jury may think proper to give to punish the wrong-doer. But if instead of an action of trespass, he elects to bring trover, where he can recover only the value of the property, it never has been supposed that, after having prosecuted the suit to judgment, and received the damages awarded him, he can then bring trespass upon the ground that he could not in the action of trover give evidence of the circumstances of aggravation, which entitled him to demand vindictive damages. The same principle is involved here. The plaintiffs show that they have sued for, and recovered in the mandamus suit, the full amount of the award; and having recovered the debt, they now bring another suit upon the same cause of action, because in the former one they could not recover damages for the detention of the money. The law does not permit a party to be twice harassed for the same cause of action; nor suffer a plaintiff to proceed in one suit to recover the principal sum of money, and then support another to recover damages for the detention. * * * Whenever, therefore, a mandamus is applied for, it is upon the ground that he cannot obtain redress in any other form of proceedings. And to allow him to bring another action for the very same cause after he has obtained the benefit of the mandamus, would not only be harassing the defendant with two suits for the same thing, but would be inconsistent with the grounds upon which he asked for the mandamus, and inconsistent also with the decision of the court which awarded it."

The same case makes exceptions to the general rule, that a proceeding in mandamus is a bar to an action for damages, or rather limits and confines it to actions against the officers who neglect or refuse to perform their duties. For it maintains that where one has been unlawfully excluded from an office, and has been compelled to resort to an action by mandamus, to procure his admission thereto, he may, notwithstanding, maintain an action of assumpsit or case, to recover the emoluments which had been received by another, or of which he had been deprived during the time of exclusion.

While all the cases agree that mandamus will not lie, where the relator has a complete, specific, and adequate remedy by action in some other form, yet there seems to be no general rule for determining when an action against the delinquent officer would be a complete, specific, and adequate remedy. The mere fact that an action will lie, does not supersede the remedy by mandamus. For although an action may be sustained, yet from the facts and circumstances of the case, it may be doubtful whether such action will afford the relator a complete remedy; in which case mandamus should be awarded.

It has been maintained as a well settled principle, that when the legislature, under the right of eminent domain, and for the prosecution of works for public use, authorize an act, or series of acts, the natural and necessary consequence of doing which will be damage to the property of another, and provide a mode for the assessment and payment of the damages occasioned by such work, the party authorized, acting within the scope of his authority, and not guilty of carelessness or negligence in executing such work, is not a wrong doer, and an action will not lie as for a tort. The remedy, therefore, is by the statute, and not at common law. And when the remedy pointed out by the statute, is an assessment of damages by the county commissioners, and they neglect or refuse to proceed and perform such duty, mandamus will lie to compel them.

This principle was recognized and applied in the case of *Dodge and another* v. *County Commissioners of Essex*, 3 *Metcalf's* (*Mass.*) *Reps.*, 380. That was an application for a writ of mandamus to the commissioners, requiring them to assess damages for the petitioners against the Eastern Railroad Company. The facts, as set forth in the petition, and admitted by the answer of the commissioners, were, that the plaintiffs were owners of a lot of land in Beverly, with a house thereon, situated near the limits of the railroad, but not within them, that the railroad was near a ledge of rocks; that the company by the necessary operation of blasting said ledge of rocks, for the purpose of grading their railroad, greatly damaged, and nearly destroyed the petitioner's house. It was contended on the part of the Railroad Company, that under the provisions of the statute respecting railroads, one cannot have compensation for damages, whose lands have not been directly taken for the site of the railroad, nor for supplying materials for its construction, and that the remedy for a damage like that of the petitioners, where no land was taken or appropriated, was not to be sought by an application to the county commissioners, but by an action at common law. The statutory remedy in such case was as follows: "Every railroad corporation shall be liable to pay all damages, that shall be occasioned by laying out, and making and maintaining their road, or by taking any land or materials, as provided in the preceding section."

SHAW, C. J., in delivering the opinion of the court, said: "The court are of opinion, that the provision is broad enough to embrace damages done to real estate, like that which the petitioners have sustained. It is like the case of a house situated on the brink of a deep cutting, so as to become insecure, and so that it is necessary to remove it. It is a damage occasioned by the laying out and making of the road. * * * "An authority to construct any public work carries with it an authority to use the appropriate means. An authority to make a railroad, is an authority to reduce the line of the road to a level, and for that purpose to make cuts, as well through ledges of rock as through banks of earth.

"In a remote and detached place, where due precaution can be taken to prevent danger to persons, blasting by gunpowder is a reasonable and appropriate mode of executing such a work; and if due precautions are taken to prevent unnecessary damage, is a justifiable mode. It follows that the necessary damage occasioned thereby to a dwelling house or other building, which cannot be removed out of the way of such danger, is one of the natural and unavoidable consequences of executing the work, and within the provisions of the statute.

"Of course, this reasoning will not apply to damages occasioned by carelessness or negligence in executing such a work. Such careless or negligent act would be a tort, for which an action at law would lie against him who commits or him who commands it. But where all due precautions are taken, and damage is still necessarily done to fixed property, it alike is within the letter and the equity of the statute, and the county commissioners have authority to assess the damages. This court are therefore of opinion that an alternative writ of mandamus be awarded to the county commissioners, to assess the petitioner's damages, or return their reasons for not doing so."

And where county commissioners refuse or neglect to estimate the damages caused by laying out a railroad, turnpike, or highway; such duty being enjoined upon them by law, a mandamus would issue to compel them to do it, that is to exercise their judgment upon the matter. But having estimated damages, if either party should be dissatisfied, and apply for a jury, the granting of the warrant would be a ministerial duty, enforceable by mandamus, when the remedy by appeal is given to the dissatisfied party. And if they refuse to assess damages because in their judgment the petitioner does not own the land, the latter is entitled to the judgment of a jury upon the question, and a mandamus lies to compel them to issue a warrant therefor, when the issuing of such warrant is necessary to enable the party to take his appeal, and it is the duty of the commissioners to issue it. (*Carpenter* v. *Bristol*, 21 *Pick.* 258; *Smith* v. *The Mayor and Aldermen of Boston*, 1 *Gray*, 72.)

And when county commissioners, in laying out a highway, or ordering specific repairs thereon, make no return of damages sustained by a party who has applied to them to estimate his damages, this is equivalent to a return that he has sustained no damage. (8 *Cush.* [*Mass.*] *Rep.*, 360.)

It has been held that the writ of mandamus is a high prerogative writ, and its being granted or refused, is within the sound discretion of the court. While this, as a general rule is correct, yet, when the relator has a clear, vested, legal right to the thing withheld, he is entitled to the remedy by mandamus, although to give him the thing, would not appear to be strictly in accordance with the principles of equity.

This doctrine was recognized and acted upon in the case of *Harrington* v. *The County Commissioners of Berkshire*, 22 *Pick.* 263. The facts were fully stated in the opinion of the court. SHAW, Ch. J., in announcing the opinion of the court, said: "The petition and answer on which this question arises, presents a novel and in many respects a peculiar and extraordinary case for the consideration of the court. It appears that the county commissioners, in pursuance of the powers vested in them by law, having given the notice required, and conformed generally to the rules of law, adjudicated upon the common convenience and necessity of a public highway, and thereupon located and laid out the same, passing to some extent over the land of the petitioner. The usual orders for making and fitting the road for public use were passed. The petitioner applied for a jury to assess his damages; and after one attempt, which proved unsuccessful on account of some informality, a verdict of the sheriff's jury, assessing his damages, was duly returned to the court of Common Pleas and accepted, and certified in due form of law to the county commissioners.

Before the proper time had arrived for granting an order on the treasury for the payment of the complainant's damages, and before his land had been entered upon, or his possession disturbed, measures were taken for the discontinuance of the highway, and subsequently an order or decree was passed discontinuing it. Therefore the county commissioners declined issuing an order for the payment of the complainant's damages, on the ground that as his land had not been entered upon, and after the order of discontinuance never could be entered upon, he had sustained no real damages, and was not entitled to claim payment according to the verdict. It is now contended for the respondents that it would be highly unjust and inequitable to require the public to pay the whole value of the land for a naked right or privilege which they have never used, and now never can use; and that it is equally unjust for the complainant to demand a sum of money by way of damage, for a loss which he has not and cannot sustain.

"If there were any middle course to be adopted, if any

apportionment could be made by which the complainant could be indemnified for the actual trouble and expense to which he has been subjected, and the public exempted from further liability, it would be more in accordance with principles of equity; but there seems to be no legal principle in which this can be done. It was suggested that he should claim damages for the discontinuance; but the discontinuance, as it relieves his estate from a burdensome service, to which it was subject by perpetual easement, is a benefit and not a damage; indeed, the damage given on laying out the road is a compensation for imposing this service upon the land. It is, therefore, a question of legal right to the sum fixed by the verdict, and the adjudication upon it, by the court having jurisdiction of the subject; and it appears to be a necessary consequence that the complainant is entitled to the whole amount or to no part of it. If the adjudication discontinuing the road vacated all the prior proceedings, including the verdict and judgment of the court of Common Pleas accepting it, that judgment is in effect reversed and annulled, and then the complainant can make no claim under it; otherwise it remains in full force, and he is entitled to the entire benefit of it. Such being the question, the court are of opinion that the petitioner, on the return and acceptance of the verdict, acquired a vested right to his damages, and that the subsequent discontinuance of the highway did not divest or defeat that right. The subsequent discontinuance of the highway is a new, distinct, substantive proceeding, which does not annul or disaffirm the former proceeding, but on the contrary assumes and acts upon it as a valid proceeding. It was a contingency contemplated at the time of laying out the highway, inasmuch as the easement for the public was always held at the will of the public, to be exercised by their competent agents. When it is exercised, it grants no new rights to the owner of the property, but simply leaves him in the enjoyment of a right which was always his, as incident to his ownership.

"The enjoyment of this latter right, therefore, cannot deprive him of his former vested right to damages—the one being entirely consistent with the other. The commissioners, therefore, were not justified in withholding from the complainant his order for the payment of his damages, conformably to the verdict accepted by the court of Common Pleas and certified to the commissioners. The court do therefore order that an alternative writ of mandamus issue, directed to the county commissioners, requiring them to draw an order on the county treasury for the payment to the complainant of the amount due to him pursuant to the verdict, or to make a return of the writ, setting forth the reasons and causes why they have not done it."

It was also maintained by the respondents that even if they were not authorized to withhold payment, yet mandamus was not the proper remedy. That the remedy by writ of mandamus was an extraordinary remedy, to be resorted to with great caution, and ought not to be had when there is any other adequate remedy in a regular course of judicial proceeding. But it was held by the court that it was, to say the least, doubtful whether any action of debt or case would lie in favor of the complainant, as the act required to be done on the part of the county commissioners was a ministerial and not a judicial act, and that, therefore, it was the opinion of the court that the complainant was entitled to the remedy prayed for.

And where a town was entitled by a statute to a jury in relation to the location of a highway, and the jury impaneled were unable to agree, and were discharged, it was held that the town was entitled to another jury, although the statute made no express provision for such a case; that the statute intended to secure to parties, situated in the condition of the petitioners, the right of a trial by jury; that such trial necessarily implies an effectual trial, resulting in a verdict; that a hearing before a jury impaneled for the purpose, but who cannot agree in a verdict, is not such trial; that a power must necessarily rest somewhere to order a new hearing in such case; that by reasonable construction of the statute and analogy to other cases, such power was vested in the county commissioners, and that as they declined to exercise it, in a case where the petitioners were entitled to the benefit of it, the writ of mandamus ought to issue. (*The inhabitants of Mendon* v. *The County of Worcester*, 10 *Pick.* 235.)

And where, by law, it is made the duty of county commissioners to take the supervision of a highway, to determine whether it should remain or be discontinued, and if they should not discontinue it, it was their duty to complete, at the expense of the county, such parts as remained unfinished, re-assess the damages on such parts, and cause the same to be paid by the county, it was held that a mandamus would lie to compel them to perform such duty.

Neither is it necessary, in such cases, that there should be any law, specifically directing them to take the supervision of that particular road.

A law providing that "whenever any highway is already laid out, or altered, in any county, which it would be the duty of such county to make, under the provisions of the law, and the working of the same is not already commenced by said commissioners of highways, or by them contracted to be made, it shall be the duty of said county commissioners to do and perform all the acts in relation to the making of the same, which it would be incumbent upon the said commissioners of highways to do and perform if this act had not been passed," imposes upon the commissioners the duty of taking supervision of a highway, previously established by a court of Sessions.

But upon the petition of a town for a mandamus to the

county commissioners to take supervision of, and to finish a part of a highway which had formerly been laid out by the court of Sessions, an alternative mandamus was issued, to which the commissioners made return that the part in question, which was a bridge, had been built by the town, with the aid of individuals, and that the expense had been voluntarily incurred by the town, and the individuals, after the enactment of the statute providing for the payment of similar expenses out of the county treasury; and that the bridge, immediately after its erection, was dedicated to the public without any expectation on the part of the town that the expense would be reimbursed by the county; it was held, that as the grant was made by the town freely and deliberately, with a full knowledge of the law, and on a good consideration, namely: the voluntary contributions of others towards an object of common and public benefit, that the return disclosed a fair legal reason for not performing the act complained of. (*The Inhabitants of Springfield* v. *The County Commissioners of Hampden*, 10 *Pick.* 59.)

Where county commissioners act in a judicial capacity upon a question properly submitted to their judgment, mandamus will not lie to reverse or control their decision. Therefore, where the petitioners represented that they were the owners of certain land; that the Blackstone Canal Company, by virtue of their act of incorporation, had located and constructed a reservoir to the Blackstone canal, by reason of which the petitioners' land was overflowed with water, and rendered good for nothing; that certain commissioners, appointed pursuant to the act, had made an estimate of the damages sustained by the petitioners, with which they were dissatisfied, and upon their application to the county commissioners, a jury was impaneled to estimate the damages; that the jury awarded to the petitioners a larger sum than the one awarded by the commissioners, and the verdict was returned to the county commissioners, and was by them accepted and affirmed; and that the petitioners, at the time of the acceptance and affirmation of the verdict, moved the county commissioners, in writing, to allow them their legal costs in the suit, but that the motion was overruled; wherefore the petitioners prayed the court to issue a writ of mandamus to the county commissioners, ordering them to allow and tax for the petitioners their costs in the suit, and to enter up judgment therefor; it was held by the court, that the action of the commissioners in the matter was a judicial act, over which the court had no power of control, and therefore a mandamus would not lie. (*Chase et al.* v *The Blackstone Canal Company*, 10 *Pick.* 244.)

So, when the alternative mandamus recited that the relator was appointed by the Secretary of State to take the census for a certain town in the county pursuant to the provisions of the statute, that he thereupon entered upon and discharged the duties of such office until the same was completed, as required by the act; that the relator was actually and necessarily employed in the discharge of the duties of said office, and in taking the census and enumeration of the inhabitants of said town as required by said act, fifty-nine days; that the relator presented his account for such services to the defendants, duly made out and verified as required by law, at a regular session of the defendants for allowance, and that the defendants refused to audit or allow the said account. It then commanded the defendants to audit and allow the said account for fifty-nine days' services as such marshal at two dollars per day, or show cause why.

The defendants returned that at the annual meeting of said board, held pursuant to law, the said relator presented to said board his account for fifty-nine days' services, which he claimed to have rendered as marshal in the town of Lima, in said county, under and by virtue of the act within mentioned; that said board, pursuant to the statute in such case made and provided, proceeded to examine, settle, audit, and allow said account, and did examine, settle, audit, and allow the same.

That upon such examination and settlement the said board ascertained and believed, found and determined, that said relator was not actually and necessarily employed as such marshal, under and by virtue of said act, fifty-nine days; and in like manner ascertained and believed, found and determined, that said relator was not so employed over forty days; and thereupon said board of supervisors audited and allowed said account of said relator for the sum of eighty dollars pursuant to the statute, and their duties in that behalf.

This return was demurred to for insufficiency. The court, however, held that in the examination and decision of the question of the number of days the marshal was actually and necessarily employed, the board of supervisors acted judicially; and if they committed an error in their decision, it found no ground for the writ of mandamus; that such determination must, in that proceeding, be regarded as final. (*The People* v. *The Board of Supervisors of Livingston county*, 25 *Barb.* 118.)

And where county commissioners, after adjudging that a town way was required by the wants of the town, and giving notice that they will lay it out, lay out only a part of it, being of opinion that the remainder has been rendered unnecessary, since the adjudication, by the construction by the town of another nearly parallel town way, will not be compelled by mandamus to complete it. The question of what the public convenience required is peculiarly within the province of the commissioners, and the court will not reverse their judgment in the matter. (*Hill* v. *The County Commissioners*, 4 *Gray*, 414.)

But where a statute creating and defining the duties of commissioners of highways provided that "all roads laid out, but not worked, at the time this act takes effect, shall be subjected to the supervision and review of the commissioners aforesaid, and the said commissioners shall have all the powers, and the counties be subject to all the liabilities in reference to such roads as are provided for new roads by this act," it was held that the legislature here had respect to roads before located by the court of Sessions, but not finished; including as well those which had been partly worked as those on which no work had been done, and they meant to transfer all authority on the subject to the commissioners; that if they deemed it proper that the road be made as laid out, it gave them power to do so; or if they thought it not proper to so work it, they possessed the power to discontinue it; and that a mandamus would lie to compel them to finish or to discontinue it, as they might think expedient. (*The Inhabitants of Springfield* v. *The Commissioners of*, &c., 4 *Pick.* 68.)

It has also been held, that where commissioners of a county have authority by statute to issue bonds, and are required to levy a tax to pay the interest coupons as they become due, and having issued such bonds, they neglect or refuse to assess the tax, or pay the interest, a writ of mandamus is the proper legal remedy, and that the Circuit court of the United States have authority to issue such writ of mandamus against the commissioners, when it is necessary, as a remedy for suitors in such court. (*Knox County* v. *Aspinwall*, 24 *How.* [*U. S.*] *R.*, 376.)

The court will not grant a mandamus when it would be fruitless and ineffectual to relieve the relator.

Therefore when a mandamus was prayed for, to issue against the county commissioners to compel them to make an order on the treasury in favor of the relator, for a sum of money due from the county to him, and the commissioners should show for cause, that there was no money in the treasury to pay the order, it was held that this was a sufficient cause. The court, in delivering the opinion of the court, said: "Why draw an order on an empty treasury? The treasurer would refuse payment, and there the matter would end. No money can come into the treasury but by tax on the county, and that tax the commissioners cannot lay, except by the co-operation of other persons, even supposing that the act authorizing the laying of a tax for the purchase of the bridge. If the object be obtainable by mandamus, the first step must be to order the proper persons to lay the tax, and it must be laid for the whole sum at once, &c." (*Commonwealth* v. *Commissioners of Lancaster County*, 6 *Bin.* 5; *Dodd* v. *Miller*, 14 *Ind.*, 433.)

To warrant the granting of a mandamus, the applicant must have a clear legal right. And therefore a bidder in proposals issued by county commissioners for estimates for any public works, acquires no legal right, or cause of action, to enforce which a mandamus will be issued, until the contract has been actually made with him. (*The People* v. *The Croton Aqueduct Board*, &c., 26 *Barb.* 240; *The People* v. *The Canal Board*, 13 *Barb.* 432. *But see The People* v. *The Contracting Board*, 27 *New York Reps.*, 378.)

The applicant must not only have a clear legal right to the thing demanded, but he must be without any other specific legal remedy. Therefore where a party overtaxed, appeals in due form from the assessors to the county commissioners, who refused to entertain his appeal, or to make any record of their proceeding in the matter, it was held that he was not entitled to a mandamus, for the reason that under the statute he might have appealed to the court of Common Pleas. (*James* v. *Commissioners of Bucks County*, 13 *Penn. State Reps.*, 72.)

And where the supervisors of a county have neglected to perform any duty required of them at their annual meeting, and they are authorized to hold special meetings for the transaction of business, at such times and places as they may find convenient, they may be compelled by mandamus to meet again, and perform it. Their neglect to perform their duty imposed by law, at the time required, cannot nullify the statute. They, or their successors, are bound to do what was required, and on failure to perform it, may be compelled by mandamus, and in some cases are liable to a penalty for their neglect. The omission to perform their duty at the proper time, does not in such case render a substantial compliance with the statute impossible, as they or their successors in office can be convened at another time. (*The People* v. *The Supervisors, &c.*, 4 *Selden's* [*N. Y.*] *Reps.*, 318.)

It would, however, be otherwise, if they were authorized to perform the duty at a specified time which had passed.

It is not necessary to the issuing of a mandamus commanding county commissioners to perform official duties neglected by them, that the complainant should have previously demanded of them to perform their duty. (*Commonwealth* v. *Commissioners, &c.*, 37 *Penn. S. R.*, 237 ; *and see same*, 277.)

Where boards of supervisors exercise both judicial and ministerial functions, and they have gone forward and performed the judicial act, and the result of such act raises an obligation on them to perform a ministerial act, which they refuse to perform, a mandamus is the proper remedy to compel performance on their part; and this may be done, although they may have reconsidered and endeavored to reverse and annul such judicial act.

Inferior jurisdictions, such as boards of supervisors, which derive their powers from the statute, have no power or authority to review, reverse and annul their own judicial action when it has once been legally exercised. It has, therefore, been held that when a board of supervisers have, by a legal quorum of their members, voted upon a resolution "concerning the raising of money," under the statutory authority to apportion the tax to be raised among the several towns and wards of the county, "as seemed to them equitable and just," and such vote has been entered by their clerk in the book of records required to be kept by them, they have exhausted their discretion over that subject; that they have thereby executed a judicial act, which is in effect a judgment final and conclusive as to any power they can exercise over it by way of review or reversal. And if the board, after having passed a resolution of that nature, which has been entered in their book of minutes by the clerk, reconsider their action by a resolution for that purpose, and by another resolution again apportion and equalize the assessment of value in the several towns and wards, upon a new and different basis, the second apportionment will be held a nullity; and the board may be compelled, by mandamus, to attach collectors' warrants to the tax books made out according to the original resolution. (*The People* v. *The Board of Supervisors of Schenectady*, 35 *Barb.* 408.)

It has also been held that mandamus will lie to compel supervisors to renew a license to a ferry owner, who is entitled to it, when such supervisors, through a mistake of the law, refuse to do so. (*Thomas* v. *Armstrong*, 7 *Cal.* 286.)

CHAPTER XVIII.

MANDAMUS TO THE OFFICERS OF A MUNICIPAL CORPORATION.

It seems that mandamus is the proper and appropriate remedy to compel a municipal corporation to make provision for the payment of interest due upon bonds issued by it in payment of a subscription to the stock of a railroad company, by the assessment and collection of the necessary taxes; and therefore where an act of assembly directed that provision be made for the payment of the principal and interest of the debt thus incurred, by the assessment and collection of a tax, the proper officers of such corporation may be compelled by mandamus to assess and collect a tax for the payment of the interest. (*Commonwealth* v. *Pittsburg*, 34 *Penn. S. R.*, 496; *State* v. *Davenport*, 12 *Iowa Reps.*, 335.)

The same doctrine was maintained in *Graham et al.* v. *Maddox et al.*, 6 *American Law Reg.* 620. It is there said that the duty of the city council, to levy and collect the tax to pay the principal and interest of such bonds, is mandatory, leaving in the city council no discretion. It was also held that it was not an available legal objection to the payment of such bonds and their interest, that the money was squandered, or that the enterprise has resulted disastrously, and the tax would therefore be onerous; that no individual could be excused from the payment of a debt because the business in which he had embarked his borrowed money had proved a failure; and that a corporation can have no immunity in this respect above an individual.

Neither is it a sufficient answer to the relator's petition for a mandamus, he being the holder of the bonds, to aver that the road has never been completed; that the company have forfeited their charter, and by gross mismanagement have placed it out of their power to comply with their engagement in this respect. (11 *B. Monroe*, 154.)

So in *Maddox* v. *Graham*, 2 *Met.* (*Ky.*) 56, it was held that where a city council is required by law to collect a tax upon the real and personal property of the city, sufficient in amount annually to pay off the interest upon bonds issued by the city in payment of a subscription of stock to a railroad company, and the council refuse to do so, and there is no specific legal remedy provided for non-performance, mandamus may be maintained to compel them to discharge that duty, at the instance of holders to whom the bonds have been passed by the company; and it seems that an express refusal in terms is not necessary to put the defendants in fault; it will be sufficient that their conduct makes it apparent that they do not intend to do the act required.

So in *Carroll* v. *Board of Police*, 28 *Miss.* (6 *Cush.*) 38, it was held that mandamus was the only remedy by which to compel the board of police to discharge their duties as public officers, in levying the tax required by law to pay the debt of the county; and the writ ought to be granted upon all occasions where the law has established no specific remedy, and where justice and good government require it.

And where a city council appointed commissioners to assess damages to private property, by reason of opening a street, who reported their assessment and a taxation of adjoining property to pay the same, and the city opened the street but refused to collect the tax, it was held that mandamus was proper to compel them to do so. (*State* v. *Keokuk*, 9 *Iowa*, 438.)

And where it is made the duty of a town or city council to elect certain municipal officers, and they neglect or refuse to do their duty in that respect, mandamus is the proper remedy. Therefore, where at a meeting of the town council the minority of the councilors present delivered voting papers to the mayor for certain persons to be elected aldermen; the mayor and the majority of the town councilors had been advised that the day was not the proper one for the election, the mayor consequently declined to proceed with the election, and no election was declared, it was in fact the duty of the council to have proceeded to the election of aldermen on that day, had they known the law. It was thereupon held by the court that the act of the minority was not the act of the town council; that the election had not been held, but that there had been no election, and that consequently a mandamus might issue, calling upon the council to proceed to elect aldermen. (*Regina* v. *Bradford*, 4 *Eng. L. & Eq. Rep.*, 194.)

And where it is made the duty of a city comptroller, upon the presentation of a certificate from the auditing board, allowing a claim against the corporation to draw his warrant on the treasurer, if he refuse to do his duty in that respect he may be compelled by mandamus. But until the auditing board has allowed the claim and certified to the comptroller, he cannot be proceeded against by mandamus, although it may appear that the relator has a valid claim against the corporation.

Therefore, where it appeared that the relator had a valid claim against the city, and the comptroller had refused to draw his warrant on the treasury, and the relator had thereupon asked for a writ of mandamus to compel him, the writ was refused, on the ground that as the law had created an auditing bureau in the financial department, with an auditor of accounts as the chief officer, whose duty it was to "audit, revise, credit, and settle all accounts in which the city is concerned as debtor or creditor," it was not the duty of the comptroller to draw his warrant on the treasury for the payment of any claim until it had been allowed by such board. (*The People* v. *Flagg*, 17 *N. Y. R.* 584.)

Mandamus is a proper remedy for one who has been illegally removed from a municipal office. But when one has practically deserted, abandoned, and repudiated an office, and followed his own pursuits not connected with, but inconsistent with the duties of the office, he cannot compel the proper authorities to reinstate him in office. Therefore, where an act was passed to establish a Metropolitan Police district, bringing into being a new system, all of whose officers were then first introduced into the administration of the authority of the State government under new names, and with greatly enlarged duties and territorial jurisdiction, and subject to the authority and control of a new board of police; and also providing that the police in the cities of New York and Brooklyn, officers and patrolmen shall hold office and do duty under the provision of the act, and as members of the police force of the Metropolitan Police district, it was held that although no acceptance or new oath of office or manifestation of consent on the part of an old member of the police force was necessary in order to entitle him to the right to exercise the duties of a patrolman under the new act, yet as the relator had withdrawn from such police force; had disclaimed taking such office and repelled its duties; had followed his own pursuits having no connection with the police service for a period of two years, a mandamus ought not to be granted to reinstate him in the office; that by his conduct he had clearly vacated the office, and that the Board of Police could lawfully fill his place. (*The People* v. *The Board of Metropolitan Police*, 26 *N. Y. R.* 316.)

The case of *Tatham* v. *The Wardens of Philadelphia*, 5 *American Law Reg.* 379, was a petition praying that a writ of mandamus be awarded commanding J. E. Harned and others, wardens of the port of Philadelphia, to cause to be defined upon the ground, at the expense of the applicant, the line of low water bounding their jurisdiction of a certain lot in Philadelphia of a certain description, bounded upon the line of low-water mark by the river Delaware. The petition recited that the petitioner was the owner of the lot of ground so described, and that he made application in writing to the board of wardens requesting them to cause said line of low-water mark to be defined, which application was refused, and that on the first day of September last he again applied to the board, asking to reconsider their rejection of the prayer of his petition which was laid upon the table by the respondents; and that they still continue to refuse to define for him the line bounding their jurisdiction upon the land mentioned in his petition.

The statute required that the board of wardens of the port of Philadelphia, on the application of the owner of land bounded by the Delaware and Schuylkill rivers within the limits of the port, shall cause to be defined upon the ground, at the expense of the applicant, the line of low-water mark bounding their jurisdictions.

It was held, that the act to be done was simple and specific; and so far from leaving it to the discretion or judgment of the wardens, the language of the law was imperative, and that the petitioner had a clear right to build his wharf to low-water mark, and that he had a right to compel the wardens to go forward and define the line in order to enable him to do so with safety.

It was further held, that the answer setting up the impossibility of fixing the line of low-water mark as prayed for by the petitioner was insufficient, as it was not pretended that an effort had been made to comply with the directions of the act, nor the nature or character of the disability set out, that the court might judge whether it was a mere disinclination to perform the duty required, or an actual impediment, which rendered it impossible for the respondents to do that which the law says they shall do.

And where the authorities of a borough are bound to keep its streets in repair, they may be compelled to do so by mandamus. (*Uniontown* v. *Commonwealth*, 34 *Penn. S. R.* 293.)

So in *Hammon* v. *Covington*, 3 *Met.* (*Ky.*) 494, it was held that where the city council is required by law to keep a street in repair, if they suffer it to so far fall into disrepair as to prevent passage thereon in carriages, and to render it dangerous for people having houses thereon to pass to and fro, and to endanger said houses, that although the abuttors thereon have cause of action by reason of the special injury done to them, yet they may also have mandamus to issue to the council to compel them to make the proper repairs. And so where an act was passed by the legislature, entitled "An act to widen Fulton street, between Red Hook lane and Court street, in the city of Brooklyn," and providing that "Fulton street, between Red Hook lane and Court street, is hereby widened as follows;" and also providing that the common council of Brooklyn might take certain steps towards carrying out the act, and bestowed certain powers upon the courts for the same purpose, it was held that shall may be substituted for may in the interpretation of a statute, when the good sense of the entire enactment would require the same; and that the rule applies when the statute establishes an improvement, and devolves upon any person or persons, or a corporation, the performance of such acts as may be requisite to insure its completion; that applying this rule to this case, the statute was peremptory upon the common council to pursue the designed improvement to its consummation, and that a mandamus would lie at the suit of a citizen and tax-payer of Brooklyn to compel them to do so. (*People* v. *Common Council of Brooklyn*, 22 *Barb.* 404.)

Mandamus is also the proper remedy to obtain possession of the seal, books, papers, muniments, &c., the property of the corporation, held in possession by an ex-mayor; and a pretended intrusion into or retention of the office of mayor will not justify the withholding of such property so as to compel the informant to resort to a quo warranto. (*The People* v. *Kilduff*, 15 *Ill.*, 492.)

And where the only pre-requisite required to entitle a person to receive from the mayor a license to engage in the business of broking emigrant passengers, was the giving of a bond of a certain description, the mayor can only exercise his judgment as to the sufficiency of the bond. If that be found by him to be sufficient, he is bound to issue the license, and if he refuse, he may be compelled by mandamus. (*The People* v. *Perry*, 13 *Barb.* 206.)

It has also been held that mandamus is the appropriate remedy when an officer of a municipal corporation undertakes to set at naught the corporate will, by refusing to execute or deliver the bonds of the corporation in payment of the price of lands purchased by the corporation; and that the writ may also be applied for by the vendor, who is beneficially interested in enforcing the contract, after a resolution has been passed by the common council directing the officer to carry out and complete the purchase. Therefore, where the relator offered to sell to the city of New York certain property, either for cash or corporate bonds, and the corporation, by resolution, accepted the offer, the payment of the price to be made in corporate bonds, it was held that this constituted an agreement whereby payment was to be made in bonds, and that mandamus would lie against the comptroller to compel him to execute them. BARNARD, J., said: "The remedy by mandamus is both appropriate and proper in this case. An officer of the corporation undertakes to set at naught the corporate will. Surely, the corporation must have some legal remedy to compel its subordinate to obey its lawful behests. It is impossible to conceive of any legal remedy adequate for the purpose other than a mandamus. Assuming that the corporation could have sued out the writ, is there any objection to allowing to the party who is beneficially interested in enforcing the corporate will expressed in his favor, the use of the same remedy which the corporation would be entitled to use? There does not appear to be any well founded objection so long as the corporation assents to the proceedings being taken against the officer." (*The People* v. *Brennan*, 39 *Barb.* 536.)

It has also been held that if there are words of permission in the charter of a public corporation, to do an act which is clearly for the public benefit, they are obligatory upon the officers of the corporation. Therefore, where a charter declared that the mayor and jurats of an ancient town might hold a court of record for the holding of pleas, but which had been long disused, the court of King's Bench granted a mandamus to compel such court to be held, at the instance of an inhabitant of the town, though he was not a corporator.

So where a charter granted to the steward and suitors of a manor power and authority to hold a court for the purpose (among other objects) of hearing and determining pleas of debt, &c., but the court had been disused for that purpose during fifty years, it was held that a mandamus would lie to compel the court to be held again for such purpose, notwithstanding the non-user. (*Rex* v. *Hastings*, 1 *D. & R.*, 148; 5 *B. & A.*, 692; 2 *D. & R.*, 176.)

CHAPTER XIX.

MANDAMUS TO OTHER OFFICERS.

Mandamus will not lie to compel public officers to perfect an incomplete contract which will be binding upon the State, especially where the subject or object of the contract has passed by sale from the State into the hands of some other person.

Therefore, where the relator set forth that in the year 1853 he made application to the then school fund commissioner to purchase certain lands then for sale in his office, and was informed by said commissioner that the lands were already pre-empted by one R., but that the relator might enter the lands subject to the pre-emptor's rights, which was done, the relator paying part of the price and taking the commissioner's receipt therefor; that said R. failed to make good his pre-emption, and that afterwards the relator applied to the commissioner for the requisite papers in respect to the title to the land, tendering performance of his duties in the premises; that said commissioner refused to issue the requisite papers, and said he should offer the lands for sale at auction; that relator refused to receive back his money, and that the respondent was the present school commissioner, it was held that the relator could not thereby obtain the aid of the court to perfect an inchoate contract which would be binding upon the State, especially as it appeared that other persons had purchased the land, in one case, of the then present commissioner without notice by him or them of the relator's claim. (*Chance* v. *Temple*, 1 *Clarke* [*Iowa*], 179.)

In fact, it seems to be a well established principle that although a mandamus may sometimes lie against a ministerial officer to do some ministerial act connected with the liabilities of the government, yet it must be when the government itself is liable, and the officer himself has improperly refused to act. It must be in a case of clear and not doubtful right. (*Reeside* v. *Walker*, 11 *Howard's Rep.*, 272.)

It is upon this principle that it has been held that a mandamus will not be issued on the application of an individual to any officer of the government, commanding him to approve of a contract, entered into with that individual by public officers, when such approval is necessary in order to make the contract binding upon the State. If the contract is complete, mandamus will lie to compel the proper officer to execute it in good faith. (*Ante*, 132–3.)

In the case of *The People* v. *The Canal Board*, 13 *Barb. Rep.*, 432, was a motion for a peremptory mandamus, to be directed to the Canal Board, commanding them to act and approve or disapprove of the contract awarded to and made with the relator, as stated in the affidavit on which the motion was founded; and to approve or disapprove of the terms upon which, and in the manner in which, the board of Canal Commissioners, State Engineer and Surveyor and division engineer had contracted with the said relator to do the work in the said contracts specified. The relator, among other things, alleged that in pursuance of an advertisement for proposals for work on certain canals therein described, and his proposal in the manner and form described in his motion, the board of Canal Commissioners, together with the State Engineer and Surveyor, and the division engineer having charge of that portion of the canal where the work was to be let, awarded to the relator a contract for certain work therein described; that he was advised by his counsel and believed, that in order to render the contracts so made with him valid or binding, it was necessary that the Canal Board should approve of the terms upon which, and the manner in which, the said Canal Commissioners, State Engineer and Surveyor and division engineer had contracted with him to do the work mentioned; that he had presented to said board his application, praying in substance that said board would examine the prices established in said contracts, and approve or disapprove of the same, but that said board had hitherto wholly neglected so to do.

Cady, J., in delivering the opinion of the court, said: "The State has not, as yet, made itself liable to the relator to execute or deliver by its officers to him any contract whatever; and I have been unable to find any case in which, on the application of an individual, a mandamus has been issued to any officer of the government, commanding him to make a contract with that individual binding on the State. If no action can be commenced and maintained against the State to compel the performance of a contract without a previous statute authorizing such action, it would seem to follow that no action can be maintained against an officer of the State to compel him to make or complete a contract on behalf of the State."

And where the constitution of the State declared that "all contracts for work or materials on any canal shall be made with the person who shall offer to do or provide the same at the lowest price, with adequate security for their performance;" and by legislative enactment it was also provided that the contracting board "shall have power, and it shall be their duty to let by contract, under such regulations as said board shall prescribe, to the lowest bidder or bidders, who will give adequate security for the performance of the contract," the repairs of any completed section of the canal. And under this law the contracting board advertised for proposals to keep a certain canal in repair for four years and a half. The notice indicated the form and character of the security which the board would consider adequate—that is, it stated that every proposal must be accompanied by a certificate of deposit in some bank in good credit; that four thousand dollars in cash had been deposited therein to the credit of the Auditor, which would be retained as security for the performance of the contract. The relator made a proposal which was somewhat lower in price than that of any other person, but it was not accepted. A contract was made with one Case, who was the next highest bidder. The relator delivered with his proposal a certificate that he had deposited in the Salt Springs Bank of Syracuse four thousand dollars payable to the order of the Auditor, but the certificate did not state, in so many words, that he had deposited such amount *in cash.* Case, whose bid was accepted, delivered a similar certificate containing, however, the words *in cash.* It was inferred by the court that this difference in the form or phraseology of the certificate was the reason assigned for rejecting the relator's bid, and accepting a higher one.

Although the court of Appeals was unable to justify such a decision of the board, yet it held that the board could not be compelled by mandamus to reverse their action, or to make a contract with the relator, after they had already made another contract with another person. (*The People* v. *The Contracting Board*, 27 *N. Y. R.* 378.)

And where the authority of a corporation to sell and convey land rests wholly upon statutory law, its provisions must be strictly complied with; and if in any part of the proceedings the provisions of the statute have not been strictly complied with, the proceedings are irregular, and the purchaser takes no title; and if any part of the proceedings have been irregular, mandamus will not lie to the officers of the corporation to compel them to complete the proceedings. Therefore, where a statute authorized the corporation of a city to sell lands for taxes, and to execute a lease of the same to the purchaser, if the owner neglected to redeem within two years from the time of sale; and it was also made the duty of the city, six months before the expiration of the two years after such sale, to cause an advertisement to be published at least once in each week for four weeks successively in two newspapers, that unless the lands sold were redeemed by a certain day, they would be conveyed to the purchaser; and the corporation failed to publish such notice after the sale as so required; it was held that the failure to give such notice made the proceedings irregular, and mandamus would not lie to the officers of the corporation to compel them to execute the lease, though the two years had expired. (*The People* v. *The Mayor, &c., of New York*, 10 *Wend.* 395.) Mandamus is the proper remedy for the neglect or refusal of a school district to raise and pay over to the district from which it has been divided the proportional amount for retaining the school house. (*School District No.* 2 v. *School District No.* 1, *Wis.* 333.)

So, mandamus lies to compel a township clerk to correct, by an amendment of his records, any errors, whether arising from design, mistake, or accident, on the application of any person interested. (20 *Conn. R.* 290.) A mandamus, however, was refused to compel a justice to amend his record, where the amount was insignificant and it was of no benefit to the petitioner. (*Hall* v. *Crossman*, 1 *Williams* [*Vt.*] *Rep.* 297.)

And a mandamus requiring the clerk of a school district to amend his records was also refused, where it appeared that he had ceased to be clerk, and had removed without the jurisdiction of the court. (*Mason* v. *Dist. No.* 14, 20 [*Vt.*] *Rep.* 487.)

But it will lie to compel him to deliver the records to his successor in office, if he refuses so to do, on the application of his successor and his showing himself to be clerk. (*Taylor* v. *Henry*, 2 *Pick.* 397; *Commonwealth* v. *Atheam*, 3 *Mass.* 287.)

So, where it is the duty of the town clerk to record deeds or other papers, or to file papers, and he refuses to do so, he may be compelled to perform such duty by mandamus. (*Strong's Case*, *Kerby's Rep.* 345; 7 *John's Rep.* 549.)

Mandamus is also an appropriate remedy to compel the collectors of the public revenue to proceed and perform their duties. For, unless there was some summary process to compel the performance of these duties, the treasury would become embarrassed, and great public mischief might ensue. And where by law it is made the duty of the treasurer, in case the collector neglects to collect a tax, to issue his warrant of distress against such collector for the amount of the tax assessed, if the treasurer refuses or neglects to so issue his warrant, he may be compelled to do so by mandamus.

Therefore where the law provided that if the tax collector failed to do his duty, the treasurer should issue a warrant directed to the sheriff, authorizing a distress of the collector's goods and chattels, and the imprisonment of his person, and the petitioners for a mandamus represented, that at a meeting of the inhabitants of a certain school district in the town of Dudley, on a certain day named, a vote was passed to purchase a convenient spot of land for a school house, and to build a new school house thereon ; that the petitioners were chosen a committee to make the purchase, and to build the house; that it was also voted to raise a certain sum named for those purposes; that the clerk of the district, in due time certified this last vote to the assessors of the town, and requested them to assess the sum mentioned upon the inhabitants of the district ; that the assessors did assess said sum in pursuance of the vote and the clerk's certificate thereof, and committed to one Ingraham, a constable and collector of Dudley, the list of the assessment, with a warrant for collecting and paying in the same to the treasurer of the town, or his successor, on or before the first of March, 1826, and certified their doings to Lee, the respondent, then and ever since, the treasurer of the town; that the petitioners purchased a convenient spot of land on a certain day, and thereafter, in pursuance of the vote of the district, contracted for the building of a school house thereon, and promised in writing to pay the builders a certain sum of money when it should be finished; that said Ingraham had neglected to comply with the warrant, and the town treasurer had refused to pay to the petitioners the before mentioned sum because the same was not collected and paid into the treasury; that the petitioners thereupon requested the treasurer to issue his warrant of distress against the collector, pursuant to the statute, but that he had refused so to do; that the school house was finished, and the expenses incurred were still due from the petitioners, as the building committee; the petitioners therefore prayed that a mandamus might issue to the treasurer, requiring him to issue his warrant of distress against said Ingraham, pursuant to the statute.

It was held that the collector ought to have proceeded in collecting the tax; and that not having done so, he had subjected himself to the warrant from the treasurer, and granted the writ accordingly.

It was also held, that a return showing that the tax was illegally raised and assessed, by reason of the insufficiency of the warning of the inhabitants of the district, of the meeting at which the tax was voted; that the tax was not assessed upon any valuation taken with a view to that tax; and that the person to whom the warrant calling the meeting was directed, had certified in general terms that he had duly warned the inhabitants, without stating the time or manner of the warning, was not a sufficient return. It was held by the court, that the treasurer was merely a ministerial officer; that he had no authority to pause in the execution of his duty, on the suggestion of errors or mistakes in the proceedings. That if the facts upon which he is to act are properly certified to him, he has no discretion, but is obliged to issue his warrant. That whether the tax be legal or illegal, whether duly assessed or not, are not subjects for him to inquire about. That if there be a tax, an assessment, a warrant to the collectors, all certified to him by assessors duly qualified to act, his duty is clear, and he is peremptorily commanded by the law to discharge it.

It was, however, maintained, that as the issuing of the writ depended in a measure upon the discretion of the court, it was proper for the court to look into the facts stated in the return of the officer against whom the mandamus is prayed, in order to determine whether the exercise of his duty, in issuing a warrant of distress against the collector mentioned in the return, ought or ought not to be compelled.

And that if it should manifestly appear that a tax was illegally granted or assessed, so that the officers required to collect it would have no authority, or the persons taxed would have a right to restitution by action, without doubt the court would withhold the exercise of its power, rather than throw the parties into an expensive field of litigation. (*Waldron* v. *Lee*, 5 *Pick.*, 323.)

And where the selectmen of the town, having authority to so do, surveyed a highway, and laid a survey thereof in writing before the inhabitants of the town, at a lawful town meeting, and the survey was accepted by the town, and recorded; but the selectmen neglected and refused to make satisfaction for the damage done to those over whose lands the highway passed, as required by law; and also neglected and refused to open the same, although the time for that purpose prescribed by law had long since passed, it was held that mandamus would lie to the selectmen, requiring them to proceed and open the highway. (*Treat et al.* v. *The Inhabitants of the*, &c., 8 *Conn.*, 243.)

A mandamus to compel commissioners of highways to open a road should not, however, be resorted to where its necessary effect would be to subject them to an action of trespass.

If, therefore, the facts shown on the application are of a character to establish a want of jurisdiction, so as to make the proceedings entirely void, they furnish a sufficient ground for not awarding the peremptory mandamus, unless, for some good reason, the parties are estopped from inquiring into these facts. (*People* v. *Commissioners of Seward*, 27 *Barb.* 94; *Ex-parte Clapper*, 3 *Hill*, 458.)

So where it is made the duty of the township treasurer to pay orders drawn on him by the township board of education out of moneys in his hands as such treasurer, if he refuses to do so, he may be compelled by mandamus. Therefore, where the board of education—acting upon a real or pretended supposition that the local directors of the sub-district were neglecting to discharge their duties—assumed the exercise of those duties, under the provisions of the statute in such cases provided, and employed the relator to teach a school in the sub-district, which he did for three months, without being notified by the local directors to desist, and at the expiration of that time the board of education gave him an order on the defendant, who was township treasurer, for his wages, pursuant to the statute, and the local directors notified the defendant not to pay it, and threatened him with a suit if he did, whereupon he refused to pay it, and the ground of the notification was that the local directors had not neglected their duties, and that, therefore, the board of education had unlawfully usurped their authority, it was held that although it was by no means certain that the board of education was justified in superseding the directors, and that the relator, to be entitled to payment for services rendered, must show that his retainer was by competent authority; yet, as in that case the retainer was by a board exercising, *de facto*, the powers of local directors, without any objection made known to the relator against their so doing, he was entitled to payment of his order, and ought not to be turned around to sue the individuals composing the board. A peremptory mandamus was therefore awarded, commanding the defendant as treasurer, to pay the order. (*Case* v. *Wresler*, 4 *O. S. Rep.*, 561.)

So where the township board of education of a certain township determined to build a new school house in one of the sub-districts of the township, selected and purchased a site therefor and instructed the local directors of the sub-district to build the house on the site so selected, and also to sell the old school house and site, and the local directors of the sub-district proceeded to build the new school house, but refused to erect it upon the site selected by the township board, but built it on the site where the old school house stood, and the township board proceeded contemporaneously with the local directors, and built a new school house on the site selected by themselves, and in the autumn employed a teacher to teach the common school of the sub-district in the new house they had built, and refused to have any school kept in the new house built by the local directors, and in the spring the board of education certified to their clerk that there was due to the relator for teaching the school so as aforesaid the sum of eighty-eight dollars, and the clerk thereupon gave to him an order on the township treasurer for said sum, and he presented the same to the treasurer, who refused to pay it, it was held that mandamus would lie to compel the treasurer to pay the order, although the local directors also employed a teacher to teach the common school of the sub-district in the new school house built by them and had given him a certificate of the amount due him for wages as such teacher, which had been presented to the clerk, who gave such teacher an order on the treasurer, and the treasurer had paid it. It was said by the court that where the local directors persisted in building a school house and keeping up a school on the old site and in refusing to build upon the new site after the township board had notified them of its resolution to sell the former, and after it had required and directed them to build upon the latter, they were guilty of a degree, not only of neglect, but of insubordination, which, under the provisions of the statute in such cases provided, justified the board in assuming all the powers and duties which would otherwise have devolved on the local directors. (*The State of Ohio* v. *Lynch*, 8 *O. S. Rep.*, 347.)

But where the return to the alternative writ showed that before the issuing and service of the writ, the defendant's term of office as township treasurer expired, and a successor having been elected and qualified, he had paid over to that successor all the public funds in his hands, and such payment was made in good faith, it was held that it was a good defense to the writ, and that the relator must be left to assert his rights against the defendant's successor in office. (*The State of Ohio* v. *Lynch*, 8 *O. S. Rep.*, 347.)

The township treasurer is, no doubt, in certain cases, justified in looking behind the order drawn on him, and if illegal, refuse its payment.

Therefore, where an alternative mandamus was issued, commanding the defendant, as township treasurer, to pay to the relator the sum of twelve dollars, for services as teacher of a union school district, composed of parts of the townships of Tallmadge and Stow, in Summit county, and Franklin and Brimfield, in Portage county, to which the defendant made return: "That no such union school district as that mentioned in said writ, as being composed of parts of the townships of Tallmadge and Stow, in Summit county, and parts of Franklin and Brimfield, in Portage county, ever legally existed; but the same as to that portion thereof which lies in the township of Tallmadge aforesaid, was embraced in said union school district without the assent of the trustees of the township of Tallmadge, at the time of the pretended formation of said union school district, and against their express dissent;" it was held, that as the statute conferring the authority to establish union school districts upon the trustees of the several townships, required a majority of each township board of trustees to concur, with a like majority of each, and of all the several township boards of trustees; and that no organized township, or any part of it could therefore be forced into a school district against the consent of its trustees; the treasurer was justified in refusing to pay the order, and the writ was dismissed. (*The State of Ohio* v. *Wright*, 17 *O. Rep.*, 32.)

Mandamus will also lie to compel township trustees to make a proper distribution of funds in their hands, to be divided among certain religious societies, if applied for before the distribution is made. (11 *O. Rep.*, 24.)

Therefore where the proceeds of certain township lands were appropriated to each religious society of the township, according to the number of its members, for that year, and it was made the duty of the township trustees to make the distribution, and they refused to distribute any dividend of the proceeds to a certain society, on the ground that it was not a religious society within the meaning of the act, it was held that if such society was in fact within the intent of the statute, the trustees might be compelled by mandamus to make a division to such society, if applied for before the funds had been exhausted. But a return by the trustees, setting forth that their predecessors in office, for the years, the proceeds for which the relators claimed a dividend, considering that the society were not entitled to any portion of the rents, had actually divided and paid out to other societies all the moneys received for those years, so that nothing of the proceeds of those years remained in the treasury, upon which orders could be drawn, it was held that the return was sufficient, and a peremptory mandamus was refused. (*The State of Ohio* v. *Trustees*, 2 *O. R.*, 108.)

So mandamus will lie to compel a town council to levy a tax to pay an indebtedness of the town. And where an incorporated town had been indebted, and afterwards the act creating the corporation was repealed, but the repealing act contained the following provision: "Provided, that the officers of said town shall have power, by their corporate name, to sue and be liable to be sued, to levy and collect all taxes necessary to discharge the present liabilities of said town; and provided further, that all rights acquired, and liabilities incurred by virtue of said act (incorporating said town) shall remain valid in all respects as if this act had not been passed." It was held by the court that the repeal of the charter did not discharge the officers of the corporation from the duties of collecting the debts due the town, and paying off the liabilities it had incurred. That it was the duty of those in office when the charter was repealed, to provide for the payment of the debts of the town, and that no resignation would absolve them from the discharge of the duties imposed. (*Gorgas* v. *Blackburn et al.*, 14 *O. R.*, 252.)

Mandamus also lies to the city council, to compel it to issue the necessary orders on the treasury, for the drawing of school funds, when the board of trustees have properly certified to the correctness of accounts, and such city council refuse to do their duty in that respect. (*The State* v. *The City of Cincinnati et al.*, 19 *O. R.*, 178.)

And where the law gives to the sheriff the right to the possession of the county jail, and the custody of the prisoners therein, and the under-keeper, who has been removed by the sheriff, refuses to give up the control and custody of the prisoners therein confined, and to vacate and surrender possession of the jail, mandamus will lie to compel him to do so. (*Burr* v. *Norton*, 25 *Conn.* 103.)

So, mandamus lies against a township school committee to compel them to admit to the public schools one who is entitled to the benefits and privileges of such schools, and who is refused admission thereto.

And where there was in a will donating a sum of money for the support of a school for the inhabitants of a certain town a clause excepting from the benefits of the school certain persons therein named, and their descendants for a term of one hundred years, it was held by the court that the clause was repugnant to the nature of the grant, and contrary to law and public policy, and was therefore "inoperative and void;" and a mandamus was allowed to compel the school committee to admit to the school a person thus excluded by the will. (*Nourse* v. *Merriam et al.*, 8 *Cushing's Rep.* 11.)

And where the trustees of a school district improperly and illegally admit colored children or immoral persons to the school, mandamus, it seems, is the appropriate remedy to compel the trustees to exclude them. But in such case it should be alleged and shown that the trustees knew that such persons were attending the school, and that there were objections to their attendance. (*Lewis* v. *Henly*, 2 *Ind.* 332.)

But where school directors are directed and empowered by law "to establish a sufficient number of common schools for the education of every individual above the age of five and under twenty-one years in their respective districts, who may apply for admission and instruction, either in person, or by parent, guardian, or next friend," and the directors meet and consider and pass upon the propriety of establishing a school at a certain point in the town, and come to the conclusion that such school would be inexpedient and injurious, they act in a deliberative capacity, and therefore mandamus will not lie to compel them to reform their decision. And this is upon the principle, that where a person acts in a judicial or deliberative capacity, he may be ordered by mandamus to proceed to do his duty; but the court cannot direct him in what manner to decide. (4 *American Law Reg.* 163.)

And where by law it is enacted, that when no special contract shall be subsisting between the borough and county relative to the prisoners sent from the borough to the county prison, the borough shall pay to the county a proportionate share of the expenses of the conveyance, transport, and maintenance of such persons, including therein repairs, alterations, and additions to the prison, it was held that where it was shown that no special contract existed, and prisoners had been sent from the borough to the county jail, mandamus would lie commanding the council of the borough to pay to the person duly appointed by the proper authorities of the county to receive it the borough's share of such expenses, &c.; and if no sufficient money should be in their hands for payment thereof, to proceed to cause a rate to be made and levied for the purpose of making payment. (*Regina* v. *The Mayor, &c.*, 20 *Eng. Law and Eq. R.* 59.)

CHAPTER XX.

MANDAMUS TO PRIVATE CORPORATIONS.

A corporation has been defined to be an intellectual body, created by law, composed of individuals united under a common name, the members of which succeed each other, so that the body continues the same, notwithstanding the change of the individuals who compose it, and which, for certain purposes, is considered as a natural person. (*Angell & Ames on Corporations*, 1.)

There are two kinds or classes of corporations. One kind is denominated public, and is founded for public purposes, and generally has for its object the government of a portion of the State, and is therefore endowed with a portion of political powers. Towns, cities and boroughs are familiar examples of this kind of corporations.

A private corporation is one created for the advancement of some private end, such, for instance, as a bank, turnpike or railroad corporation. But as their objects, to a greater or less extent, affect the whole community, and they derive their existence from the consent of the public, they in a measure partake of a public nature; so much so that they may be compelled by mandamus to perform the duties imposed upon them by law, although it is a fundamental principle that mandamus only lies in a matter of public concern. Accordingly, in case of public corporations, it has been decided that a mandamus lies to compel them to proceed to the election of a new mayor at any time after the charter day has passed without such election, where the former mayor, having power to do so, holds over and refuses to convoke an assembly for that purpose, unless, indeed, the charter restrains the right of electing to a particular time. (4 *Burr Rep.*, 2011.) The same principle would apply to other officers of a corporation. (*Rex* v. *Bedford*, 1 *East's Reps.*, 80.)

In case of a public corporation it has also been decided that if a corporation officer, duly elected, refuse or neglect to take upon himself the execution of his office, a mandamus will issue to compel him to do so, but he may show any sufficient excuse for not accepting the office. (*Angell & Ames on Corporations*, 431; 1 *East. R.*, 80.)

The law upon the right to resort to mandamus to compel a corporation to admit or restore a person to an office in such corporation is of ancient date, for in Bacon's time it was laid down as a general rule, "that where a man is refused to be admitted, or wrongfully turned out of any office or franchise that concern the public or the administration of justice, he may be admitted or restored by mandamus." And on this foundation it has been adjudged and admitted in a variety of cases, that if a mayor, alderman, burgess, common councilman, freeman, or other person, members of a corporation, having a franchise or freehold therein, be refused to be admitted, or being admitted, be turned out or disfranchised without just cause, he may have his remedy by writ of mandamus. (4 *Bacon's Abridgment*, 500.)

But in order to warrant the issuing of the writ to admit or to restore one to an office, it must appear that the office claimed is a public office. And it has often been a matter of controversy what shall be said to be a public office. It has, however, long since been decided that a town clerk, recorder, and clerk of the peace, a constable, and even a sexton, a parish clerk, and clerk of the city works, were officers of so public a character as to come within the rule.

The writ has often been made use of, in modern practice, to admit or restore to an office; and the rule, as above laid down, seems to have been unchanged. (*The People* v. *The Board of Metropolitan Police*, 26 *N. Y. Rep.* 316; *Harwood* v. *Marshall*, 9 *Ind. Rep.* 83; *Banton* v. *Wilson*, 4 *Texas Rep.* 400.)

But when an office is already filled by a person who has been admitted and sworn, and is in by color of right, a mandamus is never issued to admit another person. The proper remedy for the applicant is by a *quo warranto*. (*People* v. *Scrugham*, 20 *Barb.* [*N. Y.*] 302; *Bonner* v. *The State*, 7 *Ga. Rep.* 473; *The King* v. *The Mayor of Colchester*, 2 *Dunn & East's Reps.* 259.)

Mandamus is also the appropriate remedy to resort to when a person has been refused admission to, or has been removed from, an office in a private corporation.

Therefore, where the complaint of the relator showed that he was one of the trustees of an academic school duly incorporated by law, and that he had been removed and expelled from said office by his associate trustees, and it appeared from the return that they possessed no power to remove one of their number; or if so, that the causes of removal were entirely insufficient, a peremptory mandamus was allowed, directed to the other trustees, commanding them to restore the relator to his office as one of the board of trustees. It was also held that the place of a trustee in an eleemosynary corporation, though no emoluments are attached to it, is yet a franchise of such a nature that a person improperly dispossessed of it is entitled to redress by such writ. (*Fuller* v. *The Trustees of the Academic School in Plainfield*, 6 *Conn.* 532.)

It has also been held, that a writ of mandamus may be issued against a religious society, commanding them to restore the relator to his standing as a trustee and member of the corporation, when he has been illegally and improperly removed. (*Green* v. *The African Methodist Episcopal Society*, 1 *Serg. & Rawle's Rep.* 254; *Douglas Rep.* 158; 2 *Binn*, 441, 448; 5 *Binn*, 486; 2 *Serg. & Rawle's Rep.* 141; 10 *Barr. Rep.* 357; 15 *Penn.* 251.)

It seems, also, that a suspension from office warrants the granting of this writ as well as a removal, for a suspension is a temporary amotion; and otherwise, it is said, under pretense of repeated suspensions, an officer might be entirely excluded from the advantage of his situation. (*Angell & Ames on Corporations*, 437.)

But where it appears from the showing of an officer, that he has been justly, though irregularly removed, or in case of a financial officer for life who is suspended until he has submitted his accounts to the proper officer, and paid over the balance due, that he has refused to do so, and been guilty of contumacy and improper conduct towards those whose officer he is, a mandamus to restore, it has been decided, will not be granted.

Neither will the writ be granted to restore one who has been ousted in *quo warranto*, or who has resigned his office; since judgment in *quo warranto* is conclusive against the defendant, whether on the writ, or on the information; and after a resignation has been accepted, the corporator cannot resume his office. It has however been said, that it is no objection to the granting of a mandamus to restore, that another has been elected to the office, since the amotion of the applicant. In such case, the court will grant leave to file an information in the nature of a *quo warranto*, against the person so elected, at the same time that they award the mandamus. It has also been held, that although mandamus will not be granted to restore a deputy on the application of the deputy himself, yet it will be granted for that purpose on the application of the principal. (*Angell and Ames on Corporations*, 438, 439, 6 *East's Rep.*, 360.)

In the case of the *State* v. *Common Council*, 9 *Wis. Reps.*, 254, it is claimed to be a well settled principle that mandamus is the proper remedy to restore to office a person illegally removed; and that while the court cannot control the discretion of a board having power, to remove at discretion, yet if the power to remove be only for "due cause," the cause of removal may be inquired into by the court, as that is a question of jurisdiction. That while the board may have power to determine conclusively the truth of the charges preferred against the officer; yet it has not the power to determine conclusively that these charges if true, amount to "due cause."

The writ of mandamus also lies to compel a corporation or its officers, to do many other acts which, by general law, or by virtue of official station, they are bound to do, which the party prosecuting the writ has a right to have done, and for which there is no other adequate, specific, legal remedy. It lies also to the mayor of a city corporation, to compel him to put the corporate seal to the certificate of an officer's election, where by the constitution of the corporation, the mayor is bound to certify the election to the king for his approbation. (*Rex* v. *York*, 4 *T. R.*, 699.)

So a corporator may have a mandamus to compel the custos of corporate documents, to allow him an inspection, and copies of them, at proper times and upon proper occasions; he showing clearly a right on his part, to such inspection and copies, and refusal on the part of the custos to allow it.

It was therefore held that a board of directors of a bank

have no right to pass a resolution excluding one of its members from an inspection of its books, although they believe him to be hostile to the interest of the institution; and accordingly where the cashier of a bank had refused to permit a director to inspect the discount book, that a mandamus lay commanding the cashier to submit the book to his inspection, although the conduct of the cashier had been approved by a resolution of the board. It was also held that the mandamus might properly be directed to the cashier, and need not be directed to the board. In the decision of the case of *The People* v. *Throop*, 12 *Wend.* 183, the court say: "It must be conceded, that if the relator has a right to the inspection of the books of the bank, a mandamus is the appropriate, and the only remedy at law. If there is a right on the part of the relator to examine the books, either with reference to his own safety, or with a view to the proper execution of the trust reposed in him by the stockholders, then this is the remedy, and the only remedy in a court of law.

"The question then seems to be this: Has every director of a bank the right to know the transactions of his co-directors in relation to the management of the institution. The stating of the question furnishes the answer."

A mandamus also lies to a steward who keeps the public books of a corporation, to compel him to attend with the books at the next corporate assembly, and to deliver them up to his successor in office. Indeed it lies to any person who happens to have the books, papers, records, seal or other things, of either a private or public corporation in his possession, and refuses to deliver them up. (*Commonwealth* v. *Atheam*, 3 *Mass.*, 285; *Rex* v. *Wildman*; 2 *Stra.*, 879; 7 *Cush.*, 239; 15 *Ill.*, 492; 24 *Vet.* [1 *Deane*] 658; 2 *Pick.*, 397; 25 *Ill.*, 325.) It lies also to an executor who refuses to deliver up the books of a borough, until money expended by his testator on account of it, should be repaid. (*Angell and Ames on Corporations*, 441.) And on the refusal of the treasurer or clerk of a religious society, whose term of office has expired, to deliver the records and papers of the society to his successor in office, a writ of mandamus will be issued, on the petition of the society, to compel him to do so. (*The Proprietors of St. Luke's Church* v. *Slack et al.*, 7 *Cush. Rep.*, 226.)

In regard to a public judicial body, it is clearly settled that though no provision be made giving a binding effect to the decision of a majority, yet, where they all convene and act, the majority may decide, notwithstanding the express dissent of the minority. (*Ex-parte Rogers*, 7 *Cow. Rep.* 526.)

And this doctrine seems also applicable to corporations, both public and private. Therefore, where a certain body composed of several individuals, are by law invested with powers to perform certain acts, although it is necessary that they should all convene, yet it is not necessary that they should all concur in the decision in order to make it effective. And where the majority of such body have voted that a certain act shall be done, which is within the power conferred upon them, and in order to accomplish the act thus voted by the majority, there is some act to be done by one or more of those who did not concur with the majority, and they refuse, mandamus will lie to compel them to perform the act, and thus carry out the purpose of the majority.

Thus in the case of *Wadham College*, *Cowp.* 377, the statute provided that the wardens should not affix the corporate seal in any case without the consent of himself and a majority of the fellows. He being thus by name associated with a majority of the fellows, he insisted that he had a negative upon them. But the court of King's Bench held that he made but one with the majority of the fellows, who, with him, constituted the body that should act; and a majority of such body having voted that he should affix the seal to an answer in chancery, they compelled him to do so by mandamus, though contrary to his own vote and consent.

And in *Rex* v. *Buston*, 3 *T. Rep.* 592, a statute had authorized the church wardens and overseers of the poor to make certain contracts. They had all, with the exception of the defendant (one of the overseers), who refused to join, made a contract, and the money was in the defendant's hands to be paid upon it. On a motion for a mandamus to compel him to pay, he insisted that he was not bound, inasmuch as the statute required the contract to be made by the church wardens and overseers, without saying or a majority. They should, therefore, all concur; and he having dissented, the contract was void, and he was therefore not bound to pay the money. The motion was granted, and a rule for a mandamus entered.

And in the case of *Withnell* v. *Gartham*, 6 *T. R.*, 338, power, by law, was given to the vicar and church wardens to appoint a schoolmaster to an ancient foundation. And the only question was, whether all the church wardens must concur with the vicar. The court held that the concurrence of a majority was sufficient. LAWRENCE, J., remarked: "In general, it would be the understanding of a plain man, that when a body of persons is to do an act, a majority of that body would bind the rest."

Corporations may also be compelled by mandamus to perform those duties which are imposed by statute; this doctrine has been acted upon by the courts for a long period of time.

A turnpike company has been compelled to fence its road where it passed through the lands of private persons, and it was held no excuse that the company had made satisfaction for the damages awarded to the land owner, or that having completed their road, they had no funds with which to build the fence. (*Reg.* v. *Trustees Sutton Road*, 1 *Q. B. R.* 860.)

Corporations may also be compelled by mandamus to perform public duties and obligations which are expressly imposed upon them by the terms of their charters, and also those duties which necessarily arise from the nature of the privileges and obligations of their charters.

It has, therefore, been held that where a railway company has obtained an act of parliament reciting that the formation of a railway from A to D will be beneficial to the public, and that the company are willing to execute it, and giving them compulsory powers upon land holders for that purpose, and the company, in exercise of the powers, have taken lands and thereupon made part of their line, they are bound by law to complete such line, not only to the extent to which they have taken lands, but to the farthest point, although the statute enacts only that "it shall be lawful" for them to make the railroad. The decision seems to have been founded upon the doctrine, that when a railroad company has actually purchased lands for their road under the compulsory powers conferred upon it, that it enters into a contract with the public to construct a railway upon it. (*Reg.* v. *The York and North Midland Railway Company*, 16 *Eng. Law and Eq. Rep.* 299.)

And in the case of *Reg.* v. *The Lancashire and Yorkshire Railway Company*, 16 *Eng. Law and Eq. Rep.* 327, the court went still farther, holding that a company having obtained an act of parliament for making a railway, on representation that it will be for the public benefit, with compulsory powers for taking lands along the proposed line, is bound, from the time when such act receives the royal assent, to execute the work; that the royal assent makes the act binding as a contract by the company with the public and with the landowners, whether the clauses under which the railway is to be made be in form imperative or permissive; and that the courts will enforce the performance by mandamus, at the instance of one of the landowners, although the powers conferred upon the company are temporary, and although the company have taken no steps by issuing shares or otherwise to carry the act into execution.

But the first of these cases came before the Exchequer Chamber, and was heard at great length before all the judges, and an elaborate opinion delivered by JERVIS, C. J., of the C. B., reversing the judgment of the Q. B., chiefly on the ground that there was no implied obligation upon the company, either before or after entering upon the works, to complete it. This decision, reported in the 18 *Eng. Law and Eq. R.*, 199, is so comprehensive, and the questions so thoroughly and ably discussed, it is thought advisable to give the decision in full, although it is quite lengthy.

The court say: "Upon these facts several points arise: first, does the statute of 1849 cast on the plaintiffs in error a duty to make this railway? Secondly, if it does not, is there under the circumstances a contract between the plaintiffs in error and the land owners, which can be enforced by mandamus? Thirdly, and failing these propositions, does a work, which in its inception was permissive only, become obligatory by part performance? These questions will be found upon examination to exhaust the subject, and to comprehend every view in which the mandamus can be supported. In substance, do these acts of parliament render the company, if they do not make this railway, liable to an indictment, for a misdemeanor, and to action by the party aggrieved? For if they do not, a mandamus will not lie, and thus the question depends entirely upon the construction of the special act, and the statutes incorporated therewith. The act of 1849 may cast the duty upon the plaintiffs in error, in one of two ways; it may do so by express words of obligation, or it may do so by words of permission only, if the duty can be clearly collected from the general provision of the whole statute. The words of the third section of the act of 1849, "it shall be lawful for the said company to make the said railway," are permissive only, and not imperative, and it is a safe rule of construction to give to the words used by the legislature their natural meaning, when absurdity or injustice does not follow from such a construction. Indeed, if there were any doubt upon this subject, other parts of the statute referred to in the argument clearly show that these words were intended to be permissive only. The distinction is well put by my brother Erle; "The company are permitted at their option to take lands, turn roads, alter streams, and exercise other powers, and these matters are made lawful for them; but they are commanded to make compensation for lands taken, to substitute roads for those they turn, and to perform other conditions relating to the exercise of their powers, and these matters are required of them. It seems clear, therefore, that the duty is not cast upon the plaintiffs in error by the express words of the statute of 1849; and, indeed, it was not so urged in the argument; nor was it so put by Lord Campbell, in his judgment in the court below. But it does not follow, merely because the words of the third section are permissive only, that there is no duty cast upon the plaintiffs in error by the statute taken all together, to make this railway. This point was not relied upon in this case in the court below, but it was made the distinct ground of a decision in another case in that court (*The Queen* v. *The Lancashire and Yorkshire Railway Co.*), and was much pressed in the argument before us in support of this judgment.

"It becomes necessary, therefore, to examine the statute in its general provisions, and to consider the grounds on which the court of Queen's Bench proceeds in the case of *The Queen* v. *The Lancashire and Yorkshire Railway Co.*, 1 *E. & B.* 228; 16 *Eng. L. & Eq. R.*, 328. We agree with Lord Campbell, that the portion of the line between Market Weighton and Cherry Burton, to which the mandamus applies, is not to be considered as a separate railway, or even as a separate branch of a railway, but it is to be treated as if in its present direction it had been included in the act of 1846. The acts, then, taken together in substance, recite that it will be an advantage to the public if a railway is made from York to Beverly, through Market Weighton and Cherry Burton, according to certain plans and sections deposited, as required by the practice of parliament, and referred to in the statute, and that the plaintiffs in error are willing to make that railway. On this basis the whole provisions are founded.

"It has been proved that the work will be advantageous to the public; it is assumed that it will be profitable to the company, and that, therefore, they will willingly undertake it. Accordingly, the company are empowered to make this line. If they do make it, they may take land; but if they do take land, they must make compensation. If necessary, they may turn roads, or divert streams; but if they do, they must make new roads and new channels for the streams they alter. Similar provisions pervade the whole statute, and, throughout, the command waits upon the authority, and the distinction between 'may' and 'must' is clearly defined. But as it is manifest that such general powers must stop competition, and may, to a certain extent, be injurious to land owners on the line, the compulsory power to take land is limited to three years, and the time for making the railway to five, after which the powers granted to the company cease, except as to so much of the line as shall have been completed, and the land, if taken by the company, reverts, on certain terms, to the original proprietors. An argument might have been founded on the terms in which the latter provision is contained. By the 10th section of the act of 1849, it is enacted that the railway shall be completed within five years from the passing of this act. That section was not referred to in the argument for this purpose, but it might be said that these words were compulsory, and imposed a duty upon the company to make the line. The context of the section, however, when examined, shows that such is not the meaning of it. If not completed within five years, the powers of the act are to expire, except as to so much of such railway as shall have been completed. If the section were intended to be obligatory, it would not contain that exception which contemplates that the line may be made in part. It is inconsistent to suppose that the legislature would say to the company in the same section, you may complete a part only, if you can, in five years, and then as to that part, the powers of the act shall continue; but you must complete the entire line in that time. Upon the whole, therefore, we find no duty cast upon the company to make this railway in any part of this act of parliament. On the contrary, the legislature seems to contemplate the possibility of the railway being made in part, or being totally abandoned. In the latter case, the powers expire in three or five years; in the former, the statute remains in force as to so much of the railway as shall have been completed within that time, and expires as to the residue. This provision is inconsistent with the intention to compel the company to make the entire line, as the consideration for the powers granted by the act.

"But it is said that a railway act is a contract on the part of the company to make the line, and that the public is a party to that contract, and will be aggrieved if the contract may be repudiated by the company at any time before it is acted upon. Though commonly so spoken of, railway acts, in our opinion, are not contracts and cannot be construed as such. They are what they purport to be, and no more. They give conditional powers, which if acted upon, carry with them duties, but which, if not acted upon, are not either in their nature or by express words, imperative on the companies to which they are granted. Courts of justice ought not to depart from the plain meaning of the words used in acts of parliament. When they do, they make, but do not construe the laws. If it had been so intended, the statute should have required the companies to make the line in express terms; indeed some railway acts are framed upon this principle, and to say that there is no difference between words of requirement and words of authority, when found in such acts, is simply to affirm that the legislature does not know the meaning of the commonest expressions. But if we were at liberty to speculate upon the intentions of the legislature when the words are clear, and to construe an act of parliament by our own notions of what ought to have been enacted upon the subject; if, sitting in a court of justice, we could make laws, much might be said in favor of the course which, in our opinion, is taken by the legislature on such subjects. Assuming that the line, if made, would be profitable to the public, that benefit may be delayed for five years, during which time competition is suspended. On the other hand, if the line would pay, it probably will be proceeded with, unless the company having the power is incompetent to the task. Individual land owners may be benefited by the expenditure of capital in their neighborhood, without looking to the ultimate result; but it is not for the public interest that the work should be undertaken by an incompetent company, nor that it should be begun if, when made, it would not be remunerative. By leaving the exercise of the powers to the option of the company, the legislature adopts the safest check on abuse in either of those respects, namely, self interest. It seems to us, therefore, that these statutes do not cast upon the plaintiffs in error the duty, either by express words or by implication, that we ought to adhere to the plain meaning of the words used by the legislature, which are permissive only, and that there is no reason, in policy or otherwise, why we should endeavor to pervert them from their natural meaning.

"But it is said that the land owners are in a better situation than the public at large, and that the privilege to take their own lands is the consideration which binds the company to complete the railway. That during the currency of the three years, they are deprived of their full rights of ownership, and if not to be compensated by the construction of the railway, they would in many cases, suffer a loss, because whilst the compulsory power of purchase subsists, they are prevented from alienating their lands or houses described in the books of reference, and from applying them to any purpose inconsistent with the claim that may be made to them by the railway company. In truth they are not prevented from so doing at any time before the notice to take their land is given, if they act *bona fide* in the meantime; the notice to take their lands being the inception of the contract between the land owners and the company.

"But if this complaint was better founded, it does not follow because certain land owners are subjected to temporary inconvenience for the performance of a public good, that, therefore, the company are bound to make the whole railway. If it were a contract between the land owners and the company, it would not be just, the one should be bound and the other free. But to assert that there is a contract between the land owners and the company, is to beg the whole question; for, on this part of the case, the question is whether there is such a contract? As a matter of fact, we know that in many cases no such actual contract exists. Some few proprietors may desire and promote the railway, but many others oppose it, either from disinclination to the project, or with a view to make better terms. With the dissentients there is no contract, unless it be found in the statute, and to the statute therefore we must look to see what is the obligation that is cast upon the company, in respect of the land owners upon the line. As in the former case, the words upon this subject are permissive only. The company may take land; if they do, they must make full compensation. And in that state of things, if there be a bargain between the parties, what is the bargain? The company say, in the language of the statute, that the bargain is, that they shall make full compensation for the land taken, and no more; the prosecutors say that the consideration to be paid for the land is the full compensation mentioned in the act, and also the further consideration of the construction of the entire line of railway from York to Beverly. But if this is the price which the prosecutors are to have, each land owner is entitled to the same value; and yet by this mandamus the other proprietors on the line from Market Weighton to Cherry Burton, who, perhaps, are hostile to the application, are constrained to sell their lands for an inadequate consideration, namely, the full compensation and a part only of the line of railway, to which, by the hypothesis, they were entitled by the original bargain.

"If this were the true meaning of the statute, it would indeed, be unjust, more so than the imposition of the temporary inconvenience to which it is said the land owners may be subject, and to which we have already referred. But that that is not the true meaning is clear from the words of the statute, which are permissive, and only impose the duty of making full compensation to each land owner, as the option of taking the land of each is exercised; and further from the section to which we have already referred, which contemplates the total abandonment of the line, or a part performance of it, and makes provision for the return of the land to the original proprietors in certain cases. Upon this part of the case the authority of Lord ELDON, in *Blakemore* v. *The Glamorganshire Canal Company*, 1 *Myl. & K.* 154, was much pressed upon the court. Speaking of contracts for private undertakings, he says: 'When I look upon these acts of parliament I regard them all in the light of contracts made by the legislature on behalf of every person interested in anything to be done under them, and I have no hesitation in asserting that unless that principle be applied in construing statutes of this description, they become instruments of greater oppression than anything in the whole system of administration under our Constitution. Such acts of parliament have now become extremely numerous, and from their number and operation, they so much affect individuals that I apprehend those who come for them to parliament do, in effect, undertake that they shall do and submit to whatever the legislature empowers and compels them to do, and that they shall do nothing else; that they shall do and forbear all that they are thereby required to do and forbear, as well with reference to the interest of the public, as with regard to the interest of individuals.' There is nothing in that language to which it is necessary to make the least exception; indeed it is nothing more than an illustration of the obligatory nature of the duty imposed by acts of parliament, which do impose a duty with reference to other persons. In that case, the statute had secured to Mr. Blakemore the surplus water, and had commanded the company to do certain things that he might enjoy it. In discussing whether Mr. Blakemore's right under the statute was affected by his right before the statute, his lordship might well say he considered the statute the origin of Mr. Blakemore's right in the light of a contract, and the statute then under discussion containing express words of command, he might well add, that those who come for such acts of parliament do, in effect, undertake that they shall do and submit to whatever the legislature empowers and compels them to do. As we understand them, the words used by Lord ELDON in no respect conflict with the view we take of this case; but if they mean that words of permission only, when used in the class of cases under consideration, should receive a construction different from their ordinary meaning, because if construed otherwise, they might work injustice, with great respect for his high authority, we dissent from that proposition. We agree with my brother ALDERSON, who, in *Lee* v. *Milner*, 2 *Y. & Coll.* 611, said: 'These acts of parliament have been called parliamentary bargains, made with each of the land owners. Perhaps more correctly they ought to be treated as conditional powers given by parliament to take the lands of the different proprietors through whose estates the works are to proceed.'

"Each land owner, therefore, has the right to have the power strictly and literally carried into effect as regards his own land, and has the right also to require that no variation shall be made to his prejudice in the carrying into effect a bargain between the undertakers and any one else.' 'This,' he adds, 'I conceive to be the real view taken of the law by Lord ELDON in the case of *Blakemore* v. *The Glamorganshire Canal Company*.' There remains but one further view of the case to be considered, and that we have partly disposed of in the observations we have already made; but inasmuch as Lord CAMPBELL proceeded on this ground only in the court below, although it was not much relied upon before us in the argument, we have, out of respect for his high authority, most carefully examined it, and are of opinion that the mandamus cannot be supported, on the ground that the railway company, having exercised some of their powers and made a part of their line, are bound to make the whole railway authorized by their statutes.

"It is unnecessary here to determine the abstract proposition that a work which, before it is begun, is permissive, is after it is begun obligatory. We desire not to be understood as assenting to the proposition of my brother ERLE, that many cases may occur when the exercise of some compulsory powers may create a duty to be enforced by mandamus; and, on the other hand, we do not say that such may not be the law. If a company empowered by act of parliament to build a bridge over the Thames, were to build one arch only, it would be well deserving consideration whether they could not be indicted for a nuisance in obstructing the river, or for the non-performance of duty in not completing the bridge. It is sufficient to say that in this case there are no circumstances to raise such a duty, if such a duty can be created by the acts of plaintiff himself. The plaintiffs in error have made the principal portion of their line, and they have abandoned the residue for no corrupt motive, but because Beverly has already sufficient railway communication, and because the residue of the line passes through a county thinly populated, and if made, would not be remunerative. But it is said that the railway company are not in the situation of purchasers of land, with liberty to convert it to any purpose, or to allow it to be waste; that they are allowed to purchase it only for a railway, and having acquired it under the compulsory power of the act, there must be an obligation upon the company to apply the land to that, and to no other purpose. Subject to the qualification in the act, this is undoubtedly true. Having acquired the lands of particular land owners, the company could not retain them by merely laying rails on the lands so taken, and we agree it never was intended that the land owners should be left with a high mound or a deep cutting running through his estate, and leading neither to nor from any available terminus. The precaution against such a wasteful expenditure of capital may, perhaps, safely be left to the self-interest of the com pany, but if such work were to be done, it would not be a practicable railway, and after five years the powers of the act would expire. and the land revest in the original proprietor. It is true that he would sustain some inconvenience without the corresponding advantage of railway communication, but in the meantime he would have received full compensation in the market value of the land, and for all damage by severance or otherwise, and would receive back the land on more reasonable terms. To be a railway it must have available *termini*. When the statutes passed all persons supposed the *termini* would be York and Beverly; and if the argument be well founded and the company are bound, if they take the land upon any portion of the railway to complete the whole line, it would seem to follow that one of the proprietary, by compelling the company to take his land on the line from Market Weighton to Cherry Burton, would thus entitle himself to a mandamus to compel them to make the line from Cherry Burton to Beverly, and the acts having expired, to apply to parliament for a renewal of their powers for that purpose. But although the *termini* were originally intended to be York and Beverly, it is plain that the legislature contemplated the possibility of the line being abandoned or being only partially made, because in the one case the powers of the act were to cease, and in the other they were partially continued. An option, therefore, is given to some one. By the course taken, the Court of Queen's Bench has exercised that option, and said line is to be made, not to Beverly, but to Cherry Burton. In our opinion that option is left to the company, and the company having *bona fide*, made an available railway over the land taken, the obligation to the land owner has, in that respect, been fulfilled. The cases upon this subject are very few, and the absence of authority is very striking, when we remember how many acts have passed *in pari materia*, not only for railways, but also for bridges and turnpike roads. Notwithstanding the numerous occasions on which such proceedings might have been taken, and the manifest interest of land owners to enforce their rights, no instance can be found of an indictment for disobeying such a statute, or of a mandamus for the purpose of enforcing it. If correctly reported, Lord MANSFIELD determined this point in *The King* v. *The Proprietors of the Birmingham Canal*, 2 *Wen. B.*, 708, for he says the act imports only an authority to the proprietors, not a command. They may desert or suspend the whole work, and *a fortiori* any part of it. On the other side, the language of Lord ELDON in *Blakemore* v. *The Glamorganshire Canal Company* is referred to as an authority for this mandamus. In our opinion it does not bear that construction, although it appears that the Court of Queen's Bench took a different view of that authority in the case of *The Queen* v. *The Eastern Counties*

Railway Company, 10 *Ad. & Ell.*, 531, and was inclined to act upon it, and award a mandamus. The writ was subsequently withheld in that case, on another ground, but Lord DENMAN seems to have been of opinion that on a fit occasion a mandamus ought to go. That and the recent cases in the Queen's Bench, now under discussion, are the only cases which bear upon the subject. We feel that Lord DENMAN and Lord CAMPBELL are high authorities upon this or any other matter, and are both equally entitled to the respect of this court; but we are bound to pronounce our own judgment, and after the most careful consideration, are of opinion that the judgment ought to be for the plaintiffs in error. The result is, that the judgment of the court below must be reversed."

The Supreme Court of the State of Connecticut has, however, decided that when a railroad company has received a charter authorizing them to construct and operate a railroad between certain points, and the company go forward, construct the road, and put it in operation, and afterwards cease to run their passenger cars over a portion of their road, to the inconvenience of the traveling public, a mandamus will lie to compel them to run their cars over the entire line, in such manner as shall reasonably accommodate the public travel.

In that case the Hartford and New Haven Railroad Company was chartered to construct and operate a railroad from Hartford to the navigable waters of New Haven harbor. A steamboat company was afterwards chartered to run in connection with it to New York, and the railroad and line of steamboats constituted a route that was of great convenience to the public.

After the construction of the road, and the use of it in connection with the steamboat line for several years, the railroad company constructed a track diverging from the original track, at a point a mile and a half from its terminus at tide water, and running to the station of the New York and New

Haven Railroad Company, in the city of New Haven, and discontinued the running of passenger trains to the original terminus at tide water.

This change incommoded travelers who wished to pass by the steamboat route. The respondents in their return to the alternative mandamus alleged that they had discontinued running their passenger cars over a certain portion of their road, in pursuance of a contract made by them with the New York and New Haven Railroad Company, the object of which was, among other things, to prevent the extension of a certain railroad in the State, which would interfere with the respondents' road; by which contract they had agreed that they would not, during a certain term, run any passenger train over their road, in connection with any steamboat running between New York and New Haven, and would not during said term, run any passenger trains to or from the steamboat dock in New Haven; that said term had not expired, and that the said New York and New Haven Railroad Company insist on the observance of said contract as binding and obligatory upon the respondents, and that they should not run their trains, or transport passengers to and from said terminus, as in said order required. The court held that this contract was void as against public policy, and that a mandamus ought to issue to compel the railroad company to run passenger trains to the original terminus.

Ellsworth, J., in delivering the opinion of the court said: "We consider the return made by the respondents to the mandamus unsatisfactory and insufficient, presenting no reason why the order should not be immediately executed.

"The respondents admit that they have accepted their charter, made and completed their road as required, and for years have continued to run cars upon it for freight and passengers to and from tide water, in the harbor of New Haven, in connection with steamboats from New York; and they do not deny that they are now using that part of their road for the transportation of freight, but they refuse, and have for some time past refused, to use it for the transportation of passengers. And it is substantially admitted by the return that the public convenience will be subserved by the use of this part of the road.

"Now it is difficult to perceive upon these premises on what ground the respondents can justify their refusal to discharge their entire corporate duty; how they can expect to retain their franchise, and pay no attention to the duty it enjoins upon them. The contract with the New York and New Haven Railroad Company that they will not permit the public to enjoy the benefit of this part of their road, amounts to nothing. It is, in our judgment, an aggravation of their censurable neglect of duty instead of a legal excuse for the neglect. What right have they to covenant with that corporation, that they will not run cars to tide water, as the charter provides that they shall, and as the public accommodation requires, especially when they enter into that covenant to secure to that corporation a monopoly of the public travel to and from New York, and as an equivalent, to secure to themselves a like monopoly of all the travel in the Connecticut Valley, to the prejudice of every other corporation that might have an interest in those routes? The whole proceeding, from first to last, seems to us to be in contravention of the charter obligations of both these companies, and to present a case of odious monopoly, if not of positive oppression and wrong, which can receive no countenance from an impartial tribunal. We hardly know what doubtful principles of law are thought to be involved in the case. The respondents certainly were bound to make their road (if at all) within the time prescribed in the charter; and having made it, to put it into use—every material part of it—and keep it in use until discharged by the legislature. And this continuous duty is in no manner inconsistent with the power in the company (which has been so much dwelt upon in the argument), to regulate and control the manner of using the road by wholesome rules and by-laws. These we admit are necessary and allowable; but then they must be such as are really promotive of the original design of the charter and not such as tend to defeat that design. Under the contract in question, viewed in the most favorable light, persons traveling by railroad down the valley of the Connecticut, and desiring at New Haven to take the steamboat for New York, and those coming by steamboat from New York and designing to take the cars, must necessarily be exceedingly incommoded; while this very course of travel was well known when the charter was granted, and was intended to be secured and promoted by it.

"We forbear going into other questions raised on the trial, or commenting on the authorities cited by counsel. We think it unnecessary, and prefer to place our decision upon the simple ground of the corporate duty of the respondents. All jurists and judges will at once agree that chartered companies are obliged fairly and fully to carry out the objects for which they are created, and that they can be compelled by mandamus to do it; and it will not be questioned that in the case of public highways, whether turnpike or railroads, they are bound to keep them fit for use, and in the case of railroads, to keep them furnished with suitable cars, engines and attendants, without which they cannot be used at all. We advise the issuing of a peremptory mandamus." (*State* v. *The Hartford and New Haven Railroad Company*, 29 *Conn. Rep.*, 538.)

And in *Rex* v. *The Severn and Wye Railway*, 2 *B. & Ald.*, 646, it was held that when a railway company, after having completed their road, under an act of parliament, by which it was provided the public should have the beneficial enjoyment of the same, had no right to discontinue it, and as they had proceeded to take up the railway, a mandamus was awarded to compel them to reinstate it.

When the act of the legislature creating a railroad company

for the purpose of making a road between certain *termini* is imperative upon the company to build their road, this duty will be enforced by mandamus. (18 *Eng. L. & Eq. Rep.*, 211; 8 *W. & S.*, 365.) The same rule applies in all cases when a charter is given to a company, for the purpose of promoting some public object, and the language of the statute is imperative, and not permissive. Therefore, where an act of parliament created a company to improve the port and harbor of Bristol, by doing certain works, among which were the making, completing and maintaining a new course or channel for the Avon, from at or near the Redcliff, by a certain line into the Avon, at a point described; and one clause of the act expressly required the company to make, complete and maintain these works, it was held by the court that the act imposed upon the company the duty to keep the works in repair; that those who obtain an act of parliament for executing great public works, are bound to fulfill all the duties thereby thrown upon them, and may be called upon by the courts, by mandamus so to do. A mandamus was, therefore, awarded, commanding the company to make the repairs. (*The Queen* v. *The Bristol Dock Company*, 2 *Eng. Railway and Canal Cases*, 437.)

And where, by a railway act, a company were empowered generally to divert, raise, sink or deepen any roads, in order to carry the same over, under or by the side of the railway, subject to the provisions and restrictions of the said act; and by another act they were authorized to carry the line of the railway across a certain turnpike road, by means of a bridge of the width of thirty feet at the least, and for that purpose to lower the then present bed of the road, but in so doing, were required to leave a certain inclination on each side of the bridge, and headway under it, and to relay and reform the road. And from the alternative writ of mandamus, and the return, it appeared that the railroad company had constructed the bridge of a width exceeding the directions of the act, and the turnpike road had been excavated on each side of it, but not to the whole extent of its ancient width, it was held by the court that although the act did not specify the width which the road should be after the excavation was made, yet the language and meaning of the act imposed upon the company the obligation to extend the excavation, on lowering of the road, to the whole original breadth, and that mandamus would lie to compel a compliance therewith. (*The Queen* v. *The Manchester and Leeds Railway Company*, 2 *Eng. Railway and Canal Cases*, 520; *The Queen* v. *The Birmingham and Gloucester Railway Company*. 2 *Eng. Railway and Canal Cases*, 508.)

So, where by a railway act, it was provided that the company should not carry the railway across a certain turnpike road, except by means of a bridge of the width of thirty feet, so as to form a clear carriage road under the bridge of the width of twenty-four feet, with a foot path of six feet, and of the height of eighteen feet from the under side to the surface of the road; and that in case it should be necessary to lower the bed or surface of the road, it was to be so effected that the ascent on the road should not exceed one foot in fifty on the south side of the bridge, and one foot in a hundred on the north. That the company should make new fences and drains, and relay and reform the road; and that the alterations should be made under the superintendence and direction of the trustees of the road. And the company made a bridge over the road, and lowered the surface under the bridge to the depth of nine feet giving the required ascent on each side; but instead of making the bed of the new road forty-two feet wide (the width of the old road), they made a sunken carriage way of thirty-five and a half feet in width on the north, and of twenty-four feet under and on the south side of the bridge, leaving the foot-path at the original level, and having reduced its width in some places from six to three and a half feet, by making steps descending to the carriage road;

it was held that such works of the company were not a compliance with the act; and the rule for issuing a mandamus was made absolute. (*The Queen* v. *The Manchester and Leeds Railway Company*, 1 *Eng. Railway and Canal Cases*, 385.)

And where by a railway act, a company were required to construct a bridge over the river Y, so as to leave the same width of water-way under the same as there existed at the point where the river was crossed, and so that there should be a clear height of five feet above the ordinary level of the river; provided, that after notice given to the company by any owner or occupier of lands adjoining the railway, that the said bridge was not made according to the true intent and meaning of the act, it should be lawful for such owner or occupier to apply for and obtain an order from a justice of peace enabling such person to make such bridge accordingly, the expenses to be defrayed by the company.

The company were constructing a bridge which did not comply with either of the above provisions, whereupon a land owner gave them notice, requiring them to construct a bridge, leaving the former width of water-way, and the clear height of five feet above the water, in the terms of the act. The company replied that they would do the first and would accept process as to the second. They afterwards made the bridge the required height, and to preserve the same width of water-way, commenced cutting the banks of the river, which they afterwards discontinued. To subsequent applications to proceed with the work they returned no answer.

It was held that the above facts amounted to a refusal to do what was demanded, and that the applicant was entitled to a mandamus, notwithstanding the powers given him of applying to a justice for an order enabled him to build the bridge himself. And to the objection against issuing the mandamus on the ground that the act provided another specific and legal remedy, it was said by the court, that it would be rather absurd if a person was to have no other remedy than to pull down the bridge and build up a new one himself. (*The Queen* v. *The Norwich and Brandon Railway Company*, 4 *Eng. Railw. and Canal Cases*, 81.)

And where, by a railway act, a company was required to make proper watering places for cattle in all cases where, by means of the railway, the cattle of any persons occupying lands adjacent thereto should be deprived of access to their ancient watering places, and to supply the same with water, and it appeared from the alternative writ, and the return thereto, that the company had carried their road through certain closes belonging to the relator, and that by means thereof ancient ponds and watering places for cattle had been cut off from said closes, and that the company had been called upon by the relator to supply such watering places, which they had refused to do, the Court of Queen's Bench made the rule for a peremptory writ absolute, commanding the company, at their own proper costs and charges, to make, or cause to be made, proper watering places for cattle, in such portions respectively of the said several closes of land as last aforesaid, and to supply the same at all times with water, when made, pursuant to the aforesaid application made to them in that behalf. And although this case was afterwards taken on a writ of error to the Exchequer Chamber, and the judgment reversed, yet it was not reversed on the ground that mandamus would not lie in the case commanding the company to do that required of them by the act, but on the ground that there was nothing on the face of the writ to show that eight ponds were necessary or proper for the occupation of the eight portions of the fields that were severed from the other parts in which there were ponds before. That it was quite consistent with all that appeared on the face of the writ, that one watering place would have been sufficient and proper for the whole of them. And that as the writ ordered the company to make a pond in each of the portions of the closes, it commanded something to be done which was not shown to be required by the statute, and was, therefore, not valid in law. (*The Queen* v. *The York and North Midland Railway Company*, 3 *Eng. Railway and Canal Cases*, 562, 570.)

As there is frequently much difference of opinion as to the true meaning of the requisitions of particular statutes, the party acting under a statute should not have a mandamus moved for against him before he has had distinctly brought to his notice the precise act which he is required to do, and his attention drawn to his adversary's construction of the statute. And when a company have completed their works in a mode at all varying from the letter of their act, a party interested, and disapproving of such deviation, should not go to the court for a mandamus against the company before having made a demand to have the work done in another way. And expressions of disapprobation while the works are proceeding, though proper to be made, do not relieve such party from the necessity of specifically demanding a proper compliance with the statute after the works are done, as without it he might be supposed to have waived his objection. (*The Queen* v. *The Bristol and Exeter Railway Company*, 3 *Eng. Railway and Canal Cases*, 318.)

It seems also that the mandamus should require some particular thing to be done, and not in general terms, command that the work should be made conformably to the provisions of the act. (*The Queen* v. *The Eastern Counties Railway Company*, 3 *Eng. Railway and Canal Cases*, 18.)

A mandamus will also issue at the suit of supervisors of a town to compel a railway to build a highway or bridge, for public use, where such work is within the requirements of its charter. (8 *Watts and Sergeant Rep.*, 365; 2 *American Railway Cases*, 263; 7 *Mit.*, 70; 37 *Maine*, 461; 9 *Rich*, 247.)

It has been said that "no better general rule can be laid down upon this subject than that where the charter of a corporation, or the general statute in force, and applicable to the subject, imposes a specific duty, either in terms or by fair and reasonable construction and implication, and there is no other specific or adequate remedy, the writ of mandamus will be awarded. But if the statute, or the general law of the State, affords any other specific and adequate remedy, it must be pursued." (*Redfield on Railways*, 456.)

Although it seems mandamus will lie to enforce the payment of money awarded against a corporation, in pursuance of a statute duty, where no other specific remedy is provided (*The King* v. *Nottingham Old Water Works*, 6 *Ad. & Ellis*, 355; *Rex* v. *Trustees of Swansea Harbor*, 8 *Ad. & Ellis*, 439), yet the courts will not in this manner enforce the ordinary matter of contract or right upon which action lies in the common law courts. (*Ex-parte Robbins*, 7 *Dowl. P. Cases*, 566.)

If, however, the party have no right to execution, mandamus will be awarded to compel the payment of money, although an action at law might lie. (4 *Barn. & Ad.*, 360; 3 *Ib.*, 801; 1 *Q. B. R.*, 288.)

Thus, when the St. Katherine Dock Company were incorporated by act of parliament, which directed that all actions against the company should be prosecuted against the treasurer or directors for the time being, but that the body or goods, lands, &c., of such treasurer or director should not, by reason of his being defendant in such action, be liable to execution. An action having been brought by T. C. against the treasurer as such, and another by the company in the name of the treasurer against T. C., all matters in difference were referred to an arbitrator, who awarded that T. C. had cause of action against the defendant as such treasurer for a certain sum, and directed that the treasurer should pay T. C. that sum on demand; and as to the other suit, he awarded that the treasurer, as such, had no cause of action, and ordered him, as such treasurer, to pay T. C. the costs on demand; it was held that a mandamus would lie to the treasurer and directors, commanding them to pay the sums awarded. (2 *Shelford on the Law of Railways*, 839.)

And in *Reg.* v. *Bristol and Exeter Railway Company*, 3 *Eng. Railway and Canal Cases*, 777, the court granted a mandamus to compel a railway company to pay compensation for damages under an agreement upon which no action would lie, because it was not under the common seal of the company. But where, by an act of parliament, constituting a joint stock company, the company were to apply the first moneys received under the act in discharge of the expenses incurred in obtaining the act, it was held that the plaintiff, though a member of the company, might maintain an action of debt or case at his election, for his services and money expended in obtaining the act, and that mandamus would not, therefore, lie. (*Carden* v. *General Cemetery Co.*, 5 *Bing.*, 553; *Tilson* v. *Warwick Gas Light Co.*, 4 *B. & C.*, 962.)

And where a railway act enacted that a company established by it should, in a given event, pay a certain other company a sum not exceeding a given amount, by way of compensation for the loss of tolls by the latter company, the given event having happened, it was held that mandamus was not the proper mode of compelling the payment of the compensation money, as debt would lie on the statutory obligation. (2 *Shelford on the Law of Railways*, 840.)

So, where the act incorporating a railway company, and empowering them to build a bridge over the Ouse, recited that the building of such bridge might diminish the tolls received at a neighboring bridge over the same river belonging to another company; and it, therefore, enacted that if, in the first three years after the opening of the railway, there should be an annual decrease in the tolls of the last mentioned bridge, as compared with the tolls during the three preceding years, the railroad company should forthwith pay to the bridge company a sum equal to ten years' purchase of such annual decrease, taken upon an average of the three years in which it occurred; the decrease took place, and the compensation was claimed. It was held that an action of debt lay against the company for the amount, and that a mandamus to compel payment was not a more effectual remedy, and ought not to be granted. (*Reg.* v. *Hull and Selby Railway Co.*, 6 *Q. B. R.*, 70; 3 *Eng. Railway and Canal Cases*, 705.)

Patterson, J., delivering the opinion of the court said: "On considering this case, which was argued in the absence of the Lord Chief Justice, we are of opinion that an action of debt on the statutory obligation will clearly lie, and that remedy would be equally efficacious as the remedy by writ of mandamus. In either case the amount must be assessed by a jury. In an action, execution would go against the goods of the corporation, and a peremptory mandamus could only be enforced by distress on their goods. The present question was not raised in the argument in the case of *Regina* v. *The Great Western Railway Company, ante, p.* 700 at all. We are, therefore, of opinion that the rule for a writ of mandamus must be discharged."

Norris v. *Irish Land Co.*, 8 *Ellis & B.*, 512, was a case in which an administrator alleged that the defendants, a corporation, were bound by their charter and by subsequent deed, to keep a proper registry, in a book kept for that purpose, of the residence and number of shares belonging to each shareholder, and of changes in the ownership, which book was to be conclusive evidence as to who were proprietors of the stock, and that in case of death of a shareholder, his personal representatives might give notice of their wish so to do, and become shareholders by signing the deed and paying any arrears, and were then entitled to have their names registered as such; that he, the administrator, had complied with the terms and was entitled to have the entry made in his favor, but that the defendants refused to make it, and he claimed damages, and also a mandamus commanding the defendants to make the entry, he alleging that he was personally interested. The court held that a mandamus would lie.

That an action will lie against a joint stock company who neglect or refuse, upon proper request, to enter upon the books of the company the transfer of shares of stock, which have been purchased of a stockholder, is sustained by numerous authorities. (*Rex* v. *Bank of England*, *Doug. Rep.*, 424; *Shipley et al.* v. *The Mechanics' Bank*, 10 *John's Rep.*, 484; *Helm* v. *Swiggett*, 12 *Ind.*, 194; *Sargent et al.* v. *Franklin Ins. Co.*, 8 *Pick. Rep.* 90; *Redfield on Railways*, 62.) But that mandamus will lie to compel them to make the entry of transfer has been denied by high authority.

In the matter of *Morris Shipley et al.* v. *The Mechanics' Bank*, 10 *John's Rep.* 484, a motion was made for a mandamus, to be directed to the president, directors, and company of the Mechanics' Bank, commanding them to permit Morris Shipley and others, assignees of Samuel Kip, to transfer eight shares of the capital stock of the bank standing on the books of the company.

It appeared from the affidavits read, that Kip had been regularly discharged under the insolvent act, and that Shipley and others had been duly appointed the assignees of all his estates, real and personal, and that the shares in question were inserted in the inventory of his estate exhibited by the insolvent. The assignee applied to the company to be permitted to transfer the shares, which the company refused, on the ground that Kip was indebted to them, in the sum of $1,474.60, for money lent, &c., and at the time, held the eight shares to the value of twenty-five dollars each, which they claimed the right of retaining and applying towards paying the debt due to them from Kip.

The court said: "The applicants have an adequate remedy, by a special action in the case, to recover the value of the stock, if the bank have refused to transfer it. There is no need of the extraordinary remedy by mandamus, in so ordinary a case. It might as well be required in every case where trover would lie. It is not a matter of public concern, as in the case of public records and documents; and there cannot be any necessity, or even a desire of possessing the identical shares in question. By recovering the market value of them, at the time of the demand, they can be replaced. This is not the case of a specific and favorite chattel, to which there might exist the *pretinne affectionis.* The case of *The King* v. *The Bank of England* (*Doug.* 524), is in point, and this remedy in that case was denied. Motion denied." (*Wilkinson* v. *Providence Bank*, 3 *R. I. Rep.*, 22.)

But where, by the charter, or the by-laws of the company, it is made the duty of the officers of the company to enter in the books of the company, the transfer of shares, it is difficult to perceive upon what principle it can be successfully maintained that mandamus will not lie to compel the officers to perform their duty. An action for damages against the officers of the company, or against the company, for such neglect or refusal to perform their duty, is no more a complete and adequate remedy than is an action against public officers who refuse to perform their official duties. And an action in the latter case, as has been before observed (*ante*, 108), is of such a doubtful character as not to supersede the remedy by mandamus.

That a writ of mandamus will lie in such case, seems to be sustained by the weight of modern authority. (*Rex* v. *Worcester Canal Co.*, 1 *M. & R.*, 529; *Regina* v. *Liverpool, Manchester and Newcastle-upon-Tyne Railway Co.*, 11 *Eng. L. & Eq. R.*, 408; *Helm* v. *Swiggett*, 12 *Ind.*, 194; *Redfield on Railways*, 63.)

Where an act of the legislature is passed for the incorporation of a company, and appointing certain persons commissioners to open books of subscription to the capital stock, and authorizing such commissioners to apportion the stock among the subscribers in a certain manner, upon their taking upon themselves the duties of such commissioners, and their neglect to perform the duties by opening books of subscription, or refusal to make the apportionment of stock, mandamus lies against them to compel the performance of such duties. (*Walker* v. *Devereaux*, 2 *American Railw. Cases*, 542.)

It seems to be an admitted principle, that every endowed minister (that is, those to whose functions emoluments are attached), of any sect or denomination of christians, who is wrongfully refused admission to, or dispossessed of his pulpit, is entitled to the writ of mandamus to be admitted or restored to his functions, and the temporal rights with which it is endowed. (*Rex* v. *Barker*, 3 *Burr*, 1265; *Runkel* v. *Winnemiller*, 4 *Har. & McHen. Rep.*, 430.)

But where there is no legal right, and no endowment, and no emoluments, except such as depend on voluntary contribution, a mandamus will not lie, either to admit or to restore a minister.

It was, therefore, held by the court of Errors and Appeals of the State of Delaware, in the case of *The Union Church of Africans* v. *Ellis Saunders*, 4 *American L. Reg.*, 378, that under the voluntary system of church government in this country (except, it would seem, in cases of actual endowment), a mandamus cannot issue to compel the trustees or members of a particular church to admit a minister to the exercise of his spiritual functions, and this, though he may have been duly appointed thereto by the superior ecclesiastical authority, a Methodist yearly conference. The same doctrine is maintained in other States. (4 *Har. &. McHen.'s Rep.*, 448.)

The case of *The People* v. *Steele*, 2 *Barb. Rep.* 397, is hardly reconcilable with the cases cited above. It was there decided that where a congregation was organized, and its house of worship dedicated with a view to the preaching of the faith, and enforcing the discipline of the Methodist Episcopal church, and it was the intention of its founders to establish a Methodist Episcopal church in connection with the general church of that denomination, and to support the tenets of that church, in subjection to the ecclesiastical power thereof, the refusal of the trustees to receive a preacher appointed by the bishop was an act of insubordination to the ecclesiastical tribunals of the church, and in violation of one of the injunctions of its discipline, which authorized the issuing of a peremptory mandamus, commanding them to admit the preacher thus appointed, into the church.

It was also held that it was no excuse for the trustees to return that the relator was not the choice of the majority of the congregation, and that such majority sustained the trustees in excluding him from the possession of the pulpit.

Mandamus will also lie to compel a corporation to admit to membership one who is in law entitled to the franchise of a corporator, unless excluded by the operation of some valid regulation or by-law of that particular society. And where a party having a clear presumptive title, claims admission to the exercise of a corporate franchise, the right of immediate expulsion should be clear and unquestioned, to justify the rejection of the claim.

Therefore, where the relator was a practicing physician in the county of Erie, had received a thorough medical education, and, in virtue of his diploma from the New York Medical College, was entitled to practice, in any part of the State, the profession to which he had dedicated his life, and the statute imposed on the president of the County Medical Society the duty of notifying him to apply for admission to such society, but, for some cause not disclosed in the papers, that duty had not been discharged, though at the time the proceeding was instituted, the relator had been in active and successful practice for a period of seven years; and in June, 1859, the relator made application for admission, and proposed to comply with the conditions of membership and to subscribe to the conventional rules and regulations adopted by the society for the government of its members, and the sole ground on which his application was rejected was, that at an antecedent period he had not observed certain conventional regulations which the society had made by their code of by-laws, it was held by the court, that the code of medical ethics adopted by the by-laws of the County Society was obligatory on members alone, and its non-observance previous to membership furnished no legal cause either for exclusion or expulsion; that the relator's diploma was presumptive evidence of his professional qualifications; and that as it appeared that his private character was irreproachable, and the only qualifications for admission required by the by-laws, were "that the applicant should be a physician or surgeon, residing in the county of Erie, of temperate habits, good moral character, and legally authorized to practice physic or surgery in this State," he was entitled to admission, and an order of the court granting a peremptory mandamus to compel the society to ad mit the relator to membership, was affirmed. (*The People* v. *The Medical Society of the County of Erie*, 32 *N. Y. R.* 187.)

Mandamus will also lie to restore a member of a corporation who has been illegally disfranchised.

Every member of a corporation is understood to have a franchise or freedom; and, therefore, where the member is deprived of this franchise, or freedom, by being expelled, it may very properly be said that he is disfranchised. (2 *Black. Com.*, 37; 1 *Kyd*, 15.)

With regard to what are called joint stock incorporated companies, or indeed any corporations owning property, it seems that a member cannot be expelled, and thus deprived of his interest in the stock, or general fund, in any case, by a majority of the corporators, unless such power has been expressly conferred by the charter. (*Angell & Ames on Corporations*, 238; 5 [*N. S.*] *Law Reg.*, *No.* 7.)

But where a member of a corporation created for religious or charitable purposes, and the members of such corporation are not stockholders, and are without any pecuniary interest in the organization, disqualifies himself to assist in promoting the objects and purposes of the corporation, he forfeits his corporate franchise, and may legally be expelled. For example, if a member of a corporation created for the advancement of religion, should conduct himself in such a manner as to counteract the efforts of the other members in effecting that object, the corporation might be authorized to disfranchise or expel him. (*Angell & Ames on Corporations*, 239; *Evans* v. *The Philadelphia Club*, 14 *Wright's* [*Penn.*] *Reps.*)

The law in such cases, as it has been laid down by the Supreme court of Pennsylvania, is that a corporation possesses, inherently, the power of expelling members in certain cases, as such power is necessary to the good order and government of corporate bodies; and that the cases in which this inherent power may be exercised, are of three kinds: 1st. Where an offense is committed which has no immediate relation to a member's corporate duty, but is of so infamous a nature as renders him unfit for the society of honest men; such are the offenses of perjury, forgery, &c. But before an expulsion is made for a cause of this kind, it is necessary that there should be a previous conviction by a jury, according to the law of the land. 2d. Where the offense is against his duty as a corporator; in which case he may be expelled on trial and conviction by the corporation. 3d. The third is an offense of a mixed nature, against the member's duty as a corporator, and also indictable by the law of the land. (*Commonwealth* v. *St. Patrick Society*, 2 *Binney's Rep.*, 448; *Commonwealth* v. *Guardians of the Poor*, 6 *Serg. & Rawl.*, 469.)

In the case of *The Commonwealth* v. *Philanthropic Society*, 5 *Binn.* (*Pa.*), 486, an application was made for a mandamus to restore a member of the society who had been expelled. The return showed the expulsion and the cause. The question was whether the member had been properly expelled. It appeared that by the articles of the society, certain causes of expulsion are enumerated, which consist in being concerned in scandalous or improper proceedings, which might injure the reputation of the society. It also appeared, from the minutes of the expulsion, that he had made a demand on the society for relief, agreeably to the rules of the institution, and had presented to them a physician's bill, which he alleged he had paid, amounting to forty dollars; but in fact it was a bill which he had altered by adding a cypher to four, the amount of the real bill.

Tilghman, C. J., said: "If this was not a forgery, it was very like it. That it was a scandalous and improper proceeding is most plain. Did it tend to injure the reputation of the society? No one can doubt, unless the society is without reputation. The tendency of such conduct is self-evident." The mandamus was refused.

And where the by-laws of an incorporated medical society provided that any member of the society might be expelled from the society by a vote of two-thirds of the members present at any annual meeting, "for any gross and notorious immorality, or infamous crime under the laws of the land," and the relator had by a two-thirds vote of the society, at an annual meeting, been expelled for the alleged offense of gross immorality in having broken his solemn pledge given to one Dr. Carpenter to not practice his profession in a certain place, and he had therefore petitioned for a writ of mandamus to order the said society to restore to membership the petitioner, it was held that as the society, both by its charter and by-laws, had jurisdiction to inquire into and pass judgment upon the conduct of its members, and, in a proper case, to expel a member; and gross immorality in a professional transaction, having a tendency to bring the profession into dishonor before the community, if distinctly charged and proved, may be of such a character as to justify the exercise of their power. And as the proceedings appeared to have been conducted with deliberation, and several opportunities were given to the petitioner to be heard before the committee, and the counselors, and the vote of expulsion was unanimous; and there was no evidence of haste or prejudice against the petitioner, or that the society came to a wrong decision, or acted in violation of the petitioner's rights, the petition was dismissed. (*Barrows* v. *The Massachusetts Medical Society*, 12 *Cushing's Rep.*, 402.)

A case was decided in Pennsylvania, which arose on return to a mandamus directed to the St. Patrick Benevolent Society, an incorporated body, commanding them to restore John Binns to the rights of a member of said society. The question was whether the by-law under which the expulsion was made, was valid—the by-law providing for the dismissal of members for vilifying the corporator. In determining the question, the court considered it necessary to regard the nature of the corporation, which was an association having for its object, the raising a fund to be applied to the relief of its members in case of sickness and misfortune, and to the assistance of distressed Irishmen, emigrating to the United States. Each member paid a certain sum, on admittance to the society, and likewise an annual contribution; and each member was entitled, in case of sickness or distress occasioned by unavoidable accident, to pecuniary assistance from the funds of the society. The corporation had power to make by-laws for the good order and support of the affairs of the corporation, provided the said by-laws were not repugnant to the instrument of incorporation; and by the charter, any member who was guilty of insulting or disrespectful behavior to any of the society, should be fined for the first offense in the sum of one dollar, double that sum for the second offense, and for the third be expelled the society.

TILGHMAN, C. J., in giving the opinion of the court, after stating that the case provided for in the charter, was, from its nature, confined to disrespectful behavior in the presence of the party offended, observed as follows: "My opinion will be founded on the great and single point, on which the cause turns. Is this by-law necessary for the good government and support of the affairs of the corporation? I cannot think that it is. I have considered the case, with a mind strongly disposed to give a liberal construction to the power of making by-laws. It is my wish to give all necessary powers for carrying into effect the benevolent purposes of this society, and many others which have lately been incorporated on similar principles. But these powers must not be constrained, or the societies, instead of being protected will be dissolved. The right of membership is valuable, and not to be taken away without an authority fairly derived from the charter, or the nature of corporate bodies. Every man who becomes a member looks to the charter; in that he puts his faith, and not in the uncertain will of a majority of the members. The offense of villifying a member, or a private quarrel, is totally unconnected with the affairs of the society, and therefore its punishment cannot be necessary for the good government of the corporation. So far from it, that it appears to me, that taking cognizance of such offenses will have the pernicious effect of introducing private feuds into the bosom of the society, and interrupting the transaction of business. On mature reflection, it appears to me, that without an express power in the charter, no man can be disfranchised, unless he has been guilty of some offense which either affects the interests or good government of the corporation, or is indictable by the law of the land. I am therefore of opinion that the cause returned by the president of the St. Patrick Benevolent Society for not restoring John Binns to the rights of a member, is insufficient. (*Commonwealth* v. *St. Patrick Society*, 2 *Binney's Rep.*, 441.)

A wide distinction is made between amotion from an office in a corporation, and the disfranchisement of a member. The enjoyment of office is not for the private benefit of the corporator, but an honorable distinction, which he holds for the welfare of the corporation. But the franchise of a member is wholly for his own benefit, and a private right; for these reasons, in the former case he may be removed for neglect of duty, or the commission of any infamous offense, although not relating to the corporation; while in the latter case he cannot be expelled for minor corporate offenses, such as improper behavior to his fellow-corporators, where not so punishable by the general law of the land, or the charter of the company. (*Willcock on Mun. Corpor.*, 271.)

The old rule appears to have been, that a mandamus will lie to compel an admission or restoration to no place or office, unless it have some relation to the public; but in modern practice, the rule has been modified to a great extent, and now, it seems, the value of the matter, or the degree of its importance to the public policy, is not very scrupulously weighed.

It has therefore been held that it will lie to compel the proper officers to admit to the freedom of a corporation any of that class of persons who are possessed of an incorporate right according to the regulations of the constitution, such as apprentices who have served their time; and to take all such steps as may be necessary, preparatory to their admission.

It has also been held to lie to trading companies to admit as members those entitled to become such (*Angel & Ames on Corporations*, 432), and to restore members and trustees of private corporations for religious and charitable purposes, who have been illegally expelled. (1 *Serg. & Rawle*, 254; 2 *Serg. & Rawle*, 141; 2 *Binne*, 448.)

If it be shown that the respondents have no longer power to do the act commanded, the peremptory writ will not be allowed. It was therefore held, that a railway company could not be compelled by mandamus to purchase land to make a branch railway, where the compulsory powers of the company to purchase the necessary land had expired before the writ issued. (*Regina* v. *The London and North West-*

ern Railway Company, 6 *English Railway and Canal Cases*, 479.

In New York it has been held that as there is no special limitation upon the remedy by mandamus, it may be brought within the time fixed for the limitation of other similar or analogous remedies. (*The People* v. *The Supervisors of Westchester*, 12 *Barb.* 446.)

It has, however, been said that this rule seems liable to objection in many cases; and that the English rule, that the party should suffer no unreasonable delay, in the opinion and discretion of the court, is more just and equitable, and is countenanced by American cases. (*Redfield on Railways*, 466.)

While it is a fundamental principle that mandamus will not lie where there is any other specific adequate remedy, yet the fact that the corporation are liable to indictment for omitting to do that which is sought to be compelled by mandamus, seems to be entitled to no weight. (*The People* v. *Mayor, &c., of New York*, 10 *Wend.* 395.) For it is said that those who obtain an act of parliament for executing great public works, are bound to fulfill all the duties thereby thrown upon them, and may be called upon by the courts, by mandamus, so to do. And if their breach of contract causes a public nuisance also, that cannot dispense with the necessity of a specific performance of the obligation contracted by them. (*The Queen* v. *The Bristol Dock Co.*, 2 *Eng. Railway and Canal Cases*, 437.)

Abbott, C. J., in delivering the opinion of the court in the case of *Rex* v. *The Severn and Wye Railway*, 2 *B. & Ald.*, 646, said: "If an indictment had been a remedy equally convenient, beneficial and effectual as a mandamus, I should have been of opinion that we ought not to grant the mandamus; but it is not, for a corporation cannot be compelled by indictment to reinstate the road. The court may, indeed, in case of conviction, impose a fine, and that fine may be levied by distress; but the corporation may submit to the payment of the fine, and refuse to reinstate the road."

But where the proper remedy is in equity, and the right is an equitable right, and one not enforceable at law, but only in equity, as in matters of trust and confidence, mandamus, it seems, will not lie.

In the case of *Regina* v. *The Trustees of the Balby and Worksop Turnpike Road*, 16 *Eng. L. & Eq. Rep.*, 276, a rule *nisi* had been obtained on the part of J. F. Dawson as administrator of the estate of J. T. Dawson, for a mandamus to command the trustees of the *Balby and Worksop Turnpike Road,* which was in the province of York, to pay the applicant a year's interest on a mortgage debt of £500.

The trustees who acted under a local act, 9 Geo. 4, C. 46, had borrowed £500, at 4 per cent. interest, of one W. Dawson, on a mortgage deed (drawn according to the form given in the turnpike act, 3 Geo. 4, C. 126), which stated that the trustees, in consideration of the sum of £500, paid to the treasurer by W. Dawson, granted to the said W. Dawson, "such a proportion of the tolls arising and to arise on the said turnpike road, and the toll-gates, chains, and toll-houses erected, or to be erected, for collecting the same, as the said sum of £500, shall bear to the whole sum now or hereafter to become due and owing on the security thereof, to have," &c., "the same proportion of the said tolls, gates, &c., with the appurtenances, unto the said W. Dawson, his executors," &c., for the residue of the term of years for which the tolls were granted by the act, unless the £500, with interest at 4 per cent. were sooner repaid. W. Dawson, assigned the mortgage to J. T. Dawson, who afterwards died intestate, and the relator obtained letters of administration, and demanded payment of the interest.

One of the questions raised, was whether mandamus was the proper remedy to compel the trustees to make payment. CROMPTON, J., in announcing the judgment of the court said:

"With regard to the second question, it must be taken since the decision of *Pardoe* v. *Price*, that such a security as the present gives no legal right to the mortgagee to demand the payment of either the principal or the interest. It was decided in *Pardoe* v. *Price*, that the commissioners are merely trustees for the mortgagees as to the application of the moneys which are to be applied in the order directed by the act of parliament; and that the relation between the commissioners and the mortgagees is that of trustees and *cestui que trust*.

"The statutory provisions for the application of the money in the above case were substantially the same as those enacted by the special act in the present case; and I feel myself bound by the authority of *Pardoe* v. *Price* (which is directly in point), to hold that the applicant in the present case has no legal right, but that his remedy is in equity. If so, the case seems to fall within the general rule laid down in *The King* v. *The Marquis of Stafford*, 3 *Term Rep.*, 646, where it was held that no mandamus will lie where the right is merely equitable, and where there is no legal right. I say the 'general rule,' because I find that in *Edwards* v. *Lowndes*, 1 *Ell. & Bl.*, 92; *S. C.*, *ante*, *p.* 204, where an action on the case had been brought against trustees under circumstances very similar to those in the present case, it was said by Lord CAMPBELL, in delivering the judgment of the court that, 'the proper remedy in such case would be in equity, or if there is any remedy at law, it might, under some circumstances be by mandamus, but not by action.' Taking the general rule, however, to be as stated in *The King* v. *The Marquis of Stafford*, and finding no particular circumstances to take the case out of the general rule, even if a mandamus can ever lie where there is no legal right, the present facts showing the case to be one peculiarly for equitable relief. I must apply the general rule to this case. On both grounds, therefore, my opinion is against the application."

If, however, the right is a *legal right*, and there is no legal remedy, the party, it seems, is entitled to the writ, though he might seek redress in chancery. The principle which is said to lie at the foundation of applications for this writ, and the use of it, is, that whenever a legal right exists, the party is entitled to a legal remedy, and when all others fail, the aid of this writ may be invoked. The fact that the party may seek redress in chancery, may and should influence the court in the exercise of the discretion which they possess, in granting the writ under the facts and circumstances of the particular case, but does not affect its right or jurisdiction to grant it. (*The People* v. *Mayor, &c., of New York*, 10 *Wend.* 395.)

It however seems, that mandamus will sometimes lie, although the application concern a trust, and mere private endowment. Therefore, when, in pursuance of the will of a private person, his executor, by deed, conveyed lands to trustees for the benefit of the poor of a parish; and the deed provided that a chest, of which there should be three locks and three keys, should remain in the parish church, for keeping all writings, accounts, &c., and the trust moneys remaining unexpended; one of such keys to be kept by the receiver; the second by the parson; the third by the church-wardens. It was held that a mandamus lay to the trustees, to compel the delivery of one key to the church-wardens. (*Reg.* v. *Ottery St. Mary*, 3 *Gale & D.* 382; 4 *Ad. & E.* (*N. S.*) 157.

CHAPTER XXI.

PRACTICE IN MANDAMUS

PARTIES.

The writ of mandamus, from its very nature and definition, is "a command issuing in the name of the sovereign authority." (*Bouvier's Dict.*) And although it is substantially a civil remedy (2 *Carter's Ind. Rep.*, 423), yet in the United States it has always been issued in the name of the sovereignty by which it has been authorized. The suit, therefore, is properly prosecuted in the name of the State, on the relation of some person or persons who is called a relator. (*The State of Ohio* v. *The Commissioners of Perry County*, 5 *O. S. Rep.*, 497.)

When the remedy by mandamus is resorted to for the purpose of enforcing some matter of private interest, the relator must show some special interest in the subject matter. Otherwise, it is said, a mere stranger might obtain a mandamus officiously, and for purposes not at all desirable to the real party. (*The People* v. *Collins et al.*, 19 *Wend.* 65; *Hamilton* v. *The State*, 3 *Ind. Rep.*, 458.)

Therefore, where a committee was appointed by a town to audit the accounts of the overseers of the poor, and to demand, and receive from them the books of accounts belonging to the town, held by the overseers in their official capacity, it was held that the committee had no such property in the books as would authorize them to apply in their own names for a mandamus to compel the surrender of the books. (*Bates* v. *Plymouth*, 14 *Gray* [*Mass.*] *Rep.*, 163.)

It has been held that a private citizen has no right to apply for a mandamus to compel a public officer to perform an omitted duty, in a case where he is not directly injured by its non-performance. That where the public rights are to be subserved, it is for the public officers exclusively, to apply for the writ. (*Sanger* v. *County Commissioners of Kennebec*, 25 *Maine*, 291; *People* v. *Regents of the University*, 4 *Mich.* 98; *People* v. *Inspectors of State Prison*, 4 *Mich.* 187.)

And in a case where the petitioner for a mandamus showed an act of the assembly requiring the town borough to open an alley in said borough; that he had notified them of said law, and requested them to open said alley, which they had refused to do; that he was the owner of a lot of ground with two dwelling houses erected thereon, through which the alley must pass, and that the opening of such alley would greatly augment the value of said lot. It was held by the court, that the petitioner's interest was one in kind, if not in degree, common to all the inhabitants of the borough, and that he had no right therefore to the writ, which should be applied for by public officers. (*Heffner* v. *Commonwealth*, 28 *Penn. S. R.* 108.)

In the case of *Sanger* v. *County Commissioners*, 25 *Maine*, 291, the commissioners of the counties of Kennebec and Somerset, at a joint meeting of the two boards, adjudged "that common convenience and necessity required that the road prayed for in said petition," (and which was in both counties,) "be located and established." The commissioners for the county of Somerset thereupon duly located that part of the road lying in the county of Somerset, and the commissioners for the county of Kennebec, duly laid out that part of the same road in the county of Kennebec, which lay between the northerly end of Marston's bridge and the dividing line of the counties of Kennebec and Somerset. The residue of the same road never having been located by the county commissioners for the county of Kennebec, who afterwards upon a petition therefor, declined to lay out the same. One of the original petition ers for the road made application for a writ of mandamus to the county commissioners for the county of Kennebec, requiring them forthwith to complete the location of that part of the road lying in the county of Kennebec which they had omitted to lay out.

The respondents moved that the petition be dismissed for the reason, among others, "that the petitioner for the writ prayed for, is interested only as other citizens in opening new thoroughfares, and not entitled to the process prayed for"

TENNEY, J., in announcing the opinion of the court upon this point, said: "A private individual can apply for this remedy only in those cases where he has some private or particular interest to be subserved, or some particular right to be pursued or protected by the aid of this process, independent of that which he holds in common with the public at large, and it is for the public officers exclusively to apply, when public rights are to be subserved. (*Rex* v. *Merchant Factor's Co.*, 2 *B. & Ald.* 115.) These authorities, which are believed to be in accordance with others upon the same subject, contain the general rule of the common law upon this point. And we are not satisfied that the mode provided by the statute, to obtain the laying out, the alteration and discontinuance of public roads, which is by petition, which is often followed by proceedings, which are of an adversary character, and are sometimes followed by costs against the petitioners, can take this case from the general rule. The reason given in the original petition, for the location of the road, is, that the public good requires it." And the judgment of the joint board of commissioners for the two counties is, that "common convenience and necessity requires it." Neither the petition for the road, nor that for the writ of mandamus, allege any interest of this petitioner to be promoted, or that his rights are in any degree diminished, by the omission complained of, more than any other individual in the community, and he is not shown to have been at any trouble, or incurred any expense or liability by the proceed ings upon the original application for the road. However mistaken in their duty the county commissioners for the county of Kennebec may have been, in omitting to make effectual the judgment of the joint board of commissioners, and notwithstanding they may be exposed to a peremptory mandamus to lay out the remainder of the road, by virtue of an application by a public officer, we think this petition must be dismissed."

The better rule, however, in the absence of any statutory provision on the subject, seems to be, that where the proceedings are for the enforcement of a duty, affecting not a private but a public right, common to the whole community, it is not necessary, that the relator should have a special interest in the matter, or that he should be a public officer. This rule is maintained by high authority.

In the case of *Hamilton, Auditor*, v. *The State*, 3 *Ind. Rep.*, 452, where this question was raised and distinctly decided, the court say: "Were this a case merely for private relief, the relator would have to show some special interest in the subject matter. But here the case is different. The defendant, who was county auditor, refused to issue the legal duplicate for the collection of the taxes, and a mandamus was applied for to compel him to discharge this duty of his office. It is a case for the enforcement, not of a private, but of a public right; and it is not necessary, in such cases, that the relator should have a special interest in the matter, or that he should be a public officer. That the defendant should discharge correctly the duties of his office, was a matter in which Bates, as a citizen of the county, had a general interest; and that interest was, of itself, sufficient to enable him to obtain the mandamus in question, and have his name inserted as the relator."

So in the case of *The People* v. *Collins et al.*, 19 *Wend.* 56, it is said that in matters of mere public right, the people are the real party; that in such cases the wrongful refusal of the officers to act, is no more the concern of one citizen than another; and that while there was no doubt but that the attorney general might very properly move in the matter, yet the court could not collect from any of the books, or the reason of the thing, that he alone had the power to move. (*Rex* v. *The Justices, &c.*, 7 *T. Rep.*, 463; *Rex* v. *The Commissioners, &c.*, 1 *T. Rep.*, 146; *County of Pike* v. *The State*, 11 *Ill. Rep.*, 202.)

And when the subject matter has relation to the validity of an election, it seems that it is a matter of such public right, that any citizen may be a relator in an application for a mandamus. (*State* v. *County Judge*, 7 *Clark* [*Iowa*] *Rep.*, 186; *State* v. *Bailey*, *Ib.*, 390.)

When a suit for a writ of mandamus is prosecuted by any public officer in his official capacity, for the public benefit, and he dies, or his term of office expires before the determination of the suit, it will not abate, but may be continued by his successor. (*Felts* v. *Memphis*, 2 *Head.* [*Tenn.*] *Rep.*, 650.) Though several persons may be included as prosecutors in the same writ, at the discretion of the court, and will be when they constitute but one officer, and the object of the writ is to admit or restore such persons to such office, or when the object is to secure some private right, and all claim in the same right, as to admit, or restore several persons to the same office, in the same corporation; yet when two or more persons join. whose interest and cause of complaint are entirely distinct, it may well be doubted whether a joint application for the writ prayed for, can be sustained. Therefore, when the record showed that a certain sum was awarded to Simon Doe, and another sum to Dennis Blackwell, as damages severally sustained by them by reason of a road laid out across their lands, it was held that there was no interest common to both which would authorize them to join in an application for a mandamus, to compel the county commissioners to order and direct the damages so allowed to be forthwith paid. (*Hoxie et al.* v. *The County Commissioners*, 25 *Maine*, 333.) Neither can one and the same writ of mandamus be directed to the officers of several corporations, to compel them to perform distinct duties, growing out of distinct liabilities. (*Angell & Ames on Corporations*, 451.) It was therefore held, that one and the same writ could not be directed to the township committees of two several townships, to compel them to proceed to do their duty in the matter of a road. (*State* v. *Chester Eveshane*, 5 *Halst.* 292.)

The writ should be directed to those who are to execute it. or to do the thing required. And if it be directed to several, acting in different capacities, but the action of all is necessary for the accomplishment of the thing required, it should be taken distributively, and each are bound to obey the writ according to their several functions. (3 *Stephens' Nisi Prius*, 2321.) It should also appear, that the person to whom it is to be directed, has the power to execute it, for if he has not, it will not be issued. (*State* v. *Dunn*, *Minor*, 46; 15 *Barb.* 607; 12 *Ib.* 217.)

Where the cashier of a bank had refused to allow one of the board of directors to examine the discount books of the bank, it was held that the cashier had the possession, and control of the books, and that the writ might be directed to him, and not to the directors, although the cashier had excluded the relator from such inspection, in pursuance of a by-law passed by the board of directors, excluding the relator from all access to the books of the institution. The court also intimated that it might also be directed to the directors. (*The People* v. *Throop*, 12 *Wend.* 183.)

If the act commanded must be done by the whole corporation, or if a portion of the act by the whole corporation, and another portion by the head officer, the writ should be directed to the whole corporation, and not to the different enumerated classes, or individual members who compose it.

Thus a mandamus to compel an election of an officer in a corporation should be directed to the whole corporation, and not to the individual members. But if the act is to be done by a select body, as, for instance, certain officers of a corporation, the writ may be directed to the select body, or to the whole corporation. (*Angell & Ames on Corporations*, 451; 4 *American Law Reg.*, 163; 6 *Conn. Reps.*, 532.)

If directed to the officers by name, it should state distinctly and accurately their proper capacity. The common practice, however, is, to direct the writ to those officers of a quasi corporation who are to be required to perform the act, without giving the names of such persons. If, however, there is but a single person holding and performing the duties of the office, as an auditor, or treasurer, it may issue to such officer by name, and as such officer.

But in which ever form the proceedings may be commenced, it seems that a motion for a mandamus against a municipal or quasi corporation, is virtually a proceeding against the body, and the judgment is obligatory on the members of the board in office at the time of its rendition. And although it may assume the character of an individual proceeding, yet if it becomes necessary to enforce the orders of the court by attachment, or other process for contempt, a change in the membership of the board does not so change the parties as to abate the proceedings. The constituent parts of the board may not be the same, but the representative body remains identical. (*Maddox* v. *Graham*, 2 *Met.* [*Ky.*] *Rep.*, 56.)

A writ of mandamus, to a subordinate judicial tribunal, is properly directed to the judge or judges of the court, and especially where there may be other judges authorized to hold, or participate in holding the court. In case of disobedience to the mandate of the supervisory court, the authority to compel obedience is exercised over the judges personally having the power to exercise the functions of the court. (*Hollister & Smith* v. *The Judges of the District court of Lucas county*, 8 *O. S. Reps.*, 201.)

And where, to a writ thus directed, it was objected that the defendants were judges of the court of Common Pleas, and only as such, authorized to hold a District court, it was held that as by the Constitution and laws of the State, the judges of the court of Common Pleas, constituted the judges of the District court, and as such, clothed with full authority to hold the District court, and exercise its jurisdiction and authority, it mattered not in what form of expression the judicial power was conferred. And that, therefore, there was nothing in the objection that the writ was directed to them as the judges of the District court, instead of *the District court*. (*Ib.*)

The writ is, however, sometimes directed to the judges by name, stating their position; and when the object is to compel the signing of a bill of exceptions, perhaps this is the advisable practice. (*The State of Ohio* v. *Todd et al.*, 4 *O. Reps.*, 351.) This, however, is not universally the practice. (*The State* v. *The Judges of Common Pleas*, 1 *West. L. J.*, 358.)

CHAPTER XXII.

PROCEEDINGS IN MANDAMUS.

The proceedings in mandamus were formerly commenced by a motion in court, the grounds for which were supported by the production of affidavits, asking for a rule against the defendant, to show cause why the writ of mandamus should not issue. The hearing on the motion was *ex-parte*, and no previous notice to the opposite party was necessary; the defendant was notified of the granting of the rule, by serving upon him a copy of the rule.

It was necessary that the affidavits in support of the motion, should contain a precise statement of the facts constituting the relator's right to the writ; and it was held that they were insufficient if the allegations in them were not so positive, that an indictment for perjury could be maintained upon them if false. They should also show that the applicant is entitled to the relief he prays; that he has complied with all the forms necessary to constitute his right; that he has applied to the defendant to do that which he asks the court to command the performance of; and the refusal or neglect. (3 *Stephens' Nisi Prius*, 2318, 2319; 1 *Swift's Digest*, 564.)

The defendant might come into court, and by counter affidavits, show cause against the rule; and if, upon reading such affidavits, or hearing counsel against the rule, it became perfectly apparent that the relator was not entitled to the writ, the rule was discharged. But if his right appeared only doubtful, the court made the rule absolute, in order that the right might be tried. On the rule being made absolute, an alternative writ of mandamus was issued, in which writ it was necessary to set forth the facts which entitled the prosecutor to the relief prayed for, and the duty to be performed by the defendant, and directed to the person or persons whose duty it is to perform the act, commanding them to do the thing required, or signify some reason why they should not do it. To this writ the defendant was required to make a written return, either denying the facts stated in the writ on which the claim of the relator was founded, or setting forth other facts sufficient in law to defeat the relator's claim.

If the writ was defective, either in form or substance, the defendant could move to quash it. If the defect was of form only, the motion to quash should have been made before return made to the writ. But if the defect was one of substance in the writ, as a want of sufficient title in the relator to the relief sought, it could be taken advantage of at any time before the peremptory mandamus was awarded. (*The Commercial Bank of Albany* v. *The Canal Commissioners*, 10 *Wend.* 26; 6 *Conn.* 532; 7 *East.* 245; 4 *Cowen's Reps.* 73.)

If the return was adjudged insufficient, a peremptory mandamus was issued commanding, absolutely, the defendant to do the thing required, and if not obeyed, an attachment issued against the person disobeying it. If the return was sufficient in law, although false in fact, the relator could not traverse it, but was compelled to resort to his action for a false return.

But after the passage of the statute of 9 Anne, C. 20, the relator might reply, take issue, or demur to the return. (3 *Black. Com.* 265.)

The more common practice in the American courts is to file a formal petition, complaint, or application, as it is variously called, alleging in detail the grounds of the application, and praying for a writ of mandamus to be issued. This petition is sworn to by the applicant, or supported by the affidavits of others. If this petition and affidavits make a *prima facie* case, an alternative writ of mandamus is issued, commanding the defendant to do the thing required or to show to the court cause why it should not be done. This writ serves the same purpose as a declaration in an ordinary case, and the defendant must move to quash or demur according to the peculiar practice of the courts, or make return denying the allegations of the writ, or setting up new matter, constituting a defense to the relator's claim.

In some States, however, the practice seems to be to serve the petition or complaint upon all parties supposed to have an interest in the question involved, a sufficient time before the term to give an opportunity for taking the testimony upon notice; and upon the return of the petition the case is heard upon its general merits. In either form, if the application prevails, a peremptory madamus issues, the only proper return to which is a certificate of compliance with its requisitions, without further excuse or delay. (*Redfield on Railways*, 441; *State* v. *Smith*, 9 *Iowa*, 334.)

This general rule that the respondent must certify in answer to the writ, that he has complied with or obeyed its requirements, is subject to exceptions in case the writ has been improvidently issued, or has commanded the performance of an illegal act. (*State* v. *County Judge*, 12 *Iowa*, 237.)

In such case, a motion to vacate the rule allowing the peremptory writ and setting the mandamus aside, has been granted.

And where an agreement was made between counsel for the relator and counsel for the respondents, that all further proceedings in a mandamus cause should be stayed until the next term of the court, and notwithstanding such agreement the relator procured other counsel, and in the absence of the relator and his counsel, and before the next term of the court, procured a peremptory mandamus to be issued, the rule granting the writ was, on motion, vacated, and the mandamus set aside. (*Everitt* v. *The People*, 1 *Caines Rep.* 8.)

CHAPTER XXIII.

THE APPLICATION.

The petition for a writ of mandamus, should present to the court a *prima facie* case of duty on the part of the defendant to perform the act demanded, and an obligation to perform it; otherwise the alternative writ will not be granted. It should also appear from the petition that a demand has been made on the defendant to do the thing he is sought to be compelled to do, and that he has refused or neglected to do it. (*Stephens' Nisi Prius*, 2318, 2319; 9 *Mich. R.* 328.) And the facts and circumstances under which the petitioner claims the relief prayed, should be stated fully, clearly and unreservedly, and not inferentially. (*Commonwealth* v. *Commissioners*, 37 *Penn. S. R.* 277.) And it should also be shown that the defendant has it in his power to perform the act.

It has, therefore, been held that a complaint in mandamus against a comptroller is fatally defective if it fails to allege that there are "moneys not otherwise appropriated by law," out of which the compensation sought for, is to be paid. (*Redding* v. *Bell*, 4 *Cal. R.* 333.)

And where a petition for a mandamus alleging a contract between the petitioner and the justice of a county by which he was to be paid a certain sum for building a court house, and a certain other sum for building a jail, in monthly installments, for lumber and work, and praying for a writ of mandamus to compel the payment of what was due, without averring that any particular sum was due, was held defective, and on motion should be quashed. (*McCoy* v. *Harnett County*, 5 *Jones Law* [*N. C.*], 265.)

Where the practice is to hear the case on its merits, upon the return of the petition, the petition serves the purpose of a declaration in a civil case; and can be quashed, if it fails to present such facts, as shows the relator entitled to the remedy demanded. Where, however, the practice is to grant, on an *ex-parte* hearing of the petition, an alternative writ of mandamus, the alternative writ takes the place of a declaration, and the return motion to quash, or demurrer should be to it, and not to the petition.

The truth of the facts set forth in the petition should be shown by the oath of the petitioner, or the affidavits of others.

The petition should include, as parties defendant, all persons interested in the defense, and who are to be required to act upon the order.

CHAPTER XXIV.

THE ALTERNATIVE WRIT.

If an alternative writ is allowed by the court, it is the duty of the relator's counsel to prepare it, and not depend on the clerk of the court to draft it. As the petition upon which the writ issues is no part of the pleadings, the writ must be sufficient in itself to show precisely what is claimed, and the facts upon which the claim is made. (*Commercial Bank of Albany* v. *Canal Com.*, 10 *Wend.* 25.) To draft such writ properly, requires time, legal skill, and a knowledge of the case. (*Johnes* v. *The Auditor of State*, 4 *O. S. Rep.*, 493.)

The petitioner's rights, and the circumstances under which he claims them, must be stated unreservedly, fully, and clearly; and it has even been said, that it ought to answer all the objections that can reasonably be anticipated.

It should not only show facts sufficient to entitle the relator to the relief which he claims, but it should also show his right to all he claims. For it seems in the English practice, at least, that if the writ issue in the first instance for some things, which the defendant is not bound to do, it cannot be supported even as to those things which he is compellable to perform, and will be quashed on motion. (3 *Eng. L. & Eq. R.*, 285; 22 *Ib.*, 113; 3 *Eng. Railw. & Canal Cases*, 774.)

Nor can reference be made to the petition and affidavits on which the order was granted, in aid of the writ, in this particular.

And where a writ of mandamus commands the defendant as a judge or referee, to settle a case and exceptions by disallowing certain words and sentences, and allowing others, but contains nothing showing that the case thus settled would truly detail the events of the trial, it is not a mere defect in form, but an omission of a substantial statement or recital, essential to the relator's title to the relief claimed.

So, a mandamus issued to a railroad company, commanding them to issue their warrant to the sheriff to summon a jury to estimate the damage caused to the relator by the company, in the construction of their road, is insufficient if it use simply the general words of the statute. The writ should state specifically the nature and cause of the injury complained of. (*The Queen* v. *The Eastern Counties Railway Company*, 2 *Eng. Railway and Canal Cases*, 540.)

The court may grant the relator leave to amend his writ, by setting forth his damages fully and specifically, or perhaps to make any other proper and necessary alterations. (4 *O. S. Rep.*, 493.)

And where a mandamus was issued to compel a railroad company to proceed to purchase the lands necessary for the completing of their roads, between the points specified in their charter, and to set out and define the line of their road deviating from the line set forth in the act of incorporation, in pursuance of an act amending their act of incorporation, which writ did not aver that the company had given up their design, or had willfully exercised any injurious option, or that they were not effecting it with all convenient speed, or that even a reasonable time had elapsed, in the opinion of the prosecutor, without due preparation being made, or that it would not be more advantageous to all concerned to abide by the original line, than set out and define a different one, was held insufficient. (*The Queen* v. *The Eastern Counties Railway Company*, 2 *Eng. Railway and Canal Cases*, 190.)

And as has before been observed, the writ should demand just the remedy to which the relator is entitled, for if it demands too much, it is substantially defective. (1 *Hill's Reps.*, 50, 55; 35 *Barb.*, 110.)

Therefore, where the alternative writ was issued, commanding the respondents as a board of supervisors, to raise by tax a certain sum of money to pay the relators the whole amount to be due them for the performance of a certain contract, and it appeared that only a portion of the contract was yet performed, and therefore only a portion of the whole sum due, the peremptory writ was refused on the ground that the alternative writ demanded more than the relators were legally entitled to. That as the peremptory writ must follow the alternative, there could not be judgment for the relators for part, and the respondents for the other part. (*The People* v. *The Board of Supervisors of the County of New York*, 18 *How. P. Reps.*, 152.)

An alternative writ of mandamus, to compel the treasurer of school funds, to pay a bill, should show that the treasurer has funds from which he ought to pay the bill; and if it does not, it may be quashed on motion. (*State* v. *Slavin*, 11 *Wis.*, 153.)

It should also appear that the relator has no other specific legal remedy to which he can resort, to compel the performance of the duty, and that the party to whom the writ is to be directed, has it yet in his power to perform it. (34 *Penn. State Reps.*, 494; 20 *Ill. Reps.*, 525.) A distinct assertion, that he cannot have adequate relief without the aid of a writ of mandamus, has however been held a sufficient averment of the want of other legal remedy.

And it seems that a mandamus requiring a municipal corporation to provide for the payment of the interest on its bonds, need not set forth when the principal will become due, nor when, nor where, the interest is to be paid. Nor is it necessary that the relator's title to the bonds should be set forth; the averment of his ownership being sufficient to show his right to ask the interference of the court by mandamus. (*Ib.*)

But where an alternative writ was issued, to compel the judges of a court to vacate a rule granted by them, and no reason appeared upon the face of the writ why the rule of the court should be vacated, it was held that the writ was defective, and a peremptory writ refused, even after a return to the alternative writ had been made. (*The People* v. *The Judges of Columbia Common Pleas*, 3 *How. P. Reps.*, 30.)

The command of the writ must also be according to the duty. It was therefore held bad to require supervisors to expend a certain sum of money, in repairing a bridge; the command should be simply to repair. (*The People* v. *The Supervisors of Dutchess County*, 1 *Hill's Reps.*, 50, 362.) It must also correspond with the order, directing its issue. (*Hawkins* v. *Mone*, 3 *Pike's Rep.*, 345.)

The alternative writ, in the absence of any statutory provision upon the subject, should be served upon the defendants a sufficient length of time before the hearing to allow them to make their defense. For it is a general and well established rule, that no motion which in its operation is to have the effect of a final judgment ought to be granted without giving the party against whom it is made an opportunity of being heard. This is a common right, and to deprive a party of this right is a violation of the spirit and fundamental principles of our government. (*The People* v. *The Judges of Rensselaer Com. Pleas*, 3 *How. P. Rep.* 164.)

The allegations or recitals in an alternative writ of mandamus being in the nature of a pleading, their sufficiency to support the writ is brought in question on demurrer to the return, or any subsequent pleadings, the same as in an ordinary action, and the party must fail who commits the first error in matter of substance; and defects in these allegations are not to be aided by the affidavit on which the writ was granted. (*People* v. *Baker*, 35 *Barb. R.* 105; 10 *Wend.* 26.)

If the writ is not quashed, the defendant must make a return thereto, unless he think proper to put an end to the controversy by doing the act required.

CHAPTER XXV.

THE RETURN.

The return must, in all cases, be made by the person to whom it is directed. Where a mandamus is directed to the mayor, the mayor alone can make the return, and the other component parts of the corporation cannot disavow it, because the court cannot refuse the mayor's return, he being the officer to whom the writ is directed and to whom it is actually delivered. (*Stephens' Nisi Prius*, 2326.)

It stands as the second pleading in the action or proceeding, and must be good, tested by the ordinary rules of pleading, both in form and substance.

It must either deny the facts stated in the writ, on which the claim of the relator is founded, or must state other facts sufficient in law to defeat the relator's claim, and these facts should be stated positively and distinctly; and if instead of stating facts the return merely sets out or refers to matters of evidence from which these facts are inferred, it is objectionable. (10 *Wend.* 20; 35 *Barb.* 105; 37 *Penn. S. R.* 237; 32 *Ib.* 218.)

Therefore upon a return to a mandamus to the canvassers of an election that they rejected certain election returns because they were not made according to the statute, it was held proper to order the respondents to state the defects specifically, that the court might judge of them. (7 *Clarke* [*Iowa*] *Reps.* 390.)

And where one has been expelled from a society for an alleged violation of the rules of the society, to which rules there are certain exceptions, the return to the alternative writ must deny that the case comes within the exceptions. Therefore where the rules of a religious society provided "that all disputes between members are to be settled by arbitration, and any member who commences an action at law against another member is liable to expulsion, except the case be of such a nature as to require and justify a process at law," and the return simply set forth that the plaintiff brought suit against a member of the society in violation of the rules of the church, but did not aver that the case was not of such a nature as to require and justify a process at law, the return was held insufficient.

And where the return stated that the plaintiff was tried and expelled by a "select number of the said society, and in the presence of three deacons and a preacher," but it was not shown of how many this select number consisted, or by what authority they proceeded to try and expel a member, the return was declared insufficient.

The court say: This is a radical defect, for the power of expulsion must belong to the society at large, unless by the fundamental articles, or some by-law founded on those articles, it is transferred to a select number. It ought therefore to have been set forth from what source this select committee derived this authority, and in what manner they were selected, in order that the court might judge whether the proceeding had been conducted according to law. (*Green* v. *African Methodist*, *&c.*, 1 *Serg. & Rawle*, 254.)

So, too, it has been held not a good return to a mandamus to restore a member of a corporation, that "he consented to be turned out." This was held not a return of resignation. (2 *Raymond's Reps.*, 1304.)

And upon a mandamus to swear in two church wardens, alleged in the writ to be duly elected, a return that they were not duly elected was held bad, unless it also alleged that neither of them were elected. (*Ib.*, 1008.)

And where the writ recited that the plaintiff was duly elected, admitted and sworn into an office, and without just cause had been removed, and the return was that he was not duly elected, admitted and sworn, and therefore they could not restore him, it was declared a defective return. For if he had been admitted, although not duly elected or sworn, yet the return should show a good cause for the removal. If he had not been admitted, the return might be good; or if the return had stated that he had not been elected, admitted or sworn, it would be good. (*Douglas' Reps.*, 79.)

A return to a mandamus commanding a railroad company to purchase the lands necessary for making, constructing and completing their road, which set forth that all their power and authority given them by law for the compulsory purchase of land had expired before the writ of mandamus issued, or was applied for, was held a sufficient return. (*Reg.* v. *The London and Northwestern Railway Co.*, 6 *Eng. Railway and Canal Cases*, 479.)

The court say: "A writ of mandamus supposes the required act to be possible and to be obligatory when the writ issues. What power have the defendants now to purchase the lands necessary for making a line of railway of several miles? A peremptory mandamus going as is prayed, no excuse can afterwards be made, and the defendants must implicitly and fully obey it under pain of imprisonment. Supposing that they were bound to pay any prices which might be demanded, however extortionate, can it reasonably be supposed that all the land owners along the line will be willing to sell at any prices, and that none of them are under disability to sell? Mr. Knowles contended that the return should have shown an application to all the land owners, and a refusal by them. But such a return, and the issues arising upon it, would be highly inconvenient; and even if all had promised to sell, without binding contracts have been entered into, they might afterwards change their minds and the defendants might be subjected to perpetual imprisonment for not doing what the law forbids them to do."

But it seems not a good return, that the prescribed period

for the compulsory purchase of the necessary land has nearly expired, if there is still a period during which the company may take the requisite initiatory steps. (*Reg.* v. *The York, Newcastle and Berwick Railway Company*, 6 *Eng. Railw. and Canal Cases*, 489.)

And where a mandamus is issued, requiring a municipal corporation to provide for the payment of the interest on its bonds, and the writ avers that the relator is the assignee and owner of the bonds, a return, averring simply that the bonds were not transferred in accordance with the acts of assembly, is insufficient; it should show wherein the supposed illegality of the transfer consists. Neither is it sufficient to aver that the liability of the corporation is disputed, without setting forth facts from which the court may determine that the debt is not due. (*Commonwealth* v. *Pittsburg*, 34 *Penn. S. R.*, 496.)

Every intendment is made against a return to a writ of mandamus, which does not answer the material facts; therefore, it has been held that where it is shown that an ex-officer had the seal of a corporation on the fifteenth of June, it is not sufficient to avoid the writ, to return that he had no control over, or possession of it in July, unless he also shows how he has parted with the control. (*The People* v. *Kilduff*, 15 *Ill.*, 492.)

For the same reason it has been held that a return of a justice to an alternative mandamus to send up papers, that at the time of service his fees had not been paid, is no defense against making the writ peremptory, for they may have been paid since the service. (*People* v. *Harris*, 9 *Cal. Reps.*, 571.)

It seems, also, that an answer to an alternative writ, setting up prior proceedings on the same subject in the same court, as a justification of the defendant's action, is defective if it fails to set forth those proceedings fully, so that the plaintiff may reply thereto, and the court be enabled to judge whether the pleadings present a good defense. (*State* v. *Jones*, 10 *Iowa*, 65.)

If the return be insufficient, the relator may demur (*Gorgas* v. *Blackburn et al.*, 14 *O. R.*, 252) or move to quash it; and on motion the peremptory writ will issue. (*People* v. *State*, 2 *Barb.*, 554; *Commonwealth* v. *Commissioners*, 32 *Penn. S. R.*, 218.)

But on demurrer, motion to quash, or motion for a peremptory writ, the truth of the return is admitted (24 *Miss.*, 439.)

The return, formerly, was not traversable; but in some States the relator is permitted to plead to it, while in other States, new matter set up in the return is understood as denied, without a reply. In such case, if a reply to the return be filed, a motion to quash the reply will be granted. (9 *O. S. Reps.*, 599.)

But when the relator pleads to the return, he thereby admits that, upon its face, the return is a sufficient answer to the case made by the alternative writ; and if, on the trial, no material fact on the return is disproved, the defendant will be entitled to the verdict. (*People* v. *Finger*, 24 *Barb.*, 341.)

A return to a writ of mandamus need not be single, but may contain several defenses, or justifications; and if one of those be sufficient, the return must be allowed as to that. (*Wright* v. *Fawcett*, 4 *Burr*, 2041.)

Where, however, inconsistent causes for not obeying the mandamus are stated in the return, it must be quashed; for, taken as a whole, it is false. (*Angell and Ames on Corporations*, 457.)

In the case of *The King* v. *The Mayor, &c., of Cambridge*, 3 *Durnford & East's Reps.*, 456, the court say: "Where two causes returned to a mandamus are inconsistent, the whole must be quashed, because the court cannot know which to believe, and it is an objection to the whole return. It is like a declaration in which two inconsistent counts are joined; there the plaintiff cannot have judgment." (5 *Durnford & East's Reps.*, 66.)

But where the return was, first, that the relator was not duly elected sexton; and, secondly, that there was a custom to remove, and that he was removed pursuant to such custom, it was held by the court that the return was not inconsistent; for that he might have been elected in fact, and afterwards removed. (*Cowp.*, 413.)

So, it seems not to be inconsistent to return that the relator was not eligible to the office, and also that he was not elected. (3 *Durnford & East's Reps.*, 461.)

It, however, was held inconsistent to state in a return to a mandamus to certify the election of a recorder, supposed in the writ to be on the 15th day of January, that the corporation was not then duly assembled; and afterwards, in the same return, to state the election of another corporate officer on the 15th of January of the same year; for if it was not duly assembled, it could not have elected such other corporate officer. (*The King* v. *The Mayor of York*, 5 *Durn. & East's R.*, 66.)

But a return to a mandamus directed to the steward of the Court Leet of a borough, commanding him to admit and swear the relator a freeman of the borough, which set forth that he was not elected, and further that he was not entitled to be sworn in because he has not been previously approved of by the lord of the manor, which is essentially necessary to be done according to a custom which the steward sets forth before he can be admitted and sworn, was held consistent. (4 *Burr*, 2044.)

If a return to a mandamus consists of several independent matters not inconsistent with each other, but part of them good in law, and part bad, the court may quash the return as to such part only as is bad, and put the prosecutor to plead to, or traverse the rest. (3 *Durn. & East's Reps.* 461.)

A return to a mandamus, directed to the judge of the Probate court, commanding him to grant probate of a will, which sets up the pendency of a suit, in the proper court, to contest the validity of the will, is a sufficient return to the writ. (*Rex* v. *Dr. Hay*, 4 *Burr*, 2295.)

It has been said, that in a return to a mandamus, the same certainty is required as in indictments, or returns to writs of *habeas corpus*. (*The King* v. *The Mayor of Lynn Regis*, *Doug.*, 149.) It may, however, well be questioned, whether this is not carrying the rule too far. Lord MANSFIELD, in the case of *The King* v. *The Mayor*, *&c.*, *of Lynn Regis*, *Doug.*, 177, said: "In criminal prosecutions, technical forms are established, and ought to be followed. If, in an indictment, you say that A. forged, and caused to be forged, the proof of either fact will support the indictment; but to say that he forged, or caused to be forged, would be bad. This being determined, must be adhered to. But such nicety is not required in accusations against a corporation in a corporate court. There substantial certainty is all that is necessary."

Such certainty only is required as, upon a fair and reasonable construction, may be called certain without recurring to possible facts which do not appear. Therefore where a return to a mandamus to restore, it was stated that the party was removed by the corporate body at large, the return was held sufficient without averring that the power of removal was vested in them, because that power is incidental to such corporate body, unless given by charter, by-law or otherwise, to a select body. (*The King* v. *The Mayor of Lynn Regis*, *Doug.* 149.)

Where a mandamus was issued suggesting that the relator was, in easter week, chosen church warden, and the return was that the relator was not elected in easter week, it was held by the court that the return was sufficiently certain, because it pursued the suggestion of the writ. (*Rex* v. *Penrice*, 2 *Strange's Reps.*, 1235.)

On a mandamus to restore an officer who is in at pleasure only, it is held a good return to say it was their pleasure to remove him. (1 *Ib.*, 115.)

Ouster upon *quo warranto* is always a sufficient return to a mandamus to restore one to an office. And where the writ avers, generally, that the prosecutor has been elected, it is sufficient to answer generally in the return, that he has not been elected, or what is the same thing, that he has not been duly elected.

This general answer, however, is not sufficient if the writ sets forth certain facts, and concludes with "by reason whereof the relator was elected;" but the return in such case should traverse some material fact, on the truth of which the election is founded; or if this cannot be done, and the facts stated are nevertheless insufficient to sustain the election, it should state what is necessary to a legal election, and negative the legal nature of that set forth in the writ. (*Angell & Ames on Corporations*, 457.)

In every case of amotion or disfranchisement, the return should show precisely the cause of the same, and the proceedings had; as that an assembly of the proper persons was duly held, notice given to the prosecutor, a conviction of an offense, and an actual amotion or disfranchisement thereupon, in order that the court may judge of the legality of the cause and the regularity of the proceedings.

Accordingly if the return merely alleges that the prosecutor was duly amoved or expelled the corporation for a violation of duty, without specifying the charges upon which he was convicted, or the manner of proceeding, it is insufficient. (*Ib.*, 461; 6 *Serg. & Rawle*, 469.)

If the officer is entitled to notice before amotion, the return must specifically aver that notice was given to him to appear and defend himself, or must show that the corporation did all they could do to give him such notice; but if it is shown that the prosecutor actually appeared and defended himself, no previous notice need be alleged. (*Commonwealth* v. *Penn. Beneficial Inst.*, 2 *Serg. & Rawle*, 141.)

The return should also state specifically the charges preferred against the relator as grounds for his removal, and that they were either proved on oath or confessed. It, however, seems not necessary to aver that the amotion was under the corporate seal, or that it was entered on the corporation books, even where it is required by law that it shall be so entered on the corporation books, and under the corporate seal, because it is said that this will be implied in the general averment that he was removed. (*Angell & Ames on Corporations*, 461: *Willcock on Corp.*, 423.)

A return averring that the relator was only an officer at pleasure, and that upon due summons to choose another, another was chosen, and thereby the relator was amoved, was held good. (*Strange's Reps.*, 674.)

Where the charter of a railroad company makes it obligatory upon the company to complete their road, a return to a mandamus to compel them to complete it alleging that the road will not be remunerative to the company, is not a sufficient return. Neither would it be a good return "that the making of the same railroad would be a useless expenditure of labor and money, whilst it would be destructive of the lands through which it would go, for any agricultural or other useful or beneficial purpose."

For although the making of a particular railway, or a portion of it, may not be profitable to the company, it may be of great benefit to particular individuals, and to the public, that the whole should be completed. And in such cases it also seems not a good return to allege "that all and every, the sum and sums of money applicable for the purposes of the said act which can in reasonable probability come to the possession of or be disposable by us, the said company, will fall short by a very large sum of money of the aggregate sum necessary for the making of the railway authorized by the said act, and which we, the said company, are by the annexed writ commanded to make." To say that "in reasonable probability" they may not have funds for all the purposes of the act, is not saying positively that they have no funds which would be sufficient to enable them to do all that they are commanded to do.

Were it, however, clearly made out to the satisfaction of the court that the company, although carrying out the design with good faith, and with prudence, was from unforeseen casualties left entirely without funds, it is probable the court, in the exercise of its discretion, would refuse the application, and leave the parties to such relief as they might obtain by interposition of the legislature. (*Regina* v. *The York and North Midland R. Co.*, 16 *Eng. L. & Eq. Rep.*, 299.)

And where a mandamus recited that a railroad company had, in November, 1838 (a time after the compulsory powers given to the company for taking land had expired), cut through and taken part of a turnpike road forty feet wide, and had made a bridge thereon for carrying it over the railway, the said bridge and approaches being about thirty feet wide only, and which writ commanded the company to restore the turnpike road to the width required by its charter, it was held that a return alleging that the company could not obey the writ without taking more land, and that their compulsory powers to take land had expired before they were required by the trustees of the road to widen it, was held insufficient. (*The Queen* v. *The Birmingham, &c.*, 2 *Eng. R & C. Cases*, 507.)

The court say: "When the company avail themselves of the very great powers with which they are vested against the public, they should take care to act strictly within those powers. As to the compulsory rights of taking land having expired, that rests entirely with the company; for the act having passed in the year 1836, the works in question were not begun till more than two years after, when the power was gone."

A return to a writ of mandamus commanding the admission or restoration of the relator to the privileges and franchises of a corporation to which by law he is entitled, must set forth such matter, in the absence of any special statutory provision on the subject, as is recognized by the common law as cause of exclusion or expulsion. Of these there seems to be but three classes: 1. Violation of duty to the society as a member of the corporation. 2. Offenses as a citizen, against the laws of the country. 3. Breach of duty in respect alike to the corporation and the laws.

If, therefore, the return sets forth certain conduct of the relator before he became a member of the corporation as a cause for his exclusion or expulsion, which conduct was neither illegal nor immoral, but simply a violation of the by-laws of the society, it does not set forth a sufficient return. The by-laws are obligatory only upon those who are members of the society. At least this is the case where neither the general statute nor the by-laws of the society make the antecedent observance of this regulation a condition of membership. (*The People* v. *The Medical Society of the County of Erie*, 32 *N. Y. Reps.*, 187.)

It has before been said that formerly if the return was sufficient in law, although it should be false in fact, the court would not try the truth of the fact, but would for the present believe the return to be true, and proceed no further on the mandamus. The party injured by the false return might then prosecute an action against the respondent for his false return, and if found to be false by the jury, was entitled to recover damages equivalent to the injury sustained; and thereupon the court, upon a new motion founded upon the postea, or judgment in the action for the false return, would grant the writ of mandamus in the peremptory form. (3 *Black. Com.* 111.)

But the practice in such cases was changed by the statute of 9 Anne, c. 20, by which the relator was permitted to plead to the return, and his antagonist might reply, take issue or demur, and the same proceedings were had as if an action had been brought for making a false return; and after judgment obtained for the prosecutor a peremptory writ might issue, and a judgment for damages and costs recovered.

This statute, with some modification, has been enacted by many of the American States. And it seems that where, upon the relator's recovering judgment, he is entitled to have a peremptory mandamus granted to him without delay; and such writ is a complete remedy, and gives to the party all he is entitled to, he is permitted to recover only nominal damages.

Where, however, the relator has sustained actual damages by being deprived of his rights (as in case of expulsion from an office, or the refusal to induct into an office, whereby the relator has sustained loss by being deprived of the emoluments of the office), the relator would, in addition to his judgment for the peremptory writ, be entitled to a judgment for the amount of his damages actually sustained, and no more.

Therefore, where a mandamus had been sued out, requiring the supervisors to audit certain damages assessed by competent authority at the sum of $200, for the land of the relator taken for a highway, and to the end that the same should be levied and collected in a certain town, or to show cause, and the supervisors made a false return, and the relator had been kept out of the damages so assessed for some time, it was held that the supervisors were liable in damages to the extent of the interest upon the two hundred dollars while thus kept out of it; but that as he was entitled to a peremptory writ, commanding the supervisors to audit and allow the amount so assessed, his judgment for damages should not include the sum of two hundred dollars. And had the law permitted the supervisors to audit and allow the interest, as well as the sum assessed, it seems there would be no ground for any damages, other than nominal. (*The People* v. *The Supervisors of the County of Richmond*, 28 *N. Y. Reps.*, 112.)

A return, on leave of court, may be amended in matters

of substance, even after it has been filed and exceptions made. (*Doug. Reps.*, 135; 10 *Pick. Reps.*, 59.)

The motion, however, for leave to amend, should probably set forth specifically the points sought to be corrected. (*State* v. *County Judge*, 12 *Iowa*, 237.)

And where the return is insufficient, and in law no defense to the writ, the court may, on motion, grant the peremptory writ; yet the court will not, ordinarily, in the first instance order a peremptory writ, where there is the appearance of having a valid defense, but will direct the respondent to file a fuller and more perfect answer. (*State* v. *Jones*, 10 *Iowa*, 65.)

In the English practice, as well as in many of the States of America, questions of fact, arising on a mandamus, are tried by a jury. (1 *Eng. Railway and Canal Cases*, 317; 2 *Eng. R. and C. Cases*, 711.)

CHAPTER XXVI.

THE PEREMPTORY WRIT.

It seems that the peremptory writ may, where the moving papers preclude the possibility of any valid excuse being consistent with the facts therein contained, be issued in the first instance, and without the previous issuing of an alternative writ. (*Harkins* v. *Sencerbox*, 2 *Min.*, 344; *Knox County* v. *Aspinwall*, 24 *How.* [*U. S.*] *Reps.*, 376.)

This, however, can only be done where both parties have been fully heard, as upon motion for a rule for a mandamus, and there is no dispute about facts, and the court is perfectly satisfied of the propriety and legality of compelling the performance of what is asked. (*Ib.; The People* v. *The Contracting Board*, 27 *N. Y. Reps.*, 378; *Crary's Prac.*, 286.)

The more common practice is not to issue the peremptory writ, until after a hearing on the return to the alternative writ.

The peremptory writ should be like the alternative one, except that the words, "or show cause why you have not done so," are left out. Therefore, though the direction of the alternative mandamus was erroneous, the peremptory writ founded upon, and issuing to enforce it, must be directed in the same manner.

And where the defendant has his option to do one or the other of two or more things, a peremptory mandamus commanding him absolutely to do one of them, leaving him no option to do the one or the other, it is invalid and void.

Therefore, when the act of parliament provided that, "if the line of the railway cross any turnpike road, or public highway, then (except when otherwise provided by the special act) either such road shall be carried over the railway, or the railway shall be carried over such road, by means of a bridge of the height and width, and with the asent or descent by this or the special act in that behalf provided," it was held that a mandamus commanding the railway company to cause the said public highway to be carried over the said railway by means of a bridge of a certain height and width, was invalid in not allowing the defendants to exercise their option, to either carry the railway over the highway, or the highway over the railway. (*Regina* v. *The South Eastern R. Co.*, 25 *Eng. L. & Eq. Reps.*, 13.)

If the defendant neglects to make a return to an alternative writ of mandamus, an attachment may issue against him, under which the court may punish the contempt and enforce obedience to their writ. The court may, however, issue a peremptory mandamus, on proof of the service of the alternative writ, without compelling a return. (*People* v. *Judges*, 1 *John's Reps.*, 64.)

The relator is not entitled, as of course, to the peremptory writ, where no return has been made; but should generally proceed to enforce a return, unless there is some statutory law upon the subject. (*State* v. *Baird*, 11 *Wis. Reps.*, 260.)

The peremptory writ may be amended so as to correspond with the judgment. But the motion to amend should specifically set forth the points of variance sought to be corrected. (*State* v. *County Judges*, 12 *Iowa*, 237.)

If it be made to appear that a peremptory writ of mandamus has been unfairly obtained, it has been said that the court have such control over their own judgments that the writ will be set aside on motion. (*The People* v. *Everett*, 1 *Caines' Reps.*, 8.)

Courts enforce compliance with the peremptory writ by attachment. And if the defendant be a corporation, the attachment issues against the persons guilty of the contempt in their natural capacity. And it has been said that if the writ is directed to several in their natural capacity, unless all join in making the return, the attachment for disobedience must issue against all, whether guilty or not, though when they are before the court their punishment will be proportioned to their offense. (*Angell & Ames on Corporations*, 467.)

The application for an attachment is made by a motion upon which the defendant may show cause unless the contempt be gross, when the rule is made absolute at first. (*Tidd's Practice*, 484.) In the case of *The King* v. *Tooley*, 12 *Mod.* 312, upon affidavit that the defendant had kept out of the way so that personal service of a peremptory writ could not be made upon him, and that the writ had been left at his house, the court ordered him to show cause. And it seems that an attachment may be granted if a frivolous return is made, or if when the writ is directed to the head officer and also to the corporation, he makes a return contrary to the consent of the corporation. (*Angell & Ames on Corporations*, 467.)

A writ of mandamus is served by delivering it to the person to whom it is directed, and he, the defendant, makes his return to it. For the officer to read the writ to the person to whom it is directed, or leave with him a copy and then to keep the original writ and make his return upon it, as he would do on a summons, is not a good service or return. (3 *Stephens' Nisi Prius*, 2324; 17 *Miss.* 159.)

If the writ is directed to several persons, a copy must be served on all but one, showing the original to each at the time of service, and the original delivered to such one (*Corner's Crown Practice*, 227), the officer retaining a copy to make his return upon. (*Hempstead* v. *Underhill*, 20 *Ark.* 337.)

But where a copy of a mandamus was served without showing the original, the court refused to set the service aside, on the ground that there was no authority cited for the motion, and that the object of the service had been effected by appearance. But if no attention should be paid by the defendant to a writ of mandamus served by copy only, it is very doubtful whether an attachment would issue for a contempt. (*Regina* v. *The Birmingham and Oxford R. Co.*, 16 *Eng. L. & Eq. Reps.*, 94.)

CHAPTER XXVII.

WHAT COURTS MAY ISSUE THE WRIT.

The power to issue the writ of mandamus is in England given to the King's Bench only, as having the general supervisory power over all inferior jurisdictions and officers, and is co-extensive with judicial sovereignty. These peculiar powers were possessed by the court of King's Bench because the King originally sat there in person, and aided in the administration of justice.

It seems evident, therefore, that by the principles of the common law, this power would not, in the absence of any constitutional or legislative enactment, be incident to any court which did not possess the general superintending power of the court of King's Bench, in which the sovereignty might, by construction of law, be supposed to sit, and to exert there its prerogative powers in aid of the court, in order that a right withheld might not be without a remedy. This common law principle may be modified by legislation, in any manner that may be deemed proper and expedient. No doubt the British parliament, or the legislature of the States, might give the power to issue the writ to any judicial tribunal in the State, according to its pleasure, unless the power is vested exclusively in certain courts, by constitutional provisions; and in many of the States, this power is vested in other judicial tribunals than the highest court of original jurisdiction. (*Kendall* v. *The United States*, 12 *Peters' Reps.*, 526.)

The Constitution vests the whole judicial power of the United States in one Supreme court, and such inferior courts as Congress shall, from time to time, ordain and establish. In the distribution of this power it is declared that, "the Supreme court shall have original jurisdiction in all cases affecting ambassadors, other public ministers and consuls, and those in which a State shall be a party. In all other cases the Supreme court shall have appellate jurisdiction." It has therefore been held, that to enable the Supreme court to issue a mandamus, it must be shown to be an exercise of appellate jurisdiction, or to be necessary to enable them to exercise appellate jurisdiction and not original. That it is the essential criterion of appellate jurisdiction, that it revises and corrects the proceedings in a cause already instituted, and does not create that cause. And that although a mandamus may be issued by the Supreme court, directed to courts, yet to issue such a writ to public officers is in effect the same as to sustain an original action, and therefore appears not to be warranted by the Constitution. (*Marbury* v. *Madison*, 1 *Cranch*, 137.)

The Supreme court, in the exercise of its appellate jurisdiction, may issue writs of mandamus to inferior courts, commanding them to sign a bill of exceptions (*Ex-parte Crane*, 5 *Peters'*, 190), or to enter judgment (8 *Peters'*, 291), or to proceed to judgment (*Ex-parte Many*, 14 *How.* [*U.S.*] *Reps.*, 24), or to reinstate a cause erroneously dismissed (*Ex-parte Bradstreet*, 7 *Peters' Reps.*, 634), or to execute the mandate of the Supreme court (*Stafford* v. *Union Bank*, 17 *How.*, 275), or to permit or refuse amendments in the pleading. (*Ex-parte Bradstreet*, 7 *Peters' Reps.*, 647.)

It has also been held, that a writ of error will lie from the Supreme court, upon the judgment of the Circuit courts, awarding a peremptory mandamus to restore to an office, where the matter in controversy was sufficient to give jurisdiction to the court; that the matter in controversy in such cases is the value of the office, which must be ascertained by the salary. Therefore, an error from the Supreme court to the Circuit court for the District of Columbia, to reverse the judgment of that court awarding a peremptory mandamus, to admit the defendants in error to the offices of directors in the Columbian Insurance Company, it not appearing that the value of the office amounted to one thousand dollars, the sum required to give the Supreme court appellate jurisdiction from the final judgments or decrees of the Circuit court for the District of Columbia, the court directed the writ of error to be quashed. (*The Columbia Ins. Co.* v. *Wheelwright et al.*, 7 *Wheaton's*, 534.)

The power of the Circuit courts of the United States to issue the writ of mandamus is confined exclusively to those cases in which it may be necessary to the exercise of their jurisdiction. (*Smith* v. *Jackson*, 1 *Paine*, 453.)

Therefore, upon a motion for a mandamus to the register

of the land office at Marietta, commanding him to grant final certificates of purchase to the plaintiff for lands, to which he supposed himself entitled under the laws of the United States, it was held by the Supreme court, that the Circuit court did not possess the power to issue the writ. (*McIntire* v. *Wood*, 7 *Cranch*, 504.)

The Circuit courts of the United States may, it has been said, issue a mandamus to a State court, which refuses to transfer a cause under the act of Congress to the Circuit court. (*Spraggins* v. *County Court of Humphries*, 1 *Cooke*, 160.)

This, however, may safely be said not to be free of doubt. The Supreme court of Ohio has held, that where a suit has been instituted in a State court, by a citizen of the State, against a citizen of another State, for the recovery of over $500, and the defendant at the time of entering his appearance, files his petition, offers surety, and complies with the provisions of the act of Congress for the removal of the cause for trial into the Circuit court of the United States; and the State court thereupon, refusing to accept the surety and stay further proceedings, proceeds to trial and renders judgment in the case against the defendant, the proper remedy for the defendant is the ordinary one of petition in error, the facts being made to appear upon the record by plea to the jurisdiction, or by bill of exceptions; and that the extraordinary remedy of a peremptory mandamus, is neither an appropriate nor adequate remedy in the case.

Although the decision was based in part upon the ground that as no stay of execution was had, and the judgment had probably been executed, and therefore the court were unable to perceive wherein the relator would be benefited by the case being certified into the Circuit court, yet the leading reason given for the decision was, that the proceedings for the correction of errors was a complete and adequate remedy, and therefore mandamus ought not to lie.

SUTLIFF, J., in announcing the opinion of the court, said: "The writ of mandamus at common law was a prerogative writ, introduced to prevent discord from a failure of justice, and to be used on occasions where the law had established no specific remedy. It is, however, a general rule at common law, that the writ of mandamus does not lie unless the party applying has no other adequate legal remedy.

"The provisions of our code seem strictly consonant with this common law rule, as to the cases in which the writ of mandamus may issue. Section 570 provides that this writ may not be issued in any case where there is a plain and adequate remedy in the ordinary course of the law.

"If we look to this case as presented by the petition of relators and the answer of the defendant, it is evident that the relators had a plain and adequate remedy at law, by excepting to the holdings of the court. The relators had only to prepare, present and procure the allowance of a bill of exceptions, so as to present a statement of the facts upon the record, and by a petition in error to subject the rulings of that court to review, and if found erroneous, to reversal by a higher court. If, in fact, any error intervened in the proceedings of the court of Common Pleas, the correction of that error could have been obtained in the usual and ordinary course of proceeding provided by law in all similar cases. But the relators, for some reason, did not see fit to avail themselves of the ordinary and adequate remedy provided for the correction of errors in proceedings of the court of Common Pleas; and it is evident to us that having so neglected their appropriate and ordinary remedy, they not only are not entitled to the extraordinary remedy of a peremptory mandamus, but that, at this time, a mandamus would be inappropriate and inadequate." (*Isaac Shelby et al.* v. *B. F. Hoffman*, 7 *O. S. R.*, 451.) The motion for a peremptory mandamus was overruled.

If it be true that a proceeding in error is a complete and adequate remedy in such cases, it would seem to follow that mandamus is not an appropriate remedy. But how the action of the court in the case of *The State of Ohio* v. *The Court of Common Pleas of Fairfield County*, 15 *O. S. R.*, 377, cited and quoted in this work, page 43, is to be reconciled with the doctrines of the above cited case, is a difficulty we will leave for the courts to determine.

It is also said that the Circuit courts of the United States may issue mandamus to a District court which refuses to proceed to judgment, to compel it to do so. (7 *Cranch's Reps.*, 577.)

It seems that under the Constitution, Congress may give to the Circuit courts the power to issue the writ of mandamus in all cases warranted by the principles and usages of law, but has, for some purpose, seen fit to confine it to certain specified cases.

Mr. Justice JOHNSON, in delivering the opinion of the court in the case of *McIntire* v. *Wood*, 7 *Cranch's Reps.*, 504, said: "But although the judicial power of the United States extends to cases arising under the laws of the United States, the legislature have not thought proper to delegate the exercise of that power to its Circuit courts, except in certain specified cases. When questions arise under those laws in the State courts, and the party who claims a right or privilege under them, is unsuccessful, an appeal is given to the Supreme court, and this provision the legislature has thought sufficient, at present, for all the judicial purposes intended to be answered by the clause of the Constitution which relates to this subject."

In the case of *McCluny* v. *Silliman*, 6 *Wheaton's Reps.*, 598 the court not only sustains the doctrine maintained in the case of *McIntire* v. *Wood*, but also held that a State court cannot issue a mandamus to an officer of the United States. It seems, therefore, that without further legislation upon the subject, there is no means provided for compelling by mandamus a federal officer beyond the jurisdiction of the Circuit court for the District of Columbia, to perform a ministerial duty, when the issuing of the writ is not necessary to the exercise of the proper jurisdiction of the Circuit court, or the appellate jurisdiction of the Supreme court. That the issuing of the writ in such cases is not among the reserved powers of the States, nor has it as yet been conferred on the federal courts by the necessary legislation.

Mr. Justice JOHNSON, delivering the opinion of the court in the case of *McCluny* v. *Silliman*, before cited, said: "When we find it withholding from its own courts the exercise of this controlling power over its ministerial officers employed in the appropriation of its lands, the inference clearly is, that all violations of private right resulting from the acts of such officers, should be the subject of actions for damages, or to recover the specific property (according to circumstances), in courts of competent jurisdiction. That is, that parties should be referred to the ordinary mode of obtaining justice, instead of resorting to the extraordinary and unprecedented mode of trying such questions on a motion for a mandamus."

It has been held by the Supreme court of the United States, in the case of *Kendall* v. *The United States*, 12 *Peters' Reps.*, 526, that as the act of Congress of the 27th of February, 1801, concerning the District of Columbia, and by which the Circuit court of the District is organized and its powers and jurisdiction pointed out, declared that the laws of the State of Maryland, as they now exist, shall be and continue in force in that part of the District which was ceded by that State to the United States; and as at the date of that act the common law of England was in force in Maryland, and that the power to issue a mandamus in a proper case is a branch of the common law fully recognized as in practical operation in that State at the time the Circuit court for the District of Columbia was organized, it was thereby vested with broader powers and jurisdiction in this respect than is vested in the Circuit courts of the United States in the several States, and that it does possess the power to issue the writ of mandamus directed to United States ministerial officers when it is a fit and proper remedy.

As to what State courts are clothed with authority to issue a writ of mandamus, reference must be made to their respective Constitutions and legislative enactments.

CHAPTER XXVIII.

JUDGMENT UPON PETITION FOR MANDAMUS REVISABLE IN ERROR.

In those States where the court having jurisdiction to award the writ of mandamus is not the court of last resort, the judgment upon application for such writs is revisable upon writ of error. (*Redfield on Railways*, 468; *Columbia Ins. Co.* v. *Wheelwright*, 7 *Wheaton's Reps.*, 534.)

So in Virginia it has been held that if the Circuit court refuse to issue a mandamus in a proper case, the relator may apply to the Supreme Court of Appeals for a supersedeas, or writ of error to the Circuit court. (*Morris, ex-parte*, 11 *Gratt.* 292.)

The writ of error, however, must be prosecuted between the same persons who were the parties in the writ of mandamus. Therefore, an order for a mandamus to compel the sheriff to accept a bond for the trial of the right of property levied on under an attachment, is not such a judgment, sentence or decree as will support a writ of error sued out by the plaintiff in the attachment suit. (18 *Ala. Reps.*, 436.)

It appears that previous to the statute of Anne, c. 20, the application for a mandamus was a summary proceeding, and never assumed the shape of a common law judgment, but upon the coming in of the return to the alternative mandamus the court summarily disposed of the case by granting or refusing the motion, without inquiring into the truth of the matters alleged in the return. That statute authorized the relator to plead to or traverse the return; and if he availed himself of this privilege, the case then assumed the regular form of a common law proceeding upon which a judgment for damages and costs might be given; and upon such a judgment either party was authorized to sustain a writ of error. This statute, however, did not abrogate the former mode of proceeding, and the relator, upon the coming in of the return to the alternative mandamus, had his election either to proceed summarily by motion, or to adopt the more formal mode of proceeding by plea or demurrer under the statute. It was deliberately settled in two different causes which were brought before the house of lords a few years after the passing of the statute of Anne, that if the case was disposed of by a summary application, without plea or demurrer, no writ of error could be sustained on such decision. (*The Dean and Chapter of Dublin* v. *The King*, 1 *Bro. P. C. Tom. ed.* 73; *Pender* v. *Herle*, 3 *id.* 505.)

These two different methods of testing the validity of a return to a mandamus are recognized by the Supreme court of the State of New York, and it is also held that no writ of error lies upon the granting or refusing a mandamus upon a mere motion where no plea or demurrer to the return has been filed, as authorized by the statutes relative to writs of mandamus and prohibition. (*The People* v. *The President and Trustees of Brooklyn*, 13 *Wend.* 130.) In Iowa it has been held that although an information for a writ of mandamus should not, in that State, be entitled of a cause, nevertheless, a defect in this respect is not one upon which error will lie. (*State* v. *Board &c., of Johnson*, 10 *Iowa Reps.* 157.)

CHAPTER XXIX.

COSTS IN MANDAMUS.

Costs in all the proceedings for mandamus, unless controlled by statute, rest in the discretion of the court. By statute 1 Will. 4, C. 21, S. 6, it was provided that "in all cases of application for any writ of mandamus whatsoever, the costs of such application, whether the writ shall be granted or refused, and also the costs of the writ, if the same shall be issued and obeyed, shall be in the discretion of the court, and the court is hereby authorized to order and direct by whom and to whom the same shall be paid. (3 *Stephens' Nisi Prius*, 2332.)

By the English practice it is common to award costs against the relator and to the defendant, when the application is denied, but not always to the relator when it prevails. It is said that the more general and the more equitable rule, in regard to costs, in proceedings where the court have a discretion in that respect, is to allow costs to the prevailing party, unless there is some special reason for denying them. (*Redfield on Railways*, 444; *Fox* v. *Whitney*, 32 *N. H. R.*, 408; *Ballou* v. *Smith*, 11 *Foster's N. H. Reps.*, 413; *Regina* v. *Hardin*, 24 *Eng. L. & Eq. Reps.*, 167.)

And where a petition for a writ of mandamus is entered, and notice ordered, and at the return term the respondent appear, and the petitioner withdraws the process, the rule was held to be, that upon the withdrawal of the bill, costs should be adjudged for the respondent, unless it was shown that he was in fault. (*Anonymous*, 31 *Maine*, 591.)

In the State of New York, if the return is insufficient, the relator can demur, or move for a peremptory writ. The practice, in that State, where costs are discretionary with the court, is not to give costs, usually, on granting an alternative or peremptory mandamus on motion. If the party would secure costs, he should go to his demurrer or issue of fact. (*The People* v. *The Supervisors of Columbia*, 5 *Cow. Reps.*, 291; 6 *Wend.*, 559.)

The reason for this practice seems to rest on the fact that courts favor, and wish to encourage the more formal mode of proceeding by plea or demurrer.

APPENDIX.

FORM OF MOTION AND PETITION.

Ex-parte David Taylor.	Petition for a mandamus to the Judges of the Circuit court of the District of Columbia for Washington county.

The above petitioner moves the honorable the judges of the Supreme court of the United States, for a rule on the judges of the Circuit court of the District of Columbia for Washington county, to show cause why a mandamus should not issue commanding them to admit the appearance of the petitioner to a suit in said court by Thomas Ewing, Jr., against said petitioner; and the petitioner moves for the said rule on his petition, and the transcript therewith filed.

1. Because there is no legal cause of bail set forth in the proceedings in said suit, and by the refusal of the Circuit court to allow his appearance to be entered to said suit, he is unlawfully detained in custody by the marshal of said District.

2. Because the act of Maryland, passed in 1715, C. 46, § 3, is in force in the county of Washington, and nowise repealed; and the petitioner was by virtue of said act entitled to appear to said suit, on giving special bail in the sum of one hundred and thirty-three dollars thirty-three and a third cents. But the court refused to allow him so to appear, or to enter bail in said amount.

3. Because the petioner has a legal right to appear without bail, or upon giving bail to the amount required by the act of 1715, C. 46, § 3, and thereby to be discharged from prison, and the said legal right does not depend on the discretion of the court, but is fixed and regulated by law, and there is no other legal remedy for the petitioner in the premises.

ROBERT J. BRENT,
for Petitioner.

To the Judges of the Supreme Court of the United States:

The petition of David Taylor respectfully showeth that he is now confined in the jail in the city of Washington, at the suit of a certain Thomas Ewing, Jr., and he refers to the accompanying transcript of the record of said suit, and makes the same a part of this petition, for the better understanding of the proceedings under which he is now unjustly and oppressively detained in prison.

Your petitioner showeth, that by said record it appears he was held to bail in said suit, upon the affidavit of said Ewing, and without a copy of the declaration being served on him, as required by the act of the legislature of Maryland of 1715, C. 46, § 3.

That, at the return of the writ of *capias ad respondendum*, issued in said cause, your petitioner moved to enter his appearance without giving special bail, because of the alleged insufficiency of the affidavit to hold to bail, but said motion was overruled by the Circuit court of the District of Columbia for Washington county. That, thereupon, your petitioner moved to enter his appearance to said suit, upon giving good and sufficient special bail, in the sum of one hundred and thirty-three dollars and thirty-three and one-third cents, because of the omission to serve your petitioner with a copy of the declaration, according to the terms of the aforesaid act of 1715, C. 40, § 3; and your petitioner then and there tendered in open court good and sufficient bail, in the last mentioned sum of money. The sufficiency of said bail for said amount was fully admitted by said court, as will appear by reference to said transcript of the record; but the court overruled said application upon the express ground that your petitioner was bound to enter special bail to said action, in the amount of the sum sworn to in the affidavit of said Ewing, which sum is shown in said affidavit to be four thousand nine hundred and seventy dollars. Your petitioner is advised that the aforesaid recited act of the legislature of Maryland is in full force in Washington county aforesaid; and that, under and by virtue of said law, it was the duty of the Marshal to require no greater appearance bail, and of the court to require no greater special bail than the amount specified in said act, where no copy of the declaration is sent to be served with the writ; and your petitioner is also advised, that there is in said affidavit, no legal cause of bail whatever. Wherefore, inasmuch as the said Circuit court has refused both of said applications for an appearance on the part of your petitioner to said suit, and as the law provides no other adequate remedy in the premises, whereby your petitioner can, before the final determination of said suit, regain his personal liberty, whereof he is now illegally and unjustifiably deprived, your petitioner prays that the writ of mandamus may be issued and directed to the judges of said Circuit court, commanding and enjoining them to receive the appearance of your petitioner to said action, either without requiring special bail, or upon your petitioner causing good and sufficient special bail to be entered to said action, in the sum of one hundred and thirty-three dollars and thirty-three cents and one-third of a cent.

And, as in duty bound, your petitioner will ever pray.

R. J. B.,
for Petitioner.

Before the subscriber, a justice of the peace of the District of Columbia, in and for Washington county, personally appears David Taylor, the within petitioner, and made oath on the Holy Evangely of Almighty God, that the facts as stated in the said petition are true, to the best of his knowledge and belief. (14 *How.* [*U. S.*] *Reps.*, 3.)

J. W. B.,

December 10, 1852. *J. P.*

In some States it is the practice to issue the alternative writ, on filing the petition, without motion for a rule to show cause why it should not issue. In such case the following form will be sufficient:

ANOTHER FORM FOR PETITION.

To the Honorable the District Court within and for the County of .... and State of .... :

Your petitioners, Richard Phillips, etc., respectfully represent and state to the Court, that they constitute the board of directors of common schools for the eastern and western districts of the city of Cincinnati, which schools are established by law for the education of the colored youth residing in said city, and that in pursuance of law your petitioners rented divers rooms and established divers schools in said city for the education of said youth, and employed competent and duly qualified teachers as instructors of said youth in the schools aforesaid.

And your petitioners further state, that heretofore, to-wit., on the 15th day of March, 1850, William Disney, in his capacity as treasurer of said city, received from the treasurer of Hamilton county the sum of two thousand one hundred and seventy-seven and sixty-seven one-hundredths dollars, for the use of your petitioners and of the common schools for colored youth so by them established, the same being the proportion of the public school funds belonging to your petitioners and to the schools under their charge, as the same was apportioned by the auditor of said county in pursuance of law, which sum of money still remains in the hands of said treasurer in the treasury of said city.

And your petitioners further represent, that on the 1st day of April, 1850, there became due from them for expenses incurred in the support of said schools the sums hereinafter set forth, as follows, namely: The sum of six dollars to the trustees of the New street church, for two months' rent of the school room; the sum of seven dollars to the trustees of the Union Baptist church, for one month's rent of school room; to Martha S. Whipple, the sum of twenty dollars, for one month's salary as teacher; to Peter Clarke, the sum of twenty dollars, for one month's salary as teacher; to William R. Casey, for one month's salary as teacher, the sum of twenty dollars; and to O. J. B. Nickens, the sum of sixty dollars, for two months' salary as teacher in said schools; and that thereupon, afterwards to-wit., on the 5th day of April, 1850, your petitioners duly certified to the city council of said city the correctness of said several accounts, together with the several accounts respectively, and desired the city council to pass an order directing the treasurer of said city to pay the same out of the funds of your petitioners in his hands, to the persons entitled to receive the same; but your petitioners state that the said city council afterwards, on the first day of May, 1850, utterly refused to pass any order in relation to the payment of said accounts, and they now claim that they have no power, jurisdiction or authority to make any order in the premises, whereas, in fact and in law they have such power, and it is in fact their duty to so do.

Your petitioners further represent, that said William Disney, treasurer of said city, has no power to disburse said funds, nor any of the funds in the city treasury, without the order of said city council, signed by the city clerk, first being had and obtained, and has therefore and for that reason, refused to pay said accounts, without the order of the city council as aforesaid.

And your petitioners further state, that by reason of said refusal by said city council to pass the orders aforesaid, and of said treasurer to pay said accounts, the teachers employed by your petitioners are deprived of the compensation which is justly due them for their services, and the schools so by your petitioners established have been suspended for want of means to carry on the same, although a fund amply sufficient to sustain said schools has been provided by law, and is now in the hands of said Disney, as treasurer of said city.

And your petitioners further state, that they are entirely without remedy in the premises, unless it be afforded by the interposition of this honorable court by their writ of mandamus; and they therefore pray that a writ of mandamus may issue against the city council of the city of Cincinnati, commanding them to pass an order directing said treasurer to pay said accounts, out of said fund, and that such other order may be had in the premises as justice may require.

A. B.,
for Petitioners.

THE STATE OF OHIO, *Hamilton County.* } SS:

Richard Phillips, one of the petitioners above named, and president of the board of directors of common schools for the eastern and western districts of the city of Cincinnati, being duly sworn, saith that the several matters and things in the foregoing petition stated are true in substance and in matter of fact, to the best of his knowledge, information and belief.

RICHARD PHILLIPS.

Signed in my presence, and sworn to before me, this .... day of ...., 186... }

FORM OF THE ORDER.

The State of Ohio on the relation of ...., vs. The City Council of Cincinnati.	Petition for mandamus.

And now came the said plaintiff and presented its petition for a mandamus, against said city council, and the court being fully advised in the premises, it is ordered that an alternative writ of mandamus issue to the said city council of the city of Cincinnati, returnable to the District court, in the county of Hamilton, on the first day of its next term, commanding said city council to pass an order directing the city treasurer to pay to the trustees of the New street church the sum of six dollars; to the trustees of the Union Baptist church the sum of seven dollars; to Martha S. Whipple the sum of twenty dollars; to Peter Clarke the sum of twenty dollars; to William R. Casey the sum of twenty dollars; and to O. J. B. Nickens the sum of sixty dollars, out of funds in the hands of the said city treasurer, apportioned by the auditor of said county for the use of common schools for colored youth in the city of Cincinnati, or that said city council show cause, on the first day of the next term of this court, why they have not done so.

FORM OF ALTERNATIVE WRIT.

THE STATE OF OHIO,
Hamilton County. } SS:

To the City Council of the City of Cincinnati, Greeting:

Whereas, it has been suggested to us, that Richard Phillips, etc., petitioners, constitute the board of directors of common schools for the eastern and western districts of the city of Cincinnati, which schools are established by law for the education of the colored youth residing in said city; that in pursuance of law they rented divers rooms, and established divers schools in said city, for the education of said youth, and employed competent and duly qualified teachers as instructors of said youth in the schools aforesaid.

That heretofore, to-wit, on the 15th day of March, 1850, William Disney, in his capacity as treasurer of said city, received from the treasurer of Hamilton county the sum of two thousand one hundred and seventy-seven and sixty-seven one-hundredths dollars, for the use of said petitioners, and of the common schools for colored youth, so by them established, the same being the proportion of the public school funds belonging to said petitioners, and to the school under their charge, as the same was apportioned by the auditor of said county, in pursuance of law, which sum of money still remains in the hands of said treasurer in the treasury of said city.

That on the 1st day of April, 1850, there became due from said petitioners for expenses incurred in the support of said schools, the sums hereinafter set forth, as follows, namely: The sum of six dollars to the trustees of the New street church, for two months' rent of the school room; the sum of seven dollars to the trustees of the Union Baptist church, for one month's rent of school room; to Martha S. Whipple, the sum of twenty dollars, for one month's salary as teacher; to Peter Clarke, the sum of twenty dollars, for one month's salary as teacher; to William R. Casey, for one month's salary as teacher, the sum of twenty dollars; and to O. J. B. Nickens, the sum of sixty dollars, for two months'salary as teacher in said schools; and that afterwards, to-wit., on the 5th day of April, 1850, said petitioners, as such board of directors, certified to the city council of said city, the correctness of said several accounts, together with the several accounts respectively, and desired the city council to pass an order directing the treasurer of said city to pay the same out of the funds of said petitioners in his hands, to the persons entitled to receive the same; but that you, the said city council, afterwards, on the first day of May, 1850, utterly refused to pass any order in relation to the payment of said accounts, and now claim that said city council have no power, jurisdiction or authority to make any order in the premises, whereas in fact and in law said city council have such power, and it is in fact their duty to so do.

That said William Disney, treasurer of said city, has no power to disburse said funds, nor any of the funds in the city treasury, without the order of said city council, signed by the city clerk, first being had and obtained, and has therefore and for that reason, refused to pay said accounts without the order of the city council as aforesaid. That by reason of said refusal by said city council to pass the orders aforesaid, and of said treasurer to pay said accounts, the teachers employed by said petitioners are deprived of the compensation which is justly due them for their services, and the schools so by said board established have been suspended for want of means to carry on the same, although a fund amply sufficient to sustain said schools has been provided by law and is now in the hands of said Disney, as treasurer of said city. That said petitioners are entirely without remedy in the premises, unless it be afforded by the interposition of this court, by their writ of mandamus. Now therefore, we being willing that full and speedy justice should be done in the premises, do command you that you issue an order directing the treasurer of said city to pay the said several sums of money so certified as herein before stated, or that you appear before the judges of our District court, sitting within and for the said county of Hamilton, at the court house in said county, on the 18th day of May, 1850, at 9 o'clock A. M. of said day, to show cause why you refuse to do so.

Witness, I. G. B., clerk of our District court at Cincinnati, this 16th day of May, A. D. 1850.

I. G. B.,
Clerk.

FORM OF RETURN, OR ANSWER.

To the Honorable the District Court within and for the County of Hamilton and State of Ohio:

The city council of the city of Cincinnati for return (*or answer, as it may be called.*) to the alternative writ of mandamus heretofore issued by said court against them, on application made by Richard Phillips, etc., claiming to constitute the board of directors of common schools for the eastern and western districts of Cincinnati, for the education of colored youth in said city, say: That the board of trustees and visitors of common schools of the city of Cincinnati on the 7th day of August, in the year 1849, passed a resolution that the city should be divided into two school districts, for the colored youth of said city, to be called the eastern and western districts; and on the same day they passed another resolution that the said board should notify the colored adult male tax payers of said districts that an election for school visitors and trustees would be held in said districts on the 13th day of August, 1849, at 2 o'clock P. M.; and on the same day the city clerk was directed by said board to cause to be published in the *Globe* and *Chronicle*, notice of the election provided for in the second of said resolutions, to be held, in the eastern district, at the New street chapel, on New street, and in the western district, at Zion church, on Third street, between Race and Elm streets, which notice was given. Soon after this the said board passed another resolution to employ suitable persons to list the colored tax payers and youth of said districts, and did employ one such person for that purpose in each district.

This respondent further says, that on the 3d day of April, 1850, the accounts set forth in said application for a mandamus, some of them certified correct by John I. Gaines, some by Charles Satchel, one by William M. Nelson and one by Richard Phillips, were presented by one of the applicants for a mandamus, to the city council of said city, and put on the desk of the president of said council, with a request that said accounts should be paid. The said accounts were referred to the committee on common schools, who, on the 2d day of May, 1850, made the report, a copy of which is certified by the city clerk and hereto annexed, marked "Exhibit A," and the said report was accepted and agreed to, and the city council refused to order said accounts to be paid.

This respondent further says, that in pursuance of the order aforesaid, an enumeration was made of the colored youth in said city, and there were found to be in the eastern district, four hundred and twenty-three, and in the western district four hundred and twenty-two, making together, eight hundred and forty-five; and that the white youth of said city were also enumerated and found in the same year (1849) to be thirty-three thousand five hundred and forty-eight. A tax was levied by the city council of said city, in the year 1849, for school purposes, on all the real and personal property in said city as returned on the grand levy of the State, without any distinction being made as to the ownership of such property whether owned by white or colored persons.

The auditor of Hamilton county made a division of the school funds in the treasury of said county, to which the city of Cincinnati was entitled, derived from all sources whatever; and in making such division he appropriated a part of said funds in proportion to the number of white youth enumerated as aforesaid, thirty-three thousand five hundred and forty-eight, for the support of schools for white youth, and a part of said funds in proportion to the number of colored youth enumerated as aforesaid, at eight hundred and forty-five, for the support of schools for colored youth. The amount appropriated by this rule for the support of schools for colored youth was two thousand one hundred and seventy-seven dollars and sixty-one cents, which was paid to William Disney, treasurer of said city, out of the treasury of said county, by order of the said county auditor, on the 13th day of March, 1850.

The said city treasurer was not willing to receive said money, supposing that it was not proper for him to receive it, and he would not have received it except for the following reason, to-wit., the said county auditor refused to give him an order for the other school money unless this was also included, and all receipted for together. For this reason the city treasurer did receive said money, and deposited the same in the State Bank of Ohio, Franklin branch in Cincinnati, where the same lies, at four per cent interest, subject to judicial decision. Said city treasurer, supposing as aforesaid, that it was not proper for him to receive said $2,177.61, has not reported the receipt thereof officially to the said city council, nor to the city clerk.

Wherefore this respondent prays the judgment of the court whether the said sum of $2,177.61 has been legally levied and collected and appropriated as above set forth, and that the court will make such order in the premises as shall be required by right and justice, and that this respondent may be hence dismissed.

D. V. M.,
Att'y for Respondent.

The foregoing petition, alternative mandamus and return, are nearly the same as in the case of *The State* v. *City of Cincinnati et al.*, 19 *O. R.*, 178. Some alterations were deemed necessary in order to make them technically accurate; especially the alternative writ, which was thought to be insufficient, in not stating facts showing the obligation of the defendants to perform the act demanded. (10 *Wend.* 26; 571 *Sec. Ohio Code.*)

In Ohio, by the provisions of the Code, the peremptory mandamus should be like the alternative, except that the words "or show cause why you have not done so," are left out. In the absence, however, of any statutory provision upon the subject, the more usual practice, it is apprehended, is to also set forth the findings of the court upon the issues of law and fact, made by the return, or demurrer, to the alternative writ. The following peremptory writ was issued in the case of *Ex-parte Bradstreet*, 7 *Peters' Rep.*, 647:

UNITED STATES OF AMERICA, *ss.*

To the Honorable ALFRED CONKLING, *Judge of the District Court of the United States for the Northern District of New York, Greeting:*

Whereas, one Martha Bradstreet hath heretofore commenced and prosecuted in your court several certain real actions, or writs of right, in your court lately pending between the said Martha Bradstreet, demandant, and the following named tenants severally and respectively, to-wit., Apollos Cooper and (others, naming them). And whereas, heretofore to-wit., at a session of the Supreme court of the United States held at Washington on the second Monday of January in the year 1832, it appeared upon the complaint of the said Martha Bradstreet, among other things, that at a session of your said court lately before holden by you according to law, all and singular the said writs of right then and there pending before your said court, upon the several motions of the tenants aforesaid, were dismissed for the reason that there was no averment of the pecuniary value of the lands demanded by the said demandant in the several counts filed and exhibited by the said demandant against the several tenants aforesaid, which orders of your said court so dismissing the said actions were against the will and consent of demandant; whereupon the said Supreme court, at the instance of said demandant, granted a rule requiring you to show cause, if any you had, among other things, why a writ of mandamus from the said Supreme court should not be awarded and issued to you, commanding you to reinstate and proceed to try and adjudge, according to the law and the right of the case, the several writs of right aforesaid, and the issues therein joined. And whereas, at the late session of the said Supreme court held at Washington on the second Monday of January in the year 1833, you certified and returned to the said Supreme court, together with the said rule, that after the issues had been joined in the several causes mentioned in the said rule, motions were made therein, on the part of the tenants, that the same should be dismissed, upon the ground that the counts respectively contained no allegation of the value of the matter in dispute, and that it did not therefore appear, by the pleadings, that the causes were within the jurisdiction of the court; that in conformity with what appeared to have been the uniform language of the national courts upon the question, and your views of the law, and in accordance especially with several decisions in the Circuit court for the third circuit (*see* 4 *Wash. C. C. Reps.*, 482, 624), you granted their motions; and assuming that the causes were rightly dismissed, it follows, of course, that you ought not to be required to reinstate them unless leave ought also to be granted to the demandant to amend her counts. And whereas, afterwards to-wit., at the same session of the said Supreme court last aforesaid, upon consideration of your said return, and of the cause shown by you therein against the said rules being made absolute, and against the awarding and issuing of the said writ of mandamus, and upon consideration of the arguments of counsel, as well on your behalf, showing cause as aforesaid, as on behalf of the said demandant in support of the said rule, it was considered by the said Supreme court that you had certified and returned to the said court an insufficient cause for having dismissed the said actions, and against the awarding and issuing of the said writ of mandamus pursuant to the rule aforesaid; the said Supreme court being of opinion and having determined and adjudged of the matter aforesaid, that in cases where the demand is not made for money, and the nature of the action does not require the value of the thing demanded to be stated in the declaration, the practice of the said Supreme court, and of the courts of the United States, is to allow the value to be given in evidence; that in pursuance of this practice the demandant in the suits dismissed by order of the judge of the District court, had a right to give the value of the property demanded in evidence, either at or before the trial of the cause, and would have a right to give it in evidence in the said Supreme court, consequently that she cannot be legally prevented from bringing her cases before the said Supreme court; and it was also then and there considered by the said Supreme court, that the peremptory writ of the United States issue, requiring and commanding you, the said judge of the said District court, to reinstate and proceed to try and adjudge, according to the law and right of the case, the several writs of right and the issues therein joined, lately pending in your said court between the said Martha Bradstreet, demandant, and Apollos Cooper and others, the tenants aforesaid; therefore, you are hereby commanded and enjoined that immediately after the receipt of this writ, and without delay, you reinstate and proceed to try and adjudge according to the law and right of the case, the several writs of right and the issues therein joined, lately pending in your said court between the said Martha Bradstreet, demandant, and the said Apollos Cooper and others, the tenants herein above named, so that complaint be not again made to the said Supreme court; and that you certify perfect obedience and due execution of this writ to the said Supreme court, to be held on the first Monday in August next. Hereof fail not at your peril, and have then and there this writ.

Witness, the Honorable JOHN MARSHALL, Chief Justice of said Supreme court, the second Monday of January, in the year of our Lord one thousand eight hundred and thirty-three.

W. T. C.,
Clerk of the Supreme Court of the United States.

In some States, following the former practice, the application for the writ of mandamus is founded upon affidavits stating the facts upon which the party relies, and which show that he is entitled to the relief demanded. (1 *Johns. Cas.*, 134; 3 *Term R.*, 575.) The affidavits, where this mode of practice is adopted, should, like a petition or complaint, set forth the facts with precision. and should also anticipate and answer every possible objection or argument in fact, which it may be expected will be urged against the claim. (5 *Term R.*, 466; 2*d Johns. Cas.*, 2 *ed.*, 217.) They should not, it seems, be *entitled;* as for example, *Reuben Turner* v. *James Haight* (2 *John's R.*, 371; 2 *How. Pr. R.*, 60; 7 *Ib.*, 124), and if so entitled, they will not be permitted to be read. The affidavits having been prepared, application is made to the court either that a peremptory mandamus issue at once, or that an alternative mandamus issue, or for an order to show cause in the nature of an alternative mandamus, why the particular act sought to be commanded should not be performed. The peremptory writ will, however, seldom be granted in the first instance; although, where both parties are heard on the application, and there is no dispute about the facts, and the law is with the applicant, the court will permit the peremptory writ to issue at once. (7 *Cowen*, 524; 4 *Abb. P. R.*, 36; 14 *Johns*, 325.) It will also be permitted to issue at once where it is apparent that no excuse can be given for the non-performance of the act, and the party's rights might be endangered by delay.

FORM OF AFFIDAVIT.

[The following forms are particularly adapted to the State of New York.]

THE STATE OF ...., }
County of .... } ss:

A. B., of ......, in said county, being duly sworn, says: That [*set forth the facts, as before directed*].

A. B.

Sworn to before me, and subscribed in my }
presence, this .. day of ...., A. D. 18... }

In the case of *The Albany Water Works* v. *The Albany Mayor's Court*, 12 *Wend.* 292, the court say, that in future, a motion for a mandamus, or a rule to show cause, will not be entertained without notice to the party to be affected by the proceedings; and although it seems that this rule has not been strictly followed (3 *How. P. R.*, 164), yet undoubtedly it is the better practice to do so. If a peremptory mandamus is applied for, the notice is indispensable.

FORM OF NOTICE.

To ....:

Sir: You will take notice that upon affidavits, copies of which are herewith served, I shall move the Supreme court, at the next special term thereof, to be held at the court house in the village of ...., on the .... day of ......, A. D. 18.., at the opening of the court on that day, or as soon thereafter as counsel can be heard, for an order that a writ of mandamus issue out of the said court directed to you, and commanding you that [*state the object of the writ*], and for such other or further relief as the court may be pleased to grant. (*See McCall's Forms*, 119.)

Dated .... A. B.,

by C. D., his Att'y.

ORDER THAT A MANDAMUS ISSUE.

IN THE SUPREME COURT.

The People *ex rel.* A. B.,
vs.
E. F.

At a special term of the Supreme court held at the court house in ...., in and for the county of ...., on the .... day of ...., A. D. 18... *Present*, O. P., Justice,

On reading and filing affidavits, and on motion of C. D., Esq., counsel for the relator, and after hearing N. M., counsel for E. F., in opposition thereto, it is ordered that a mandamus issue out of and under the seal of this court, directed to the said E. F., commanding him forthwith to [*state what is to be done*], or that he show cause to the contrary, before this court, at the court house in the city of ...., on the .... day of ...., A. D. 18... (*McCall's Forms*, 141.)

Although it would be irregular to *entitle* the affidavits on which the writ is allowed, yet it is otherwise with the rule granting the writ, which may properly be entitled in the cause. (2 *How. P. R.*, 60.)

ORDER TO SHOW CAUSE WHY MANDAMUS SHOULD NOT ISSUE

IN THE SUPREME COURT.

The People *ex rel.* A. B.,
vs.
E. F.

At a special term of the Supreme court held at the court house in ...., in and for the county of ...., on the .... day of .... , A. D. 18.., *Present*, O. P., Justice,

On reading and filing affidavits, and on motion of C. D., Esq., counsel for the relator, it is ordered that E. F., above named, show cause at the next special term of this court, to be held at the court house in ...., on the .... day of ...., A. D. 18.., why the said E. F. should not be compelled forthwith to [*state the matter required to be done*], or why an alternative mandamus should not issue, directed to him, and requiring him to do the acts above stated, or to show cause to the contrary.

And it is also ordered, that a copy of this order, with a copy of the affidavits on which the same is founded, be served on the said E. F., ... days before the time above mentioned. (*See Crary's Practice*, 588.)

The service should be made at least eight days before the hearing. (3 *How. Pr. R.*, 165.)

ALTERNATIVE MANDAMUS TO RESTORE ONE OF THE COMMON COUNCIL OF A CITY.

THE PEOPLE OF THE STATE OF ...., *to E. F., &c., the Common Council of our city of* ...., *and to every of them, Greeting:*

Whereas, A. B. was duly elected, sworn and admitted into the place and office of one of the common council of our said city of --------, in which said place and office he the said A. B. always behaved and governed himself well, yet you the said citizens of the common council of our said city, without any reasonable cause, have unjustly removed the said A. B. from the said place and office of one of the common council of our said city, in contempt of us, and to the no small damage and grievance of him the said A. B., as we have been informed from his complaint made to us in that behalf; we therefore, being willing that due and speedy justice be done in this behalf to the said A. B. as it is reasonable, do command you, that immediately after the receipt of this our writ, you do restore, or cause to be restored, the said A. B. into the said place and office of one of the common council of our said city of ------, together with all the liberties, privileges and franchises to the said place and office of one of the common council of our said city belonging and appertaining, or that you show us cause to the contrary thereof, that the same complaint may not, by your default, be repeated to us; and how you shall have executed this our writ, make known to us at --------, on --------, there returning to us this our said writ.

Witness, C. D. E., Justice of the Supreme court, at [L. S.] --------, the ---- day of ------, A. D. 18--. (2 *Johns. Cases, note* 217, 89.)

N. B., *Clerk.*

[*Indorsed*] By the court.

A. B., *Clerk.*

ANSWER, OR RETURN, TO SUCH ALTERNATIVE WRIT OF MANDAMUS.

The answer of E. F., &c., the Common Council of the city of ......, within mentioned.

We, the said E. F., &c., common council of the city of ......, for answer to the alternative writ of mandamus heretofore issued against us on the relation of A. B., say it is not true that said A. B. was duly elected, sworn or admitted into the place and office of one of the common council of the city of ...., as by the said writ is alleged; and, therefore, we could not restore, or cause to be restored, the said A. B. into the said place and office of one of the common council of said city, as by that writ we were within commanded.

E. F.

If the facts in the return, or answer, are denied, or an issue of fact exists in any other way on the pleadings, the case, in New York, must go down to the Circuit for trial. (7 *Wend.* 175.) After the facts of the case are settled, either by an issue and verdict, or by default of one of the parties, the relator obtains a peremptory mandamus by motion to the court, on notice to the opposite party, upon the return, pleadings, verdict, &c. (3 *How. Pr. R.*, 379.) For form of judgment record in such case, see *Crary's Practice*, 591.

PEREMPTORY MANDAMUS.

THE PEOPLE OF THE STATE OF ...., *to E. F., &c., the Common Council of our city of ...., and to every of them, Greeting:*

Whereas, A. B. was duly elected, sworn and admitted into the place and office of one of the common council of our said city of ...., in which said place and office he the said A. B. always behaved and governed himself well, yet you the said citizens of the common council of our said city, without any reasonable cause, have unjustly removed the said A. B. from the said place and office of one of the common council of our said city, in contempt of us, and to the no small damage and grievance of him the said A. B., as we have been informed from his complaint made to us in that behalf, and which complaint we have adjudged to be true, as appears to us of record.

Now therefore, we being willing that speedy justice should be done in this behalf to him the said A. B., do command and enjoin you, that immediately after the receipt of this writ, you do restore, or cause to be restored, the said A. B. into the said place and office of one of the common council of our said city of --------, together with all the liberties, privileges and franchises to the said place and office of one of the common council of our said city belonging and appertaining, lest in your default complaint should again come to us; and how you shall have executed this our writ, make known to us to our justices of our said Supreme court, at the --------, on the ---- day of ------, A. D. 18--, and have you then and there this writ.

Witness, Hon. I. H., one of the justices of our Supreme [L. S.] court, this ---- day of --------, A. D. 18--. (2 *McCall's Forms*, 93.)

A. B., *Clerk.*

[*Indorsed*] By the court.

A. B., *Clerk.*

INDEX.

A.

D.

H.

I.

J.

K.

L.

M.

N.

O.

P.

Q

R.

S.

T.

V.

W.